Offshore Practice and Administration

ROBIN McGHEE
Dip FS, FCIB, TEP, Dip Distance Ed, MInstD, MIMgt

THE INSTITUTE OF FINANCIAL SERVICES
c/o The Chartered Institute of Bankers
Emmanuel House
4-9 Burgate Lane
Canterbury
Kent
CT1 2XJ
United Kingdom

Institute of Financial Services Publications are published by The Chartered Institute of Bankers, a non-profit making registered educational charity, and are distributed exclusively by Bankers Books Limited which is a wholly owned subsidiary of The Chartered Institute of Bankers.

Copyright © The Chartered Institute of Bankers 1997

Printed by Communications in Print, Essex

ISBN 0-85297-428-0

CONTENTS

About the Author

Robin McGhee began work in the trust industry in 1979 when he joined the trustee department of a major UK clearing bank in Canterbury, Kent. By the age of 22 he had completed the CIB's Trustee Diploma and went on to successfully complete the more advanced Financial Studies Diploma.

In 1988 Robin was appointed Trust Manager with a large firm of solicitors in the UK. He later returned to the banking sector, this time offshore, and worked initially in the Cayman Islands, before moving to the Isle of Man in 1991. At the time of going to press, Robin heads up a trust company in the Cayman Islands.

During his career, Robin has given numerous talks and lectures on a variety of industry specific subjects and has also taught part-time at colleges in London, the Cayman Islands and the Isle of Man. He was involved in the development of the Certificate in Offshore Administration, which is offered by the colleges in Jersey, Guernsey and the Isle of Man and in 1995 was appointed Chief Examiner of Offshore Practice and Administration. In the following year he was appointed Moderator of Offshore Investment Planning and Advice, one of the subjects in the newly created Professional Investment Certificate and also wrote the study text for students.

Robin was made a Fellow of the CIB in 1996. He is a member of STEP (serving on the Central Education Committee as well as the Isle of Man's local Committee) and is also a member of the Institute of Directors and the Institute of Management. Robin also holds a diploma in training issued by the Association of European Correspondence Schools.

He is married to Davina and they have a son, David.

Acknowledgements

I would like to thank my wife, Davina, for all her help with the preparation of this book.

I should also like to pass on my appreciation to the Financial Supervision Commission in the Isle of Man for their assistance with regard to the provision of information for Unit 5.

My thanks also to Alan Smith for his support and encouragement.

Dedication

To Davina and David.

Introduction

The Concept of the Course

This is a practical course written for students studying for banking and finance qualifications and also for practitioners in the financial services industry who are looking for a practical refresher. This study text is structured so that many will find it to be the most coherent way of learning the subject.

This book is the set text for the Offshore Practice & Administration option of the ACIB-Degree link and the Diploma in Trusts and Estates Practice (DTEP)

Each Unit of the Study Text is divided into sections and contains:

- Learning objectives
- An introduction, indicating how this subject area relates to others to which the reader may have cause to refer
- Clear, concise topic-by-topic coverage
- Examples and exercises to reinforce learning, confirm understanding and stimulate thought
- Usually, an exam-style question to try for practice.

Exercises

Exercises are provided throughout to enable you to check your progress as you work through the text. These come in a variety of forms: some test your ability to analyse material you have read, others see whether you have taken in the full significance of a piece of information. Some are meant to be discussed with colleagues, friends or fellow students.

Each of the main Units consists of study notes designed to focus attention upon the key aspects of the subject matter. These notes are divided into convenient sections for study purposes.

At the end of each Unit there are self-assessment questions. These comprise a number of short answer questions. The answers to these questions are to be found at the back of the book in Appendix 1. Full specimen exam questions can be found in Appendices 2 and 4, with model answers in Appendices 3 and 5 respectively. Students should remain aware of the fact that the examination itself will comprise questions drawn from across the whole Chartered Institute of Bankers syllabus; the key sections of which for this subject are:

- Offshore Company Management
- Trustee Business
- Offshore Investment Management.

Although the workbook is designed to stand alone, as with most topics, certain aspects of this subject are constantly changing. Therefore it is of great importance that students should keep up to date with these key areas.

It is anticipated that the student will study this course for one academic year, reading through and studying approximately two Units every three weeks. However, it should be noted that as topics vary in size and as knowledge tends not to fall into uniform chunks, some Units in this workbook are unavoidably longer than others.

The masculine pronoun 'he' has been used in this Workbook to encompass both genders and to avoid the awkwardness of the constant repetition of 'he and/or she'.

Study Guide

In the next few pages, we offer some advice and ideas on studying, revising and approaching examinations.

Studying

As with any examination, there is no substitute for preparation based on an organised and disciplined study plan. You should devise an approach which will enable you to get right through this Study Text and still leave time for revision of this and any other subject you are taking at the same time. Many candidates find that about six weeks is the right period of time to leave for revision, enough time to get through the revision material, but not so long that it is no longer fresh in your mind by the time you reach the examination.

This means that you should plan how to get to the last chapter by, say, the end of March for a May sitting or the end of August for an October sitting. This includes not only reading the text, but making notes and attempting the bulk of the illustrative questions in the back of the text.

We offer the following as a starting point for approaching your study.

● Plan time each week to study a part of this Study Text. Make sure that it is equally' study time: let everyone know that you are studying and that you should not be disturbed. If you are at home, unplug your telephone or switch the answerphone on; if you are in the office, put your telephone on 'divert'.

● Set a clearly defined objective for each study period. You may simply wish to read through a chapter for the first time or perhaps you want to make some notes on a chapter you have already read a couple of times. Don't forget the illustrative questions.

● Review your study plan. Use the study checklist a couple of pages on to see how well you are keeping up. Don't panic if you fall behind, but do think how you will make up for lost time.

● Look for examples of what you have covered in the 'real' world. If you work for a financial organisation, this should be a good starting point. If you do not, then think about your experiences as an individual bank or building society customer or perhaps about your employer's position as a corporate customer of a bank. Keep an eye on the quality press for reports about banks and building societies and their activities.

Revising

The period which you have earmarked for revision is a very important time. Now it is even more important that you plan time each week for study and that you set clear objectives for each revision session.

- Use time sensibly. How much revision time do you have? Remember that you still need to eat, sleep and fit in some leisure time.

- How will you split the available time between subjects? What are your weaker subjects? You will need to focus on some topics in more detail than others. You will also need to plan your revision around your learning style. By now, you should know whether, for example, early morning, early evening or late evening is best.

- Take regular breaks. Most people find they can absorb more this way than if they attempt to revise for long uninterrupted periods of time. Award yourself a five minute break every hour. Go for a stroll or make a cup of coffee, but do not turn the television on.

- Believe in yourself. Are you cultivating the right attitude of mind? There is absolutely no reason why you should not pass this exam if you adopt the correct approach. Be confident, you have passed exams before so you can pass this one.

The examination

Passing professional examinations is half about having the knowledge, and half about doing yourself full justice in the examination. You must have the right technique.

The day of the exam

- Set at least one alarm (or get an alarm call) for a morning exam.

- Having something to eat but beware of eating too much; you may feel sleepy if your system is digesting a large meal.

- Don't forget pens, pencils, rulers, erasers and anything else you will need.

- Avoid discussion about the exam with other candidates outside the exam hall.

Tackling the examination paper

First, make sure that you satisfy the examiner's requirements.

- Read the instructions on the front of the exam paper carefully. Check that the exam format hasn't changed. It is surprising how often examiners' reports remark on the number of students who attempt too few - or too many - questions, or who attempt the wrong number of questions from different parts of the paper. Make sure that you are planning to answer the right number of questions.

- Read all the questions on the exam paper before you start writing. Look at the weighting of marks to each part of the question. If part (a) offers only 4 marks and you can't answer the 12 marks part (b), then don't choose the question.

- Don't produce irrelevant answers. Make sure you answer the question set, and not the question you would have preferred to have been set.

- Produce an answer in the correct format. The examiner will state in the requirements the format in which the question should be answered, for example in a report or memorandum. If a question asks for a diagram or an example, give one. If a question does not specifically asks for a diagram or example, but it seems appropriate, give one.

Second, observe these simple rules to ensure that your script is pleasing to the examiner.

- Present a tidy paper. You are a professional and it should always show in the presentation of your work. Candidates are penalised for poor presentation and so you should make sure that you write legibly, label diagrams clearly and lay out your work professionally. Markers of scripts each have dozens of papers to mark; a badly written scrawl is unlikely to receive the same attention as a neat and well laid out paper.

- State the obvious. Many candidates look for complexity which is not required and consequently overlook the obvious. Make basic statements first. Plan your answer and ask yourself whether you have answered the main parts of the question.

- Use examples. This will help to demonstrate to the examiner that you keep up-to-date with the subject. There are lots of useful examples scattered through this study text and you can read about others if you dip into the quality press or take notice of what is happening in your working environment.

Finally, make sure that you give yourself the opportunity to do yourself justice.

- Select questions carefully. Read through the paper once, then quickly jot down any key points against each question in a second read through. Reject those questions against which you have jotted down very little. Select those where you could latch on to ëwhat the question is about' - but remember to check carefully that you have got the right end of the stick before putting pen to paper.

- Plan your attack carefully. Consider the order in which you are going to tackle questions. It is a good idea to start with your best question to boost your morale and get some easy marks ëin the bag'.

- Read the question carefully and plan your answer. Read through the question again very carefully when you come to answer it.

- Gain the easy marks. Include the obvious if it answers the question and do not spend unnecessary time producing the perfect answer. As suggested above, there is nothing wrong with stating the obvious.

- Avoid getting bogged down in small parts of questions. If you find a part of a question difficult, get on with the rest of the question. If you are having problems with something the chances are that everyone else is too.

- Don't leave the exam early. Use your spare time checking and rechecking your script.

Don't worry if you feel you have performed badly in the exam. It is more likely that the other candidates will have found the exam difficult too. Don't forget that there is a competitive element in exams. As soon as you get up and leave the exam hall, forget the exam and think about the next - or , if it is the last one, celebrate!

Don't discuss an exam with other candidates. This is particularly the case if you still have other exams to sit. Put it out of your mind until the day of the results. Forget about exams and relax.

Unit 1

Summary of the Attractions Usually Associated with Holding Assets in an Offshore Centre

> ### Objectives
>
> **At the end of this Unit you should be able to:**
>
> - **Explain to a client what is meant by the term 'offshore'**
> - **Describe the main features of an 'offshore centre'**
> - **List five offshore centres located in Europe**
> - **List eight offshore centres located in the Atlantic and the Caribbean**
> - **List five offshore centres located in Asia and the Pacific**
> - **Explain what is meant by the term 'fiduciary services' and list five examples of such services**
> - **Summarise the general taxation treatment of offshore services provided for non-residents of offshore centres**
> - **Comment on the possible attraction of minimal reporting requirements and regulatory controls in offshore centres**
> - **Comment on the importance of an offshore centre having political and economic stability as well as locally available expertise**
> - **State ten possible benefits of placing assets offshore**

This first Unit provides a useful yet essential start to the course. It does not cover any practical administration issues nor does it contain any 'technical' content. This Unit concentrates on a few of the fundamental issues of offshore finance which many students ignore in their studies. We start by looking at a few terms and go on to look at some of the advantages commonly associated with investing or holding assets offshore. Some of the features which clients and their advisers commonly look for in an offshore centre are also explained.

1 Definition of the Term 'Offshore'

1.1 The term 'offshore' is widely used in financial planning circles but despite its popularity it might come as a surprise to some that 'offshore' has no legal definition.

1.2 Instead, the term has come to be applied to the situation where a financial transaction is carried out from a jurisdiction which is at least one step removed from the client who has initiated that transaction. In addition, the jurisdiction chosen for the transaction will usually have low rates of personal and corporate taxation.

2 Definition of the Term 'Offshore Centre'

2.1 Generally speaking, an offshore centre is one which offers concessionary rates of taxation usually for, but not necessarily restricted to, individuals, corporate entities and trusts. The rates of taxation would be considered to be concessionary if they are lower than those prevailing in 'onshore' centres such as the United Kingdom, the United States of America, Canada and Germany (to name but a few examples).

Student Activity 1

Before you read the next section of this Unit, list five offshore centres in Europe, five in the Caribbean and five in Asia and the Pacific. Of the centres which you have chosen, which is the jurisdiction with which you have the closest connection or most knowledge?

2.2 There are in the region of 60 jurisdictions which could be classified as offshore centres and the following is a list of those which are perhaps the most widely known and used:

Centres in Europe

2.3 Alderney, Canary Islands, Cyprus, Gibraltar, Guernsey, Ireland, Isle of Man, Jersey, Liechtenstein, Luxembourg, Madeira, Malta, Monaco, Switzerland.

Centres in the Atlantic and the Caribbean

2.4 Anguilla, Antigua, Aruba, Bahamas, Barbados, Belize, Bermuda, British Virgin Islands (BVI), Cayman Islands, Netherlands Antilles, Nevis, Panama, Seychelles, St. Vincent, Turks and Caicos.

Centres in Asia and the Pacific

2.5 Cook Islands, Hong Kong, Labuan, Mauritius, Singapore, Vanuatu, Western Samoa.

2.6 The majority of offshore centres are islands which have their own legal systems, the autonomy to introduce their own laws and the power to introduce their own systems and rates of taxation. Such centres can therefore implement legislation which is designed to attract foreign investors.

2.7 That is not to say, however, that onshore centres cannot provide possible tax saving opportunities. An example of this is the United Kingdom where certain taxation planning opportunities exist for individuals who are UK resident but not UK domiciled.

2.8 Now that we have defined what we mean by 'offshore' and 'offshore centre' we shall look at the type of financial services which are conducted offshore and also some reasons why clients may want their assets invested or held in an offshore centre.

3 Financial Services Provided by Offshore Centres

3.1 There are a variety of financial services which are provided from offshore centres although it must be noted that not all the centres provide all of these services. The following is a list of the most commonly used financial services:

- Banking
- Trustee services
- Company incorporation and company management
- Investment management
- Custody of investments
- Creation and administration of investment funds
- Captive insurance
- Pension funds
- Ship registration and management

We cover each of these services in detail in later Units.

3.2 It is worth mentioning that although offshore centres provide a variety of different financial services it is generally the provision of fiduciary services which have sparked the growth in this very specialised industry. A fiduciary service is generally considered to be one where the service provider owes certain duties to the person on whose behalf he is holding the assets or he has certain responsibilities which he must fulfil. The two most commonly quoted examples are trustee services and company management services, as trustees and directors are considered to act in a fiduciary capacity as they owe duties and responsibilities to the beneficiaries and members respectively.

4 Benefits Offered by Offshore Centres

4.1 The following is by no means a definitive list of what clients or their advisers might consider to be a benefit or reason to place assets offshore. However, the list does contain the most commonly quoted.

Student Activity 2

Before you read the following section, prepare your own list containing five reasons why you think offshore services are so popular with clients from onshore centres.

Reasons for using Offshore Services

Taxation

4.2 A client might decide to place his assets in an offshore centre for a number of reasons but arguably the most common is to reduce his potential tax liabilities. This is because offshore centres impose only a low or in some cases a nil rate of tax on structures or accounts which have been created locally for the benefit of non-residents. You will no doubt have come across the term 'tax haven' in relation to offshore centres, a direct reflection of the possible tax benefits which they can create. We shall return to the subject of taxation in a later Unit.

Exchange controls

4.3   Exchange controls are in place in a few onshore locations (most notably perhaps in South Africa), and their effect is to restrict the flow of assets. Such controls can make it illegal for cash or other assets to be transferred or transported out of the country where the rules exist and can also make it illegal for citizens of that country to own foreign assets. Any foreign assets which are held could be subject to a forced sale and the eventual repatriation of the proceeds to the 'home' country.

4.4   Exchange controls are not imposed in offshore centres on assets which are held for international clients. Funds can therefore flow freely into and out of offshore centres although investors should be aware that if restrictions are in place in the investor's 'home' country, the 'home' country would consider it illegal to transfer funds out of that country and into an offshore centre.

Client confidentiality

4.5   Confidentiality is another important consideration for all clients. Many believe that because of the reporting requirements in some of the major onshore centres it is advisable to have their finances managed and controlled from an offshore centre, where the reporting requirements are much less onerous (if in place at all). Some centres, such as the Bahamas and the Cayman Islands, also offer legislation which makes the release of client information a criminal offence (unless there are exceptional circumstances which dictate that information should be made available).

4.6   However, as we shall see in a later Unit, any confidentiality laws which exist offshore, or any rules and regulations introduced by service providers, cannot be used to protect clients who use offshore centres or offshore services for criminal activities.

Minimal reporting requirements

4.7   Generally speaking, the regulators or authorities in most offshore centres will not require information on the clients or investors who are conducting business in that centre. Instead, they will rely upon (and indeed expect) the service providers in their centre to perform thorough checks on the suitability and integrity of the clients on whose behalf they perform or provide financial services. This 'self policing' can appeal to many clients, especially those who are interested in remaining as 'anonymous' as possible.

4.8   That is not to say, however, that there are no reporting requirements in offshore centres. For example, certain details relating to a locally incorporated company would usually have to be reported to the Registrar of Companies (or an equivalent department) in that centre although often the beneficial ownership details will remain confidential. In addition, service providers will usually be under a duty to report clients who they suspect of money laundering activities (an area which we return to in a later Unit).

Legal system

4.9   It is important that an offshore centre possess a first class legal system which contains clear and precise laws governing both domestic and international issues. The vast majority of offshore centres have based their legal systems on English common law

4

principles but have added local provisions which are designed not only to suit the local region but also, and more importantly, to attract investors and international business.

4.10 Many of the enhancing provisions which affect trust and company business are covered in detail later in this study text.

4.11 Through their legal systems, offshore centres can provide an opportunity for international clients to protect their assets from claims or legal actions which may arise from foreign countries. For example, a foreign country might have the power to expropriate assets of its citizens and to obtain legal ownership of those assets. However, if those assets were held offshore through, perhaps an offshore trust or company, those assets would usually be protected by the laws of the offshore centre concerned. The laws of most offshore centres would usually fail to recognise, let alone defend, the laws and claims of foreign governments in relation to the forced seizure of property.

4.12 In addition, many offshore centres have introduced legislation which is specifically aimed at defeating claims which may arise from the provisions of local law in the client's 'home' country (e.g. forced heirship protection trusts which we look at later in this study text).

Local expertise

4.13 Most offshore centres boast a high standard of local expertise in respect of their service providers. Indeed, in the majority of centres there are now a good spread of international banks, trust companies, legal firms, accountants and brokers, making the servicing of the clients' needs much easier and more efficient and also adding to the growing reputation of the professionalism of offshore service providers in general and offshore centres in particular.

4.14 The attitude of the local authorities to 'ex-pat' workers is an important factor in relation to the availability of local expertise. Although an available local pool of labour is an essential requirement for the growth and development of not only service providers but also the centre as a whole, it is equally important for the local immigration authorities to realise that in some instances the local labour market will not be able to provide the specific expertise which a local employer may require. In such cases it should be a relatively simple process for the employer concerned to obtain the necessary work permit to enable him to recruit the particular skills required from outside the centre.

Regulation

4.15 It is generally true to say that financial services in onshore centres are regulated to a greater extent than financial services which are provided from offshore centres. However, a growing number of offshore centres now impose some degree of regulatory control over their finance sectors, usually by requiring service providers to be licenced to conduct certain types of activities, such as taking deposits, providing investment services and acting as trustees.

4.16 Regulation appeals to many clients as they will have the comfort of knowing that the service provider they have chosen will be accountable locally for their actions and that they must meet certain 'fit and proper' requirements. On the other hand, regulation

5

can also be a deterrent and if the controls are too tight it might restrict business development. We shall return to regulation at various stages of this study text, particularly when we cover specific financial services.

Communications

4.17 The majority of offshore centres have excellent fax and telephone links and also have sophisticated computer technology to assist with the preparation and flow of information. Most centres are also served by excellent air and/or sea links which can also be an attraction to clients and their advisers.

Geographic distance

4.18 To some clients, the appeal of an offshore centre will be how far away it is from their 'home' country. There is a perception that with distance comes greater confidentiality. This may be true in some cases but should not be relied upon.

Attitude of local government

4.19 The governments of the vast majority of offshore centres are aware of the importance which their finance sectors have in relation to the future growth and development of their jurisdictions and are therefore keen to ensure that the industry receives the support which it needs to expand. For example, this could take the form of capital expenditure programmes (perhaps to improve the local infrastructure or communication systems) or the introduction of legislation requested by service providers (designed to make the centre more attractive to foreign investors).

4.20 It is generally accepted that those centres which have supportive governments are seen as a more suitable and better long-term choice than those centres which struggle to gain the support of their ruling authorities.

Political and economic stability

4.21 Many offshore centres are able to boast a long history of political stability and strong local economies, both of which help to build confidence in those centres. After all, if a centre has recently undergone civil or political unrest there might be a risk attached to the safety of the assets which have been placed there. Similarly, if the local economy was weak, unemployment might be a problem which could affect the availability of a suitable workforce. In addition, the cost of the services might increase (making the centre less appealing) and the general mismanagement of the jurisdictions financial affairs could affect its overall reputation.

Student Activity 3

List the five factors which, in your opinion, you think are the most important for a client or his adviser to consider in the selection of an offshore centre.

5 Additional Factors in the Selection of an Offshore Centre

5.1 Although we have already covered many of the main benefits which are provided by offshore centres there are additional factors which a prospective client should consider before placing his assets in a particular jurisdiction. These are covered in this Section.

Language

5.2 It is advisable that a centre is chosen which uses the same language as the client (and possibly the client's adviser). There is no point in basing a structure in a jurisdiction only to discover that it is impossible for the client to communicate with his service providers because they do not speak the same language! In view of the number of centres and their geographic spread it should be possible for a client to find a jurisdiction which speaks his language.

Costs

5.3 This is often a consideration but should not be the main criteria on which a decision is based. Generally speaking, the costs for the provision of financial services has decreased over the years. This is mainly a result of the increase in the number of offshore centres and the resulting increase in the number of service providers.

5.4 Although it is important for clients to receive value for money in relation to the services which they choose, it is equally important for them to remember that the choice of centre should be made based on a number of factors and not just on fees and expenses. These include the suitability and attractions of the local laws (such as on trusts and companies), the quality of the service providers and often more importantly the reputation of the centre.

5.5 In some cases (although not always), it is the more expensive centres which provide certain clients with the greater tailored benefits and planning opportunities.

Reputation of the Centre

5.6 There are a great many offshore centres to choose from and making a choice can be difficult as there will often be many similarities between each location. The reputation of a particular centre can therefore play an important part in the selection process. After all, a client will be less likely to place his assets in a structure in a centre which has suffered recent economic or political problems or worse still, a financial scandal.

5.7 The older and more established offshore centres often benefit in this area as many can boast a trouble-free past without serious incident. This adds to their reputation as a solid and respectable offshore centre. On the other hand, the newer or developing centres have no proven track record as they are new to the industry, and as a result, have little or no reputation which can be marketed to attract potential clients.

Same Time Zone

5.8 The ability of a client to pick up the telephone and speak to his offshore service provider at a reasonable hour can be an important factor in the selection process and as a result a centre might be required which is situated in the same time zone as the client. This may still mean there will be a choice between centres in that same zone but at least the search will be narrowed down.

7

Climate

5.9 Do not forget that there are clients who will weigh up the pros and cons of different centres and then make their final decision based on the relative merits of the climate of the centre chosen. You might be surprised at the number of clients who choose a jurisdiction in the Caribbean in which to place their hard earned wealth because they like the sunshine!

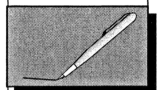

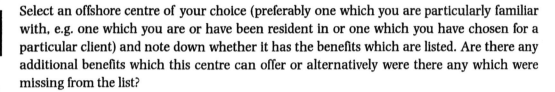

Student Activity 4

Select an offshore centre of your choice (preferably one which you are particularly familiar with, e.g. one which you are or have been resident in or one which you have chosen for a particular client) and note down whether it has the benefits which are listed. Are there any additional benefits which this centre can offer or alternatively were there any which were missing from the list?

Summary

Now that you have read this Unit you should be able to:

● Explain what is meant by the term 'offshore'

● Describe to a client what is meant by the term 'offshore centre'

● Name five offshore centres located in Europe

● Name eight offshore centres located in the Atlantic and the Caribbean

● Name five offshore centres located in Asia and the Pacific

● Describe the term 'fiduciary services' and provide five examples

● Describe to a client how offshore centres generally tax non-resident investors

● Offer an opinion on the possible attractions of minimal reporting requirements and regulatory controls in offshore centres

● Comment on the importance of an offshore centre having political and economic stability as well as locally available expertise

● Explain ten reasons why a client might want his assets held offshore

Self-assessment Questions

1.   Write a short definition of the term 'offshore'.

2.   Briefly explain what would usually make a centre an 'offshore' centre.

3.   Describe what is meant by the term 'fiduciary services' and provide two examples of the type of services which the term could be applied to.

4.   List ten possible benefits usually associated with holding assets in an offshore centre.

5.   Apart from the benefits mentioned in Question 4 above, provide five further factors which a client might want to consider before choosing an offshore centre.

6.   Describe, in general terms, the taxation treatment in offshore centres of assets which are held for the benefit of non-residents.

7.   Describe, in general terms, the regulation which exists offshore in relation to the provision of financial services.

8.   Comment on why the attitude of the local government of an offshore centre can be an important factor in the development of the finance sector of that centre.

9.   Explain why the political and economic stability of a centre are important factors when choosing where to base an offshore structure.

10.   Costs can be an important factor for many clients. On what basis would you recommend that a client chooses a more expensive offshore centre?

Unit 2

General Taxation Concepts

Objectives

At the end of this Unit you should be able to:

- Explain the importance of residence in relation to the taxation of an individual

- Describe the usual residency requirements which an individual must meet in order to be considered resident in a particular country

- Briefly explain the concept of domicile

- Highlight possible planning opportunities for individuals who are UK resident but not UK domiciled

- List the main types of taxation usually imposed on individuals

- Describe how the residence of a trust would usually be determined

- Describe how the residence of a company would usually be determined

- Highlight the usual tax treatment of non-residents in offshore centres

- Explain the basis of the tax treatment of offshore companies

- Describe the difference between tax evasion and tax avoidance

Under the terms of the syllabus students are required to have an understanding of the general taxation principles which are applied in the major onshore centres. Students are not required to have a detailed knowledge of taxation in one or more of these major onshore centres (although from a work perspective it might be useful to have a working knowledge of the basis of taxation and the reliefs and allowances available in either the USA or the UK, depending on which market is closer) and candidates will not be expected nor indeed required to provide their views on specific tax matters in the examination.

This Unit concentrates on general rather than specific tax issues and also looks at how tax is generally applied, if indeed it is, in offshore centres.

You will realise after reading this Unit that no attempt has been made to provide any advice or insight into how to create a tax-efficient offshore structure. To do so would be reckless as there is no easy or tried and tested 'offshore solution'. What might constitute an efficient and effective tax saving structure for one client might create a higher tax liability for another. Be wary of those financial advisers who are keen to sell a particular structure to clients (or service providers) on the basis that it has worked well for some and therefore it must also work for everyone.

Always suggest to a potential client that they obtain specfic taxation (as well as legal) advice before creating any vehicle or transferring funds offshore. Avoid providing tax advice yourself, unless you are fully trained and experienced in this field.

1 The Usual Basis of Taxation 'Onshore'

1.1 Before we look at some of the possible taxation benefits of placing funds offshore we must first look at how taxation is generally imposed in onshore countries (e.g. in the USA, the UK and other major centres traditionally and collectively referred to as 'onshore').

Let us start by considering the taxation of individuals before we move on to how trusts and then various types of corporate vehicles are generally assessed to tax.

The Basis of Taxation of Individuals

1.2 The basis for deciding who is liable to taxation will vary from country to country. However, in general terms, if a person is resident in a particular country he will be subject to the local system of taxation which is applied in that country which may mean he will have a tax liability to pay to the tax authority (or revenue body) in that centre.

Let us now look at how being resident in a particular country might be determined.

Residence for tax purposes

1.3 To be considered resident in a country for tax purposes a person will, in general terms, have to fulfill one or more residency qualifications.

These could include, but are not necessarily restricted to, the following:

a) He must have lived in that country for a qualifying period (e.g. for at least 6 months);

b) He must have made regular visits to that country and the length of his stays over a period of years must have exceeded a certain time (e.g. more than 3 months a year over 4 years);

c) If he lives outside of a particular country but he has accommodation available for his use there (e.g. he owns realty in that country) and he then visits that country during a tax year;

d) He must be a citizen or national of that country and is only living outside of that country as a temporary measure (e.g. not to work but perhaps to travel short-term).

1.4 If a person is resident in a country he will, in most cases, be liable to pay tax on his world-wide income and gains and not just in respect of the income or gains which are generated in that country. We shall look at the different types of taxation later in this Unit.

Student Activity 1

Select an onshore centre (perhaps one in which you have lived or currently work) and find out the basis on which an individual is deemed to be liable to personal taxes in that centre. Compare it with the list above. Are there any similarities/differences?

Another factor which might have to be taken into account is the individual's domicile, which we cover next.

Domicile

1.5   Domicile is a concept which is not applied in all onshore countries although those of you who deal with UK clients should be familiar with its effect.

1.6   In simple terms, a person is considered to be domiciled in the country where he was born (referred to as his domicile of origin). He may decide to change his domicile and acquire one of choice rather than keep his domicile of origin but to do this he would usually have to undertake a number of steps designed to sever all links with his domicile of origin and instead create new and substantial links with his intended new domicile. This might involve selling his house and resigning from any clubs or associations of which he was a member in his country of origin and purchasing a house in the new intended location.

1.7   If a person is resident in a country which recognises the concept of domicile but is not actually domiciled there, he may be able to receive certain taxation benefits and reliefs which would not otherwise be available to him if he were both resident and domiciled in that country. The UK is a good example of this as it provides a number of planning opportunities for persons who are UK resident but not UK domiciled. The main opportunities are briefly mentioned below.

Benefits of being UK resident but not UK domiciled

1.8   i)   The person is only subject to UK taxation on the income or capital gains which are actually remitted to the UK;

ii)   The person is only liable to inheritance tax (referred to as death duties in some countries) on assets which are situated in the UK.

Now that we have identified the usual basis of assessment, we can look at the nature of taxation which can be imposed on individuals in onshore centres.

Common Types of Taxation on Individuals

1.9   There are a number of ways in which individuals can be assessed and liable to taxation in onshore countries but the following are the most common types.

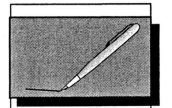

Student Activity 2

Before you read this section, list five ways in which an individual is taxed in an onshore centre which you are familiar with. Try to find out what the current rates of tax are and compare them with the rates which are payable in an offshore centre of your choice.

Tax on income

1.10 Income tax (as it is commonly termed) is assessed on receipts which are of an 'income' nature, such as dividends and interest payments from investments, bank interest, pension payments and salaries. Various personal allowances will usually be available to reduce a person's taxable income.

1.11 The rate of tax will vary between centres and often the more income a person receives, the higher their rate of income tax will be. The top rate of tax could be in excess of 70%.

Tax on capital

1.12 Capital taxes are generally levied on receipts of a 'capital' nature, such as the profits or gains on the sale of an investment or real estate. Various personal allowances will usually be available.

1.13 Again, rates will vary but sometimes a flat rate of tax will apply (which might be in excess of 50%).

Taxes on death

1.14 Death duties (or inheritance taxes) are usually calculated on the value of a person's estate (less their liabilities). Once again, allowances and reliefs will often be available to reduce the tax payable and usually the rate of tax will be determined by the value of the estate. Rates between 40% and 60% are common.

Lifetime transfer tax

1.15 Many onshore countries impose a transfer tax which would usually be payable on the transfer of assets during an individual's lifetime. As before, allowances to reduce the taxable amount will be deductable. Lifetime transfer tax might arise on, for example, the creation of a trust (usually when the assets are transferred to the trustees) or on the transfer of assets into a company by the beneficial owner.

1.16 The rate of tax might be determined by the value of the assets transferred or sometimes a fixed rate will apply.

Tax on investment income

1.17 In addition to charging income tax on investment income, some countries also impose an additional tax (which is effectively a surcharge) on income of this nature.

1.18 Dividends which are paid by companies may also have withholding tax deducted at source by the company. This tax is paid to the tax authority in the country where the company is resident and in some circumstances it may be possible for an individual to offset the tax which has been deducted from his own income tax bill.

Stamp duty

1.19 Some transactions may also give rise to a stamp duty liability. This type of tax can often be payable on the acquisition of an asset (such as realty or investments) or perhaps on the execution of a trust deed and is usually charged at a nominal, or in some cases fixed, rate. It is the execution of particular types of deeds or instruments which gives rise to this duty.

Indirect taxation

1.20 This is a tax on expenditure. In Europe it is often referred to as value added tax (in the UK the rate is currently 17.5%) and in America the term often used is sales tax. The provision of certain financial services may be liable to indirect taxation.

Taxation of Trusts

1.21 In general terms, it is the residence of the trustees which will usually determine where a trust is to be taxed in respect of its income receipts as well as its capital gains. In some cases, one of the trustees being resident in a particular country will make that trust resident there for income tax and possibly capital gains tax purposes, whereas in other countries it is where the majority of trustees reside which will be the deciding factor.

1.22 Tax will generally be assessed on the trustees and not on the trust on the basis that a trust is not a legal entity. Tax will be payable on the world-wide income and realised capital gains received by the trustees on the trust assets. Often the allowances which are available to individuals will not be available to trustees, or if they are available they will usually be at reduced rates.

1.23 It is also possible that the settlor of a trust might be assessed to tax in respect of the income and gains which arise in the trust. This will depend on the type of trust which the settlor has created, the residence of the settlor and also who stands to benefit under the terms of the trust deed.

1.24 Distributions out of trust property to a beneficiary will not usually have any tax implications for the trustees although the beneficiary might be liable to tax in respect of the funds which he receives. For example, in the normal course of events an income payment from a trust would give rise to income tax considerations for the recipient whereas a capital distribution might not be taxable. However, if regular capital payments are made to the beneficiary the revenue might consider that the payments are of an income rather than a capital nature and assess him to income tax. In addition, some countries levy tax on capital distributions by tracing back the payment to gains which the trustees have made. The beneficiary who receives the distribution might then have to pay tax based on the realised capital gains made by the trustees.

Taxation of Companies

1.25 It is widely accepted that a company will be considered to be resident for tax purposes where its management and control lies. As management and control should be held by the directors it is therefore common for the residence of the directors to determine the residence of the company.

1.26 As is the case for trustees, one director being resident in a particular country might be the required criteria for determining where that company might be assessed to tax, although in some countries the key factor will be either where the majority of directors reside or in which country the management function is performed (e.g. where directors' meetings are held).

1.27   Companies will usually be liable to tax on their world-wide income and profits and the calculation and basis of allowances available will usually be different from those which are available to individuals and trustees.

Taxation of Partnerships

1.28   In general terms it is not usually a partnership which is assessed to tax but it will instead be the partners themselves. Where the partners reside will therefore usually determine the basis of assessment, which will take into account the profits and income made by the partnership less any allowable losses or expenses.

2   The Usual Basis of Taxation 'Offshore'

2.1   Although each offshore centre will have its own system and basis of taxation it is fair to say that the following will usually apply offshore.

No Direct Taxes on Non-Residents

2.2   Generally speaking, offshore jurisdictions do not impose income tax, capital gains tax, transfer tax or death taxes on individuals, trusts, companies or partnerships which are not resident in the jurisdiction concerned.

In this context, non-resident is taken as meaning that the entity concerned is not based, resident, managed or trading in the offshore centre concerned.

Low or No Tax on Residents

2.3   A number of centres (mainly those in Europe) do, however, impose income tax on resident individuals and trusts which benefit local residents, and also corporation tax on resident companies. These are often referred to as low tax centres.

2.4   Some jurisdictions (notably those in the Caribbean) impose no tax at all on their residents and on entities which have been created locally. These are usually referred to as 'no tax centres' although often stamp duty and certain indirect taxes, such as sales and import duties, would still be payable.

Taxation of Trusts and Companies in Low Tax Centres

2.5   After reading the previous section you may wonder what benefit there could be in creating a trust or company in an offshore centre which is a low tax, as opposed to a no tax, jurisdiction.

2.6   We have already seen that it is generally the residence of the trustees which determines the residence of a trust and that equally it is the residence of the directors which often determines the residence of a company. In those centres which don't have capital or income taxes, the fact that the management and control of those types of vehicles lies in their centre is not an issue.

2.7   However, if the same principles were to be applied to low tax centres, local trusts and companies would be subject to local tax.

2.8   To prevent this happening and to maintain a taxation advantage, such centres have introduced legislation which generally excludes local trusts and locally incorporated companies from local taxation provided that they have been created solely for the benefit of non-residents. In relation to companies, most of the centres concerned do require the payment of an annual duty (sometimes referred to as tax or an exemption fee) in return for this favourable tax treatment.

We shall return to how such companies can be granted this favourable tax treatment in a later Unit.

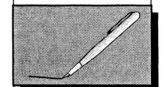

Student Activity 3

Before you proceed with the next section, summarise what you believe to be the main taxation advantages which offshore centres generally offer. Once you have done this, compare your views with those of the text.

3   The Potential Taxation Advantage of Offshore Centres

3.1   After reading the previous sections it should be apparent to you that there are tremendous offshore tax planning opportunities available to individuals or corporate entities who are resident in a high tax onshore centre and who place their assets offshore where the rates of tax are less.

3.2   However, life and taxation are not that simple and there will be many factors which will need to be taken into account to determine whether an offshore structure can provide a client with legitimate tax saving possibilities. The fact that a person's assets are held in a centre with a zero rate of tax does not necessarily mean that the client himself will be free from tax on those assets. The tax laws where the client is resident must be considered, as indeed should whether the client can enjoy the benefit of, or control, the funds which he has placed offshore.

3.3   The timing of the creation of an offshore structure can also be important. This is particularly the case with individuals who are in the process of moving to a different country, either to live or work. If they transfer their assets offshore before their arrival in the new country, they may save tax which might otherwise be payable on those assets in the new country and at the same time they may also be able to take advantage of allowances to reduce their tax bill in the country which they are leaving.

4   Tax Avoidance v. Tax Evasion

4.1   It is very important that those who are involved with the creation and administration of financial structures be aware of the difference between tax avoidance and tax evasion.

4.2   Tax avoidance is essentially what happens when a taxpayer attempts to reduce a potential tax liability by taking advantage of legislation, exemptions or allowances which are legally available to him. The avoidance of tax is at the heart of legitimate tax planning.

4.3 Tax evasion, on the other hand, is illegal and involves the non-payment of tax which is due and payable. Usually, evasion takes the form of the taxpayer not declaring assets, income or gains which he has received or acquired to the revenue department or authority which has the legal right to receive such information. Never forget that tax evasion is a crime!

4.4 It is unfortunate but also true that offshore centres have been (and are being) used in tax evasion schemes by unscrupulous clients. So too, are onshore centres. However, in the vast majority of cases the financial services provider will not be aware that his client is using his services to further this kind of criminal activity. After all, it is not usually the responsibility, nor indeed the duty, of the service provider to notify the client's tax district of his client's business. In the majority of situations the responsibility to notify rests with the taxpayer.

4.5 If an offshore service provider suspects, or indeed knows, that a potential new client wants to use his services to evade tax then he should not accept the business, as to do so might amount to conspiracy to evade tax on the part of the agent. Indeed, he may be under an obligation to report the intention to evade to the local authorities, depending on the nature of the business which was proposed and whether tax crimes fall within the centre's list of reportable offences.

4.6 There are similar issues to consider if the service provider suspects, or knows, that an existing client is evading tax. Usually, if an offshore centre is a no tax jurisdiction, tax evasion might not be a crime in that location as the concept of 'dual criminality' would not apply (on the basis that if there is not tax payable locally, tax crimes elsewhere would not be recognised). However, the argument of 'dual criminality' not applying should not necessarily be relied upon and it would be fair to suggest that the relationship with the client should be terminated if the client is evading tax.

5 Controlled Foreign Company Legislation

5.1 Some onshore centres tax foreign subsidiaries of local companies if the tax rate in the foreign centre is below a certain level when compared to that of the home country. This is essentially what controlled foreign company (or CFC) legislation attempts to do. For example, in the UK, taxes are levied on the profits of foreign subsidiaries where the foreign rate of tax is less than 75% of that which prevails in the UK.

5.2 Some countries will, however, exempt the profits of a subsidiary if they are taxed in the country in which they are located. This has provided a useful planning opportunity in relation to offshore international companies which many of the European centres can provide. As we shall see later in this study text, such companies can impose a rate of taxation, usually up to 35%, which can, in certain circumstances, prevent tax being levied in the home jurisdiction on the profits of the foreign subsidiary.

6 Double Taxation Treaties

6.1 Finally in this Unit it is worth mentioning the existence and effect of double taxation treaties.

These are tax agreements between two countries which basically allow tax deducted at source from payments from one country to be offset against tax which would otherwise be payable by the taxpayer resident in the other country.

6.2 These treaties determine in which country tax should be payable and ensure that a taxpayer is not assessed to tax twice on the same 'foreign' income. This is particularly useful in relation to the payment of investment income on overseas holdings where withholding tax is deducted at source.

6.3 Without the existence of a double taxation treaty between the country where the company paying the dividend is resident and the country where the investor is resident, it would be difficult, if not impossible, for the investor to set off the tax deducted from his dividend against his local tax liability.

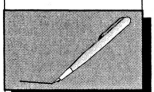

Student Activity 4

How many offshore centres can you name which have negotiated double tax treaties with onshore countries? Compare your list against the one which follows. Were you surprised at the number?

Examples of Offshore Centres Which Have Double Taxation Treaties

6.4 Below is a list of some of the offshore centres which have negotiated double tax treaties with onshore centres. The list is of course subject to change and only a few of the arrangements have been covered. However, the list should provide students with an indication of the importance which some offshore centres have placed on such treaties, and the potential tax planning opportunities which are available for 'treaty shoppers':

BVI	: Switzerland, Japan
Cyprus	: Germany, Russia, Czech Republic, USA, UK
Guernsey	: UK, Jersey
Ireland	: Australia, Canada, Cyprus, France, Germany, India, Japan, USA, UK
Isle of Man	: UK
Jersey	: UK, Guernsey
Labuan	: Australia, Canada, China, France, Germany, USA, UK
Madeira	: Brazil, France, Germany, Italy, Spain, UK
Malta	: Australia, Canada, Germany, India, USA, UK
Mauritius	: China, France, Germany, India, UK
Singapore	: Australia, Canada, China, Germany, Israel, UK
Switzerland	: Australia, Canada, Germany, S. Africa, Spain, UK

Summary

Now that you have read this Unit you should be able to:

● Explain the importance of residence in relation to the taxation of an individual

● Describe the usual criteria applied to determine the residency of an individual

● Describe the concept and effect of domicile

● Outline possible planning opportunities for individuals who are UK resident but not UK domiciled

● List how individuals can be assessed to tax

● Determine the residence of a trust

● Determine the residence of a company

● Describe the usual tax treatment of non-residents in offshore centres

● Describe how offshore companies are generally taxed locally

● Outline the difference between tax evasion and tax avoidance

Self-assessment Questions

1. You are in a meeting with a potential new client who is not sure where he is resident for tax purposes. Explain to the client how his residence might be determined.

2. The same client is unsure of his domicile. Advise him how this would usually be determined.

3. List six types of taxes or duties which an onshore centre might impose.

4. How is the residence of a trust for tax purposes usually determined?

5. Briefly describe the taxation issues which a trustee should consider when planning a distribution of capital from a trust.

6. Explain the effect which the management and control of a company may have on the tax situation of a company and describe how the management and control is usually determined.

7. Briefly describe the usual tax treatment of non-residents in offshore centres.

8. The residence of a trust is usually determined by the residence of the trustees. If a trust is created in an offshore centre which has a system of taxation, and the trustees are resident in that centre, explain the criteria which that trust must meet to enable it to offer possible tax planning benefits.

9. A potential client advises you that he would like to create an offshore structure with the intention of saving tax. He advises you that he does not intend to notify his tax district of the creation of this structure nor does he intend to declare any of the profits which he hopes to derive from it. How would you proceed?

10. Briefly explain what a double taxation treaty is and provide an example of how such a treaty can be of benefit to an investor.

Unit 3

Offshore Banking Services

Objectives

At the end of this Unit you should be able to:

- List five reasons why a bank might decide to open an offshore operation

- List five further considerations a bank might take into account before deciding whether to open an offshore operation

- Describe the possible attractions to clients in opening an offshore bank account

- Briefly explain the different types of banking licences usually available in offshore centres

- Understand and explain what is meant by the term 'managed bank'

- Summarise the usual requirements which a bank must fulfill in order to apply for an unrestricted licence

- Briefly describe the role of the Offshore Group of Banking Supervisors

- Comment on the arguments in support of opening a branch or a subsidiary

- Outline the usual common law confidentiality provisions

- Summarise those circumstances when the bankers' duty of secrecy would not usually be applied

This Unit concentrates on the provision of banking services in offshore centres. There have been many texts written on this very important area of finance and a detailed discussion is outside the scope of this examination subject. However, the practical nature of this course does require us to look at this topic from the perspective of the offshore service provider and we shall therefore concentrate on some of the issues which would affect and directly relate to them. We shall also look at banking confidentiality and how it is generally applied in offshore centres.

1 Considerations and Possible Benefits for Service Providers

1.1 The principle reasons why a bank or similar institution might decide to provide banking services from an offshore centre are as follows:

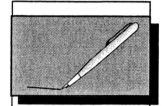

Student Activity 1

Prior to reading the following list, prepare your own schedule of reasons why an offshore banking operation might be more appealing and compare your views with the matters which are covered.

a) There is likely to be a lower rate of taxation on the profits of the bank in the offshore centre;

b) There is likely to be less stringent regulation and supervision compared with that which would usually be imposed in an onshore location;

c) There are occasions when it would be cheaper to operate in an offshore centre rather than in an onshore location. For example, the cost of premises and staff are generally cheaper in, say, the Isle of Man than they are in New York or other onshore capital cities;

d) Most offshore centres have a developed infrastructure and available workforce to support a banking operation.

1.2 In addition to these possible advantages there are other considerations which a service provider might wish to consider before locating a banking operation offshore:

e) The reputation and standing of the offshore centre;

f) The nature and extent of the competition in the centre;

g) Investor protection and the existence of a possible compensation scheme might also affect the decision to locate in a particular centre;

h) The availability and cost of suitable premises;

i) The attitude of the local centre in relation to admitting foreign workers and the ease with which work permits are granted.

At this stage we should, perhaps, quickly cover those features of offshore banking which might appeal to clients.

Possible Attractions for Clients

1.3 a) There is likely to be no tax deducted at source on deposit interest;

b) Some centres have statutory secrecy provisions in place which are in addition to the usual common law provisions which also apply onshore;

c) There is likely to be less stringent regulation and supervision in an offshore centre which might enable the institution to offer higher rates of interest;

d) The offshore banking network contains a large number of internationally known and highly respected institutions;

e)   Some offshore banks do not have operations in onshore centres. This can appeal to clients who suspect that some onshore branches might release information regarding offshore clients to onshore authorities.

2   Supervision of Offshore Banking Operations

2.1   Usually, banks or similar institutions providing banking services will be licenced by a local regulatory body in the offshore centre (such as a Financial Supervision Commission or similar department or section). They will be expected to provide regular reports and financial accounts confirming the nature of the business which they conduct and their financial standing.

Offshore Banking Licences

2.2   Those offshore centres which provide banking services usually offer different types of banking licences.

Domestic unrestricted licences

2.3   These will usually be issued to branches or subsidiaries of first class international banks which have a fully manned operation in the offshore centre. There would not usually be any limitation on the type of banking business which this type of licence holder could undertake. Sometimes such licences are referred to as 'A' licences.

Domestic restricted licenses

2.4   These would usually be issued to banks which only want to deal with banking business for clients who are resident outside the centre where the bank is to operate. The operations which such banks can perform are therefore restricted. Often they are referred to as 'B' licences.

Offshore banking licences (managed banks)

2.5   This type of licence would usually cover the activities of managed banks. These are entities which are permitted to engage in certain restricted types of banking business in the offshore centre under the management of an approved bank which will usually have to be an unrestricted domestic licence holder.

2.6   Usually, a managed bank is not allowed to employ staff, it must operate from the premises of the approved manager and there will be a minimum capital requirement.

2.7   Offshore banking licences may also be unrestricted (allowing deposit taking from clients outside of the centre) or restricted.

Student Activity 2

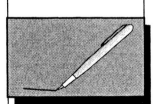

Select two offshore centres (preferably ones which you have had dealings with) and list the types of banking licences which are available in each centre.

Usual licencing requirements

2.8 The local statutory requirements will vary depending upon the type of licence which is issued and also whether the operation is to be a subsidiary or a branch. The following is a list of the criteria which banks wishing to acquire a full, or unrestricted, banking licence must fulfill:

a) There will be a minimum capital requirement (e.g. an authorised share capital of GBP5 million with a paid-up share capital – in cash – of GBP1 million);

b) It must meet the required risk : asset ratio (which the Basle Committee set at 8%, although some centres demand 10%);

c) It must meet the required gearing ratio (which is the ratio between liabilities to depositors and third party creditors, and the capital base), often the maximum ration will be 80 : 1 and the minimum 50 : 1;

d) The bank must produce and file with the regulators audited accounts (and the auditor must be approved by the regulators);

e) There must be adequate internal controls and management information systems in place (this is a 'fit and proper' test);

f) Often there will be requirement that the business of a bank be managed by at least two suitably experienced individuals (commonly referred to as the 'four eyes' test);

g) Changes in the directors or managers of the bank must be notified to the regulators, who may refuse to accept such changes;

h) Details of proposed charges over the banks assets must be notified to the regulators;

i) Regular reports on the financial standing and operation of the bank must also be submitted to the regulators;

j) Bank licences will usually be renewable annually.

Student Activity 3

Using the two centres which you researched in Student Activity 2, list the bank licencing requirements which both have in place. How do they compare with each other (and also the above mentioned list)?

3 Regulation of Offshore Banking Operations

General Cross Border Regulation

3.1 In the light of the Basle Committee findings following the BCCI collapse cross border regulation has increased making it possible and easier for information to be passed between regulators in different centres. This has helped the authorities to have a better understanding of the activities of institutions which are operating from more than one location.

3.2 There is a restriction on the type of information which can be divulged and usually this would be restricted to information which would enable the regulator to do his job and to prevent possible problems occurring. Any information which is released to outside regulators must remain confidential and be used only for regulatory purposes.

Offshore Cross Border Regulation and Supervision

3.3 The Offshore Group of Banking Supervisors was created in 1980 with its principal aim being to improve the supervisory systems and the general exchange of information which occurs offshore.

3.4 This Group currently has 19 members and includes centres such as the Bahamas, Bermuda, the Cayman Islands, Cyprus, Gibraltar, Guernsey, Hong Kong, the Isle of Man, Jersey and Singapore. Through discussions and mutual agreement it has helped its members to identify and clarify such matters as:

i) What information should be exchanged with onshore authorities;

ii) How to prevent money laundering and the use of offshore banks for criminal purposes generally;

iii) The importance of the role of external auditors in assisting with supervision;

iv) The criteria to be applied to assess a bank's financial position.

3.5 Only those centres which can show that they have implemented suitable legislation and controls in relation to regulatory issues are allowed to be admitted to this Group.

Offshore Depositor Protection

3.6 The UK has legislation in place which is designed to provide depositors with a level of protection should the bank or building society where they have deposited their funds become insolvent. However, this protection will not necessarily extend to offshore branches or subsidiaries of UK banks or building societies. (The differences between establishing a branch or a subsidiary in an offshore centre are covered later in this Section.)

3.7 Depositor protection is essentially a matter for the regulatory authorities in offshore jurisdictions and generally there is no cover available. However, an exception to this is the Isle of Man which has its own compensation scheme.

3.8 There are a number of possible reasons why a centre might decide not to provide a compensation scheme to investors but usually the main reason is the objections which the service providers themselves may have. After all, they will be expected to contribute to the scheme to cover possible claims, and if the industry was properly regulated (as most are) there would be no need for a scheme to be implemented as investors would be protected under the licencing requirements.

4 Choosing Between an Offshore Branch or Offshore Subsidiary

4.1 It can be a difficult process to decide whether a bank or similar financial institution should establish an offshore branch or a subsidiary. There are sound arguments in support of both options and the following is a summary of the main points which merit consideration:

a) Offshore regulators will usually be happy to accept the level and standard of the regulatory and supervisory controls of a branch of a bank from a major onshore centre (such as the UK) as they will be aware that in most cases the regulations and controls in place will be based on detailed requirements and legislation;

b) A branch may create taxation advantages in the early stages as start-up costs could be offset against the group's profits;

c) Onshore systems and technology could be employed in an offshore branch;

d) After start-up it might be advantageous to create a subsidiary so as to enable the profits to be assessed to tax locally. In addition, there may be tax benefits if a subsidiary remitted funds to its onshore parent by way of dividend rather than by a branch remitting funds back to an onshore parent.

5 Banking Confidentiality and Reporting

Common Law Provisions

5.1 Under common law, confidentiality may be regarded as arising in the following circumstances:

i) By virtue of an express contract;

ii) By virtue of a special relationship such as between a client and his lawyer or accountant;

iii) By virtue of the law of tort under which, for example, information with commercial value can, under certain circumstances, be protected.

These provisions are generally applied in offshore centres by banks and other financial institutions.

Banker's Duty of Secrecy

5.2 The basic duties of a bank were set out in the case of *Tournier v. National Provincial and Union Bank of England* (1924). This case established that the relationship between a banker and his client gave rise to a legal duty of confidence which involved non-disclosure of the client's affairs even after an account has been closed.

5.3 However, this duty would not apply in the following circumstances:

i) By virtue of an express rule of law, such as a court order or a statute such as the UK's Criminal Justice Act;

ii) Where there is a public duty to disclose, which would occur in cases of serious crime such as money laundering, drug trafficking, etc;

iii) Where the interests of the bank would require disclosure, such as a situation where a bank might sue a customer and state how much the customer owes in the writ;

iv) Where the client provides the bank with an expressed or implied authority to disclose, such as providing references or status enquiries.

5.4 The findings in the *Tournier Case* are also relevant to offshore banks. Indeed, there was a case in the Cayman Islands (the matter of *ABC Limited* [1985] FLR 159) which raised an issue concerning the consent required to release information. In that case it was held that a consent to the release of information had to be given voluntarily and freely in the exercise of an independent and uncoerced judgement. It was also held that a foreign court should not be permitted to obtain confidential information so as to undermine the Cayman Islands' statutory confidentiality provisions.

Statutory Confidentiality Provisions in Offshore Centres

5.5 Most advisers would probably think of the Cayman Islands when asked to recommend a centre which has statutory client protection. Under its Confidential Relationships (Preservation) Law 1976 (amended 1979), anyone who is in possession of confidential client information commits a criminal offence if it is divulged to any person who is not entitled to it. It is also an offence to make use of such information without the client's consent for one's own benefit or for the benefit of another.

5.6 The Bahamas, BVI and Gibraltar are examples of other centres which have similar provisions.

Student Activity 4

Returning again to the two centres which you selected for student Activities 2 and 3, find out the local provisions for client confidentiality and secrecy and compare them with the topics which have been covered in the previous section. How do you rate those centres in this area?

Setting Aside of Confidentiality Provisions Offshore

5.7 It is a common misconception amongst many clients and some onshore advisers that client information cannot be released by an offshore bank or service provider. It is generally true that it is harder to obtain information from offshore jurisdictions and as has already been discussed, some centres have passed legislation which can make it a criminal offence for a bank to divulge client information.

5.8 However, in certain circumstances client information can be released and the *Tournier Case* provides a useful summary of these instances. These have already been covered earlier in this Unit but it might be useful to return to a couple of the most common reasons why confidentiality can be broken.

By virtue of an express rule of law
5.9 Many centres have introduced legislation which has been based on the UK's Drug Trafficking Offences Act 1986 and the UK's Criminal Justice Act 1988.

5.10 If a warrant or similar court order is served on a bank in those centres, then under their respective local drug trafficking legislation information must be provided to the police or other specified authority. The release of such information would not be treated as a contravention of the usual contractual confidentiality obligations imposed in common law (such as those which are found in relation to client agreements etc.).

Where there is a public duty to disclose
5.11 If a client is suspected of being involved in serious crime, such as drug trafficking, serious and large scale fraud or terrorism, and a warrant or similar court order is served on it, the bank is under a duty to release information relating to that client to the police or other specified authority.

5.12 In some instances, a bank might receive a request for information from onshore investigators based on a suspicion that a particular client might have connections or dealings with serious crime. The bank might be asked to exercise its judgement on the basis that it would be in the public interest to disclose information relating to that client.

5.13 This is a difficult area for the bank, as releasing details without the authorisation of a court order could contravene the common law secrecy provisions as well as any local secrecy legislation which is in place. In such a situation it would be usual for the bank to refuse such a request and instead suggest that if the investigator has sufficient proof he should obtain the necessary court order.

We return to money laundering in Unit 5.

Summary

Now that you have read this Unit you should be able to:

● Describe the potential advantages to a bank in opening an offshore operation

● List the considerations a bank might have in deciding whether to open an offshore operation

● Describe the usual benefits to clients in opening an offshore bank account

● Describe the different types of banking licences usually available in offshore centres

● Explain what a 'managed bank' is

● Understand the requirements a bank would usually be expected to fulfill in order to apply for an unrestricted licence

● Outline the role of the Offshore Group of Banking Supervisors

● Comment on the arguments in support of a bank opening a branch or a subsidiary in an offshore centre

● Outline the usual confidentiality provisions under common law

● Explain, with examples, the circumstances when a bankers' duty of secrecy would not usually be required to be enforced.

Self-assessment Questions

1. Write brief notes on the possible benefits which a bank might experience by opening a banking operation in an offshore centre.

2. Briefly describe the attractions to a client of opening and maintaining an offshore bank account.

3. Describe the main differences between a domestic licence, restricted licence and an offshore licence.

4. List five of the requirements which a bank would usually be expected to fulfill in order for it to apply for an unrestricted banking licence.

5. Outline the purpose of cross border regulation.

6. Summarise the role of the Offshore Group of Banking Supervisors and list five of the members of this Group.

7. Under common law, describe how confidentiality is usually regarded as arising.

8. Briefly describe the bankers' duty of secrecy and name the legal case in which it was defined.

9. Provide two examples of situations where the bankers' duty of secrecy would not be expected to apply.

10. Name two offshore centres which have implemented confidentiality provisions under local statute and summarise the level of protection afforded.

Unit 4

Offshore Captive Insurance, Limited Partnerships and Ship Registration

Objectives

At the end of this Unit you should be able to:

- Describe the usual purpose and activities of a captive insurance company
- List five usual advantages associated with an offshore captive
- Explain the usual benefits of an offshore managed captive
- Outline how offshore captives are generally regulated
- Describe the usual structure of a limited partnership
- Comment on the usual tax treatment of an offshore limited partnership
- Outline at least two possible uses of an offshore limited partnership
- Define the term 'flag of convenience'
- List four possible advantages of registering a ship offshore
- Briefly outline the usual process of registering a ship

In this Unit we look at the provision of captive insurance services, limited partnerships and ship registration in offshore centres.

It should be pointed out that none of the services which are covered in this Unit are specifically mentioned in the syllabus, although students should be familiar with the various types of entity that can be operated offshore.

In due course the syllabus will be re-written to include specific reference to the topics which we shall be covering here but in the meantime, all that students will be required to know is the basic operation of, as well as the usual advantages (and potential disadvantages) associated with, these particular services.

1 Captive Insurance Companies

Purpose of a Captive Insurance Company

1.1 A captive insurance company is a corporate entity, usually a private insurance company, which is created and controlled by either a parent company, a professional association or a group of businesses. The purpose of the captive insurance company will be to provide insurance for that parent company, professional association or group of businesses against certain risks.

1.2   The risks which will be insured will usually relate to the business of the parent company etc. and the captive will usually accept the insurance from the parent or association and then pass some of the risk to a reinsurer. This is because captives are usually only authorised to deal with small amounts of risk, whereas reinsurers are able to spread the risks which they accept.

1.3   Captives can also be used to provide general risk insurance for their parents and can be used to cover insurance needs such as those required in the travel business, to cover against bad debts, and to provide professional indemnity cover.

Offshore Bases

1.4   Not all offshore centres are suitable bases from which to establish and provide captive insurance company services. Generally, it is only those centres which have introduced specific insurance legislation and regulation which should be considered (e.g. Bermuda, the Cayman Islands, Dublin, Guernsey, the Isle of Man and Luxembourg).

Student Activity 1

Before you read the next section, write a list of the possible benefits of creating a captive insurance company in an offshore centre. Try to base this list on the purpose of captives (covered above) and the general advantages of offshore financial services (covered earlier in this study text).

Possible Benefits of an Offshore Captive Insurance Company

1.5   There are a variety of reasons why an offshore captive insurance company might be chosen although the following are the most commonly quoted:

Cost savings

1.6   A captive can reduce insurance expenditure as this method of cover is often cheaper to arrange than commercial insurance. This is because all of the group's insurance can be arranged by the one entity which is usually more cost-effective than having each part of the group making their own arrangements. Greater economies of scale are therefore possible.

1.7   In addition, this type of cover provides access to the wholesale insurance market and as a result there are no marketing or sales fees to pay, which are often built into the premiums paid under conventional insurance arrangements.

1.8   Premiums which are also due to the captive can be settled at a time and in a manner which best suits the parent company or group as a whole.

1.9   It is also more economical to hold the cash within the group which would otherwise have been paid to cover commercial insurance premiums.

1.10 Finally, some risks are also very expensive to cover under conventional insurance policies and captives provide a relatively inexpensive alternative.

Centralisation of risk management
1.11 As the captive will usually be part of an organisation or group, it provides the opportunity to centralise risk management and for the organisation to review or formulate its central policy on risk.

To provide cover against risks
1.12 Captives can be used to provide cover which is not currently in place (as an alternative to conventional insurance arrangements). They can also be used to provide cover which conventional policies will not cover (such as high risk activities or natural disasters, strikes, war, product recall or pollution).

Cash flow
1.13 Those captives which reinsure a portion of the risk usually do not have to pay a premium to the reinsurance agent in advance as it would generally only be required to pay on an 'earned' basis. This enables the captive to retain the use of the cash it has received in respect of its premium income which aids its cash flow situation. Such monies can also be invested which should increase its returns. In addition, the payment of premiums can also be delayed by the parent so as to further improve its cash flow situation.

Tailoring of insurance cover
1.14 A captive insurance company can enable an organisation to arrange and provide cover which is tailored to its particular needs.

Clarity of legislation
1.15 It is generally true to say that the insurance legislation which most offshore centres have introduced is clear and concise. There will be less onerous reporting and regulatory requirements than those which are applied to onshore insurance companies enabling the managers to conduct their business affairs in a much more flexible manner.

Taxation
1.16 This possible advantage has been left until last as taxation should not in itself be a reason for deciding to establish a captive insurance company. Other considerations (as we have discussed above) should be the driving forces in determining whether a company should create a captive insurance operation.

1.17 Having said that, there can be taxation benefits which are associated with such an operation as the following indicates.

a) The insurance premiums paid by the parent to its offshore captive could be tax deductible in the parent's 'home' country;

b) A captive would not normally be assessed to tax in the offshore centre on the premiums received from the parent company, nor would it be liable to tax on any capital gains which are realised on the sale of assets purchased with the premium income;

c) Surplus income and capital gains built up by a captive could be returned to the parent company at a time which would be tax advantageous to the parent company.

Possible Disadvantages of an Offshore Captive
Cost

1.18 Although a captive can save costs in the long-term it can be an expensive option in the short-term as it would not only have to be funded by the parent company but it would also usually have to be capitalised.

1.19 The captive will also have to be fully resourced, although we shall return to this point
   - when we look at managed captives in a later Section of this Unit.

Risk

1.20 Although it is possible to limit the risk to the captive insurance company by passing some risk to the reinsurer, it is still exposed to claims which may arise, and as a result, the captive should try to limit risks to those where a good claims record has been previously achieved and is contemplated.

Fiscal restraints

1.21 Some onshore centres have legislation in place which is designed to restrict the taxation benefits offered by captives in offshore centres. In some countries, for example, local taxation is levied on some insurance premiums which are paid to overseas insurance companies which do not have a place of business in that country.

Offshore regulation

1.22 Generally, the regulation of offshore captive insurance companies is not as onerous as the regulation of onshore insurance business. This can be an advantage as it enables the captive to be more flexible in terms of its business undertakings, but it can also be a major problem if the parent or group is too flexible in its approach to the risks which it wants the captive to take on board.

Managed captives

1.23 There are two alternatives to setting up a captive insurance operation in an offshore centre. The group or parent could either set up its own operation in an offshore centre or it could instead decide to have its operation managed by an insurance broker which is resident in an offshore centre.

1.24 Having a 'real' presence can be expensive and can also create administration problems, such as how to move experienced staff into the offshore centre to service the proposed business. It is therefore common practice for captives to be managed in an offshore centre by a local agent.

1.25 The agent appointed to manage the captive operation must be carefully chosen and although there is a wide choice in some centres, in others there are only a few service providers who one would consider as suitable. It is essential that, as with other types of agent, the manager of the captive is an experienced and reputable service provider with the resources to handle both the type and volume of work which is envisaged.

1.26 Costs can often be reduced by using a manager as the agent will already have the structure, premises, equipment, expertise, experience and staff in place to handle the business, thus saving the capital costs which would have been incurred if a captive operation had been started from scratch.

Regulation and Supervision of Offshore Captives

1.27 A growing number of offshore centres have introduced legislation which governs the provision of insurance-related services and such legislation will generally cover the creation and administration of captives.

1.28 Each centre will have their own particular requirements but generally the following areas will usually be covered in the captive insurance regulations.

i) An application will have to be made to the local regulatory authority (e.g. the Insurance Supervisor) to create a captive insurance company. Usually, only a locally incorporated company can apply, but sometimes a request can be made on behalf of a company which is to be incorporated in the offshore centre concerned.

ii) The company wishing to conduct captive insurance business must meet certain capital requirements (which could range from between GBP50,000 to in excess of GBP250,000 in respect of the issued share capital required).

iii) A business plan (usually covering at least three years) must be prepared and sent to the regulatory authority and contain such information as the type of insurance to be arranged, projected cash flows as well as details of the owners of the company which is to provide the captive services.

iv) There will usually be a requirement to prove that the directors and officers are 'fit and proper' to act and that they have the technical experience and competence to undertake the positions to which they are to be appointed. Resident directors may also be a requirement.

v) Regular reports and accounts may have to be submitted to the regulatory authority and there may also be a requirement that accounting details be kept in the offshore centre.

vi) Annual accounts would usually have to be prepared and audited locally.

vii) Certain liquidity requirements will usually have to be met to ensure that the company remains solvent.

viii) A licence will usually be issued to those service providers or companies who are authorised to conduct captive insurance business (including those who act as managers of managed captives). Often the licence will be restricted solely to the provision of this type of insurance business.

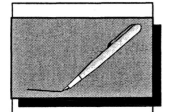

Student Activity 2

Select an offshore centre which has an active captive insurance sector and compare the regulatory requirements with those covered in the above mentioned section. How do they compare/contrast?

2   Limited Partnerships

Nature of a Partnership

2.1   A partnership is a type of business entity which is usually formed when two or more persons wish to carry on a business together with a view to making a profit. Although the same reason could exist for establishing a company, the individuals concerned will have decided that the features and benefits of a partnership structure would best suit their needs.

Types of Partnerships

There are essentially two types of partnerships:

General partnerships

2.2   These are perhaps the most commonly used type of partnership and are popular mainly in onshore jurisdictions. Each partner will be involved with the day-to-day running of the firm and each will be responsible for the actions of the others. The partners will all be personally liable for the debts of the partnership without limit.

Limited partnerships

2.3   This type of partnership is becoming increasingly popular in offshore centres. They can be structured with two types of partners, namely:

a)   Limited Partners who take a passive role in the firm and their liability is limited to such amounts as are set out in the partnership deed (which will usually be the amount they contributed to the partnership funds); and

b)   General Partners who will be the partners who manage the firm and whose liability will be unlimited. General partners are often referred to as managing partners.

The Structure and Possible Taxation Benefits of Offshore Limited Partnerships

2.4   Generally speaking, a partnership is not assessed to tax but instead it is the individual partners who will be issued with assessments in respect of their shares of the income and profits of the partnership. A partnership is therefore transparent for tax purposes; it does not exist as a taxable entity as the liabilities and profits would be attached to the individual partners.

2.5   A number of offshore centres (such as Jersey, the Isle of Man and the Cayman Islands) have introduced legislation which allows a partnership to be formed which can be comprised of limited partners as well as general partners. The limited partners would not be involved in the day-to-day business of the partnership and may be non-resident individuals, non-resident companies, international companies (or whatever the local equivalent may be), or a combination of any of the aforementioned.

2.6 The general partner will often be a locally incorporated resident company which has a resident director (and in some cases a suitably qualified company secretary). In those centres which impose taxation on corporate entities, it would be usual for such a company to be permitted to apply for tax-exempt status (or the equivalent tax status) in the offshore centre concerned.

2.7 A limited partnership would usually be treated as a separate entity for tax purposes and in those centres which have corporation tax, would be able to pay a nominal fee to the local tax authority or relevant government authority in exchange for local tax exemption. In some centres this fee can be as little as £300 per annum. In centres which impose no direct taxation, an annual 'registration' fee would be payable instead.

2.8 Partners of locally established limited partnerships would not be assessed to local tax on their share of the profits and in addition, no withholding taxes would be payable on distributions made to non-resident partners, nor would those partners be subject to any non-resident tax.

2.9 The limited partnership would not normally be permitted to carry on certain prescribed activities in the offshore centre, which would cover such activities as manufacturing and undertaking banking or investment business.

2.10 Not all offshore centres have specific legislation which covers the use of limited partnerships as international planning vehicles although the number of centres which do allow such entities is growing.

Formation of Limited Partnerships

2.11 Although the formation procedure will vary between centres, the following is a list of the usual paperwork which is required to be lodged with the Registrar of Companies (or similar department) to create a limited partnership in those offshore centres which permit this type of vehicle:

a) A copy of the partnership deed;

b) Confirmation of the name of the partnership and the intended location of its registered address (which must be in the offshore centre concerned);

c) The full names and addresses of the general partners;

d) The full names and addresses of the limited partners;

e) Details of the contributions which are to be made by the limited partners;

f) A declaration that the partnership will not conduct business locally in the offshore centre where it is registered.

The paperwork must also be accompanied by the required filing fee, the amount of which will again vary between centres.

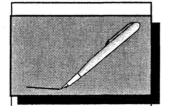

Student Activity 3

Select two offshore centres which have legislation in place which covers the creation and administration of limited partnerships and compare the formation requirements in both centres and also against the above mentioned list.

Annual Requirements

2.12 Usually, a limited partnership must file an annual return with the Registrar (or equivalent) which contains the same type of information that is required on registration, plus a declaration that the partnership has not undertaken business locally. There will also be an annual fee (as we have already mentioned).

Limited Partnerships as Investment Vehicles

2.13 A limited partnership can be used as a vehicle for collective investment schemes in much the same way as a unit trust or an open-ended investment company.

2.14 The investors would become the limited partners (rather than shareholders) and the manager of the scheme would be the general partner. The limited partners would share in the profits (or losses) of the scheme whilst the general partner would receive a fee for managing the funds.

2.15 The tax transparency of the partnership, which would result in any realised gains or losses being treated as the gains or losses of the limited partners, would also create further planning opportunities. For example, the partnership could be used as an 'investment' vehicle by a group of international corporate investors wishing to 'pool' their exposure to high risk investments (such as venture capital schemes or derivatives). By using a tax efficient offshore vehicle in such a manner it could allow them to offset any realised gains or losses against other gains or losses made as a result of their other business activities.

2.16 Another feature which would appeal to those wishing to use a limited partnership as an investment vehicle, is the fact that there is no limit imposed on the number of partners.

Limited Partnerships as Asset Protection Vehicles

2.17 A number of advisers, particularly those in the USA, have marketed the limited partnership as an asset protection vehicle. This has proved to be popular with those clients who are unfamiliar with, or dislike, the common law trust concept.

2.18 Usually, the structure comprises an offshore trust which receives assets from the client. The trustees then enter into a limited partnership whose general partner will be a company which is beneficially owned or otherwise controlled by the client. The client is therefore able to exercise some control over the assets in the structure. However, one of the potential problems which this sort of arrangement could create is the fact that the client could be deemed to have the management and control over the trust property which could undermine the possible benefits.

Limited Partnerships as a Type of Trust

2.19   Finally, offshore limited partnerships can also be used as a type of trust, employing a structure which is similar to the way limited partnerships can be used as an investment fund. Assets would be transferred into the partnership and the limited partners would receive a share of the profits. They would be the 'beneficiaries' of the structure. The general partner would control the timing of the distributions and he would also manage the assets. He would therefore be the 'trustee'.

Limited Liability Partnerships

2.20   Before we leave the subject of limited partnerships, we should briefly mention a variation of this type of vehicle known as a limited liability partnership (LLP).

2.21   Although an LLP retains many of the features of a traditional limited partnership, liability is restricted to the assets of the partnership and the individual partners will not be personally liable for any of the debts of the LLP.

2.22   Such a vehicle can create advantages for partners in law firms and in the accountancy profession. It remains to be seen whether the limited liability aspect will receive widespread acceptance from the regulators of such professions.

2.23   Jersey is an example of an offshore centre which offers LLPs.

3   Ship Registration in Offshore Centres

3.1   Ship registration and also ship management are very specialised areas and a detailed discussion of the rules and requirements is outside the scope of this course. However, students should be aware of the reasons why offshore centres are regularly used as a location to register ships as well as some of the basic administration issues which service providers should be aware of.

Flags of Convenience

3.2   This is a term which is often applied to those offshore centres which provide facilities for ships to be registered in their jurisdiction. In general terms, a 'flag of convenience' is often used to describe the situation where a vessel is registered in a country or state which is not the country or state where it was originally built or registered.

3.3   Ship owners therefore have the option to choose the laws and regulations of another marine administration rather than be governed by those of their 'home' country.

3.4   However, by the same token there is also the possibility that the centre chosen to register the ship will not have the same level of safety standards or manning requirements, etc. which would generally be expected by shipping unions and safety watchdogs.

3.5   A large number of offshore centres now have their own shipping registers and the following are some of those which can be used for this type of business: the Bahamas, Bermuda, BVI, the Cayman Islands, Cyprus, Gibraltar, Isle of Man, Liberia, Madeira, Malta, Netherlands Antilles, Panama, Singapore and Vanuatu.

3.6   With the exception of the Isle of Man, all of the above centres are generally considered to offer flags of convenience.

Possible Benefits of Offshore Ship Registers

3.7   There are a number of possible reasons why it might be advantageous to register a ship in an offshore centre but the following are perhaps the most commonly quoted:

Confidentiality

3.8   The ownership of the vessel could remain confidential.

To avoid political problems in home country

3.9   Offshore centres are usually free from any political unrest or problems whereas many onshore centres experience political situations which could have an effect on the reputation and also the security of the ships which are registered under those flags.

To circumvent local legal issues

3.10   Some countries demand that a certain percentage of the crew and officers be nationals of the home country. This would generally mean that local employment conditions must be applied (such as a minimum wage and maximum hours) which could be expensive for the ship owners to maintain. Generally, offshore ship registers impose no requirements in relation to the nationality of, or terms and conditions imposed on, the crews which ships employ.

Taxation

3.11   There could be taxation benefits on the basis that the offshore centre will be a no or low tax centre. In addition, some centres have double taxation agreements in place with certain onshore countries which might create planning opportunities in relation to the cost of building a vessel.

Lower costs

3.12   It is often cheaper to register a ship offshore and usually the management costs will be less than those charged onshore.

Potential Problems of Offshore Ship Registration
Relaxed safety regulations

3.13   Some perceive an offshore shipping register to be an attempt to compromise safety and quality for possible tax benefits. This should not of course be the case although some workers' unions do boycott ships which fly a flag of convenience.

Insurance

3.14   Some insurance companies might be concerned that the local management and regulations in place in offshore centres (especially in terms of seaworthiness) will not be as stringent as those which are imposed in the more 'recognised' ship registers. Some might refuse to provide cover for ships registered offshore.

Registration Procedures

3.15   The following is a summary of the type of requirements which must usually be met before a ship can be registered in an offshore centre. Usually, this information must be provided to the local Registrar of Ships (or equivalent):

i)   The name (or proposed name) of the ship;

ii)   A certificate of survey detailing the parameters of the ship (type of ship, size, tonnage etc.);

iii) Evidence of title of ownership;

iv) If the ship has not been registered previously, a copy of the Builder's Certificate will usually be required;

v) Details of the current registry (if applicable);

vi) The proposed use of the ship;

vii) Details of the company which owns (or is to own) the ship, such as a copy of the certificate of incorporation and full names and addresses of the directors and officers. Some centres allow limited partnerships to be registered as ship owners and details of the structure of the partnership would have to be provided;

viii) Payment of the fees to the appropriate government department.

Student Activity 4

Compare and contrast the registration procedures of two offshore centres which encourage ship registration. Also try to find out how many ships are registered in each centre and comment on why one is more popular than the other.

Local Ownership

3.16   There will usually be a requirement that ships which are registered in an offshore centre must be owned (at least in majority) by a local company.

3.17   Those centres which are classified as British Dependent Territories (i.e. Bermuda, BVI, the Cayman Islands, Gibraltar and the Isle of Man) usually allow ships to be registered locally which are either owned by a local company or are instead owned by a company which has been incorporated in any of the other British Dependent Territories.

Local Management

3.18   Often there will be a requirement that the functions of effective management of locally registered ships be undertaken by a ship management company which is based in that centre.

Summary

Now that you have read this Unit you should be able to:

- Outline the usual purpose and activities of a captive insurance company

- Comment on the usual advantages associated with an offshore captive

- Explain the role and benefits of an offshore managed captive

- Describe the regulation of offshore captives

- Describe how a limited partnership would usually be structured

- Explain how an offshore limited partnership would usually be treated for tax purposes

- Outline at least two possible uses of an offshore limited partnership

- Explain what is meant by the term 'flag of convenience'

- List four possible advantages of offshore ship registration

- Outline the usual requirements to register a ship in an offshore centre.

Self-assessment questions

1. Describe, in general terms, the purpose of a captive insurance company.

2. 'Taxation saving is the prime reason why multinational corporations create offshore captive insurance companies.' Discuss.

3. One of your clients is considering creating an offshore captive but he is unsure whether he could afford to set up a fully staffed operation. What advice could you give him?

4. Prepare a list detailing the type of information which would usually be required to enable a captive insurance company to be created in an offshore centre.

5. Compare and contrast the roles of the general partners with those of a limited partner in a limited partnership structure.

6. Briefly describe the usual taxation treatment of a limited partnership which has been created in an offshore centre.

7. Explain how a limited partnership could be used as an investment vehicle.

8. Describe what is meant by the expression 'a flag of convenience' and list five offshore centres which have been categorised as offering this type of service.

9. List five possible reasons why it might be beneficial to register a ship in an offshore centre.

10. List the information which is usually required to register a ship in an offshore centre.

46

Unit 5

Money Laundering and its Prevention in Offshore Centres

Objectives

At the end of this Unit you should be able to:

- Describe the various stages of money laundering

- Provide an example of how banking services might be used for laundering funds

- Provide an example of how corporate services might be at risk from money launderers

- List five investment transactions which might arouse suspicion that a client is laundering money

- Describe the main proposals suggested by the Basle Committee in 1988

- Comment on the purpose of FATF and the Caribbean Financial Action Task Force

- List the usual information which a service provider would require about an individual who wishes to open an offshore account

- List the usual information required by a service provider to open a trust

- Understand the usual reporting requirements

- Be aware of the usual penalties which exist if convicted of money laundering activities

Those of you who are employed in the finance sector in an offshore centre will have a legal obligation to be on your guard against money lauderers. As we shall see later in this Unit, the duties which are expected can be exercised in a variety of ways and failure to do so could make you personally liable to criminal conviction.

Take the time to familiarise yourself with the anti-money laundering provisions and laws which exist in your centre (or in a centre with which you have a close connection). They are there, amongst other things, for your protection!

1 Definition

1.1 Money laundering can generally be defined as the procedures and actions which are carried out to alter the identity of illegally obtained funds and to make it appear that they have been received from a legitimate source. It is a criminal's way of transferring the proceeds of criminal activities back into in the financial system (usually the banking system) in an attempt to make 'dirty money' look as though it has come from legitimate activities.

1.2 When referring to money laundering, most people will automatically think of the movement of proceeds derived from the illegal drug trade. Although drug trafficking is perhaps the main activity which recent anti-money laundering legislation has attempted to stem, students should be aware that laundering and anti-laundering measures have also been extended to other criminal activities such as terrorism, serious fraud, extortion and kidnapping. Some centres have also introduced laws which categorise tax offences, notably tax evasion, as criminal activities which also come within the money laundering net.

1.3 Those of you who deal with business from South Africa might also be advised to consider the fact that exchange control violations are a criminal offence in South Africa and as a result, moving cash illegally out of South Africa might constitute money laundering in those countries which have widened the definition of laundering to extend to all (or most) crimes.

1.4 Similarly, many people believe that money laundering is an 'offshore problem' affecting a few centres, most noticeably those which are located in the Caribbean. This is not the case. Money laundering is a world-wide problem, the size and extent of which should not be underestimated. Did you know, for example, that one estimate has put the amount of funds which are laundered each year at between GBP200 and GBP325 billion?

1.5 Leading onshore financial centres, such as London and New York, are perhaps more obvious targets for the launderers as the amount of funds which pass through their markets and institutions each and every day makes it much harder for sophisticated crimes to be spotted and reported. However, that is not to say that the criminals do not widely use (or try to use) offshore institutions, because they do.

1.6 Indeed, some offshore centres (which shall remain nameless) have until recent years been a virtual haven for the launderers, and have built their finance sectors on a general 'no questions asked' philosophy to international business. Fortunately, times have changes and so too have the attitudes of the regulators and service providers. Often you will find that the criteria to open an account in some offshore centres is more onerous than that which is imposed onshore!

1.7 Nevertheless, the threat of the launderers is never far away and in this Unit we shall look at how criminals might use offshore financial services to launder their criminal proceeds and also what steps have been, and can be, taken to reduce this problem.

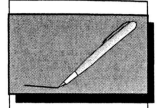

Student Activity 1

Write down what you understand to be the stages of money laundering to be and compare them with the list which follows. Of the stages which you mentioned, which one do you think is the easiest and which is the hardest for administrators to detect?

2   The Stages of Money Laundering

2.1   Money laundering is transaction-based and there are three stages in the process:

Placement

2.2   This stage is the physical disposal of the cash proceeds which have been received from the illegal activity (e.g. paying the cash into a bank account).

Layering

2.3   This stage involves creating a complex layer of financial transactions in order to hide the true identity of the source of the funds (e.g. instructing the bank to wire the funds to an account with another bank and then instructing that second bank to transfer the funds on again).

Integration

2.4   If the layering stage has been a success, the illegally obtained funds will now be integrated into the financial system and will appear to be legitimate funds.

3   Offshore Services at Risk from Criminal Activities

3.1   It is a sad fact that all financial services are at risk from the money launderers. The following are examples of how certain offshore services could be abused by the criminals.

Banking Services

3.2   A bank account is perhaps the prime target for criminals. After all, this is the vehicle through which transactions are passed, such as wire payments, bank drafts and also the receipt of funds.

3.3   Lending facilities are also open to attack. For example, illegal funds might be deposited as collateral against new borrowing and the borrowed funds might then be used to purchase goods or other assets. The illegally obtained funds which were being held as collateral could then be used to repay the loan, thus layering and possibly integrating the funds.

3.4   Letters of credit in international trading operations might also be a potential target in the laundering process, as too might the purchase of travellers cheques.

Trust Services

3.5   A person might try to launder funds by creating a trust. Placement would occur if illegally earned cash was handed to the trustees or if assets which had been purchased using illegally obtained cash (such as investments or realty) were transferred to the trustees. Subsequent distributions of trust property to the beneficiaries would complete the integration of the funds back into the banking system.

Corporate Services

3.6 Offshore private limited companies could also be used as money laundering vehicles. Particular care should be exercised by service providers in relation to trading companies (a classic front for a money laundering scam) as in some cases large receipts of funds and subsequent onward payments would not be uncommon, or indeed unexpected.

3.7 Cash or assets could also be transferred into a company, perhaps by way of a loan from the beneficial owner, and then lent on or perhaps used to purchase investments or other assets. This would effectively layer the proceeds or even integrate them back into the financial system.

Investment Services

3.8 Investments (such as stocks and shares) could be purchased using illegally obtained funds and once the holding has been sold, the proceeds would be integrated back into the system.

Collective Investment Schemes

3.9 Such services could be used in a similar manner as that covered in 3.8 above in that a client could invest in an offshore investment fund using the profits from his criminal activities.

Insurance Services

3.10 Insurance based services can also be acquired or created by using illegally obtained funds. Once the insurance provider has received the funds and issued a policy or similar product the illegal funds would have been placed and integrated into the financial system.

4   Examples of Suspicious Transactions

4.1 Now that we have established that all offshore financial services are at risk from money launderers we should look at some examples of transactions or requests for services which should alert the diligent administrator that a client might be attempting to launder money.

4.2 This is not to say, of course, that if a client does conduct any of the following transactions he is involved in a criminal activity. Nor is the list exhaustive. However, as the saying goes, 'forewarned is forearmed' and the following list is only an indication of when the warning bells should start to sound.

Cash Transactions

4.3 The following are examples of how cash might be being launderered:

a) Unusually large cash deposits are made by an individual or company, whose main business activities would usually only generate cheques or other instruments;

b)   There are substantial increases in cash deposits of an individual or a business, without apparent reason. Such deposits may subsequently be transferred within a short period out of the account and/or to a destination which is not normally associated with the customer;

c)   A customer deposits cash by means of numerous credit slips so that although the total of each deposit is unremarkable, the total of all the credits is significant;

d)   A customer constantly deposits cash to cover requests for bankers drafts, money transfers or other negotiable money instruments;

e)   A customer seeks to exchange large quantities of low denomination notes for those of a higher denomination;

f)   A customer frequently exchanges cash into other currencies;

g)   A customer transfers large sums of money to or from overseas and then requests that the funds be collected in cash.

Student Activity 2

Before proceeding, make a list of the ways in which you think a bank account could be used to launder money and compare them with the danger signs quoted below.

Bank Transactions

4.4   The following transactions across a customer's bank account might arouse suspicion:

a)   The customer wants to maintain a number of trustee or clients' accounts which are not consistent with the type of business which he has conducted in the past;

b)   The customer has numerous accounts and pays in amounts of cash to each of them to hide the total of the credits (which when viewed in isolation would not be a large amount but when added together are substantial);

c)   An individual or company whose account shows little or no business-related activities, receives or disburses large sums which bear no relation to the previous activity of the account (e.g. a substantial increase in turnover on an account for no apparent reason);

d)   There is a reluctance to provide routine information when opening an account, perhaps providing minimal or fictitious information or providing information that is difficult or expensive to verify;

e)   The customer has accounts with several financial institutions, all within the same locality;

f)   There is a matching of payments out with credits paid in by cash on the same or previous day;

g)   There are large cash withdrawals from a previously dormant/inactive account, or from an account which has just received an unexpected large credit from abroad.

Investment Transactions

4.5   Investment services could be being abused by the money launderers as follows:

a)   Purchasing of securities to be held by the financial institution in safe custody, where this does not appear appropriate, given the customer's apparent standing;

b)   Back-to-back deposit/loan transactions with subsidiaries or affiliates of overseas financial institutions in known drug trafficking areas;

c)   Requests by customers for investment management services where the source of the funds is unclear or inconsistent with the customer's apparent standing;

d)   Large or unusual settlements of securities in cash form;

e)   Buying and selling of a security with no discernible purpose or in circumstances which appear unusual.

Employees

4.6   In addition to the above, it is also important that financial institutions be aware of the danger that their own staff may be assisting clients to launder money. After all, the criminals would be able to launder their illegal proceeds more efficiently if they had an accomplice working for them in the institution where their 'dirty money' is being transferred to or being held. The following are some examples of suspicious actions or strange behaviour of an employee which might alert their employer to the possibility that they are assisting in the laundering process. Once again, the following actions do not necessarily signify a criminal activity.

a)   A noticeable change in the employee's characteristics or lifestyle, e.g. he starts taking expensive holidays or buys an expensive car or house which is inconsistent with his salary level. Perhaps he refuses to take vacation time from work, insisting instead that he has to be present in the office to personally handle important or large transactions on behalf of a particular client or account;

b)   Changes in his work performance, e.g. a salesman selling products for cash has a remarkable or unexpected increase in his performance figures;

c)   The employee has taken on a particular piece of business or opened an account which is contrary to internal policies and rules;

d)   Be on the look out for employees who have received a gift or benefit from a customer for no apparent reason. Of course, some clients like to show their appreciation for a job well done by rewarding the person who has assisted them, but would this extend to paying for airline tickets or expensive holidays!

4.7   It has also been known for empoyees of large organisations to be offered financial incentives in return for a blank piece of their organisation's letter head. This can be seen as a harmless offer to junior or inexperienced members of staff. After all, the paper will have a nominal value and would not be missed from the stationery records. However, that piece of paper could (and probably would) be used to forcify a reference or forge a payment introduction and could therefore be crucial in a money laundering exercise. Offers which seem too good to be true usually are and such 'deals' should never be entered into. Instead they should be reported to management, who may decide to report the incident to the police or possibly take legal action against the person who made the suspicious offer.

5   The Prevention of Money Laundering

5.1   So far we have defined money laundering, discussed the type of services which are at risk and provided examples of transactions which might be laundering activities. Now we shall turn our attentions to the ways in which we can combat this illegal activity.

5.2   In recent years a number of initiatives have been implemented on a world-wide basis with the purpose of reducing money laundering activities. The following is a summary of the main initiatives which students should be aware of.

The Basle Committee

5.3   The Basle Committee on Banking Supervision was established in 1975 by central bank governors of the Group of Ten countries. It now comprises senior representatives of regulatory authorities and central banks from various onshore countries including Canada, France, Germany, Japan, Switzerland, the UK and the USA.

5.4   In December 1988 the Committee issued a Statement of Practice which outlined a number of initiatives and policies which it suggested providers of financial services should implement in a combined attempt to combat the problem of money laundering. The following are the suggestions which were made:

Implementation of a 'know your client' policy

5.5   The Committee stated that when opening an account or relationship for a client the service provider should make suitable efforts to determine the true identity of the client and also ascertain certain basic information about his affairs and the need for the services requested.

The need for compliance with local laws and guidelines

5.6   It suggested that business should be conducted in accordance with local laws and regulatory codes.

Co-operation with national law enforcement authorities

5.7   Institutions should co-operate fully with national law enforcement authorities to the extent permitted without breaching customer confidentiality provisions.

Implementation of record keeping and transaction recording

5.8   Institutions should implement procedures for retaining internal records of transactions.

Staff training

5.9 Institutions should create a staff training programme to make employees aware of how to spot and then prevent money laundering activities.

The Vienna U.N. Drug Convention

5.10 Also in December, 1988 the United Nations Convention against Illicit Traffic in Narcotic Drugs and Psychotropic Substances (usually referred to as the Vienna U.N. Drug Convention) was signed by over 100 countries. The Convention came into force in November, 1990 and contained provisions which encouraged closer international co-operation in the fight against drug trafficking and also established money laundering and the aiding and abetting of money launderers as criminal offences.

The Financial Action Task Force ('FATF' or 'GAFI')

5.11 In July, 1989 the Group of Seven ('G7') countries (there are in fact 26 member countries which include the UK, USA, France, Germany, Australia, Spain and Switzerland) created the Financial Action Task Force (also referred to as 'GAFI' or 'FATF') which committed its members to implementing a set of 40 recommendations designed to combat money laundering.

5.12 Those recommendations were very similar in nature to the ones suggested by the Basle Committee and indeed expanded upon the points which we covered in the Section entitled 'The Basle Committee'.

5.13 The Task Force also recommended that each country should criminalise drug money laundering. It suggested measures to enable illegal drug funds to be confiscated or seized.

5.14 The Task Force has produced reports at various stages of its existence to assess the success which it has achieved and to evaluate the measures which it implemented and suggested. The most recent, at the time of writing, was published in June, 1996 which essentially updated the recommendations which it made in 1989. Of these revisions, perhaps the one which will be of most interest to administrators is that which requires governments to criminalise money laundering from all serious crimes (such as fraud and possibly tax offences).

Mutual Assistance Treaties

5.15 A number of countries and territories have teamed up to try and attack money laundering activities by allowing information to be freely exchanged in relation to known or suspected money launderers. Not all of the treaties which are in existence cover every laundering activity (e.g. in some cases the proceeds from tax evasion are not covered). Of the treaties which are in place perhaps the following will be of particular interest to students of this subject:

United Kingdom/United States of America Assistance Treaty

5.16 This came into force in April, 1989 and provides the framework for the flow of information relating to known or possible money launderers and also allows for the freezing of the proceeds of drug trafficking. The treaty extends to any territories whose international relations are the responsibility of the UK.

You should check whether the centre where you work or reside is a party to any similar mutual assistance treaties with onshore countries.

European Union Council Directives

5.17   Under the Council Directive of June, 1991 the members of the European Union (EU) created a system of mutual co-operation among member states on the prevention of the use of the financial system for the purposes of money laundering.

5.18   The members agreed that the laundering of funds from the illegal drug trade would be criminalised and in addition, money laundering would extend to other crimes, such as terrorism and serious fraud. The 'know your client' requirements were reinforced and emphasised.

5.19   In June, 1996 the European parliament agreed to update the 1991 Directive and in the main, aimed at extending the legislation beyond banking institutions to cover casinos and currency exchange outlets.

Caribbean Financial Action Task Force (CFATF)

5.20   This Task Force includes a number of Caribbean centres (such as the Bahamas, the BVI, the Cayman Islands and the Turks and Caicos) as well as certain onshore centres (such as the USA, the UK, France and Brazil). In 1992 the CFATF essentially adopted the FATF recommendations and also implemented its own provisions and by doing so, the members agreed that they would make money laundering a criminal offence in their respective countries and that they would increase co-operation between member states in the fight against the launderers.

Restrictions on Cash Flow

5.21   Some countries have imposed limits in relation to the amount of cash which can be taken into or out of that jurisdiction. Of particular note here is the USA where cash sums in excess of US$10,000 have to be reported.

5.22   In addition, under the EU Directive of June, 1991 the threshold for which financial institutions must demand proof of identity of occasional customers was set at ECU15,000 (approx. US$20,000).

The Role of Interpol

5.23   Interpol has provided much of the support and impetus for the implementation of many of the international anti-money laundering measures which exist and is also responsible for conducting and co-ordinating many of the on-going training programmes which are carried out, especially in the Caribbean and Latin America.

Local Centre Legislation

5.24   Most onshore and offshore centres have introduced their own legislation designed to make money laundering a criminal offence. Once again, some centres have included in their laws the laundering of funds from all criminal activities (including tax offences), whereas others extend mainly to drug trafficking, terrorism and serious fraud (and expressly exclude tax evasion). The provisions and regulations are generally similar in nature as they have all to a large extent been based on the suggestions of the Basle Committee and the FATF recommendations.

5.25   In the UK the principal legislation has been the Drug Trafficking Offences Act 1986, the Prevention of Terrorism (Temporary Provisions) Act 1989, the Criminal Justice Act 1993 and the Money Laundering Regulations 1993.

5.26 A number of offshore centres, such as Bermuda, Isle of Man, Jersey, Gibraltar and Guernsey, as well as UK dependent jurisdictions in the Caribbean, such as the Cayman Islands, BVI, Anguilla and the Turks and Caicos Islands, have based their anti-money laundering laws and policies based on those of the UK.

We shall now look at some of the general provisions which offshore centres have, in the main, introduced to counter money laundering activities.

6 Summary of the Common Anti-Money Laundering Requirements and Provisions in Offshore Centres

6.1 The exact requirements and provisions which are in place will of course vary between the centres although the general essence of the legislation and rules will be the same, which is that the responsibility for spotting and bringing money laundering activities to the notice of the authorities lies with the service provider and his employees.

6.2 The following is a summary of what is usually expected of service providers to help them in the fight against money launderers in offshore centres. Those of you who have experience of working in an onshore centre will notice similarities with the rules which you have probably encountered in that onshore location.

6.3 Students should be familiar with the provisions which are in place in the centre where they work. Indeed, it may be a local requirement that you have a duty to do this. If you do not work in an offshore centre you should at least be familiar with the rules in place in the centre with which you have the closest contact.

Identification of Clients ('Know Your Customer')

6.4 In most offshore centres, the providers of financial services will generally be required to be in possession of fairly extensive information on a potential new client before they can provide any of the services which may be required. This information would usually centre on certain personal details relating to the client as well as details of his general financial position and his motives for wanting to place assets offshore.

The information which is obtained will enable the service provider to 'know their client'.

6.5 Most regulatory bodies in offshore centres do not carry out their own due diligence checks on clients who wish to conduct business in their jurisdiction, and instead rely on the service provider concerned to perform this function.

6.6 The following lists cover the information which would usually be required to verify the identity and credentials of a potential new client. This is only the minimum information which would usually be required and in some instances a common sense approach would lead you to request further details which go beyond the details listed below.

Private individuals

6.7 a) A copy of the client's current passport, preferably certified as being a true copy (to include the date and place of issue, his photograph, his nationality, the date of expiry of the passport and the client's date of birth).

b) If there is no passport the client might be asked to produce a certified copy of another type of identification document which bears a photograph, such as an Identity Card.

c) Two satisfactory references, usually one from a bank and the other from a professional contact, such as a lawyer or accountant would be required. Note the word 'satisfactory'. There is no point proceeding on receipt of a reference from an institution which purports to be a bank if you are unable to verify that the bank exists. Always follow up references, particularly if they are from sources which are not known to you or your employer. Do not be affraid to write to or telephone the person who has supposed to have issued a reference. After all, references can be forged!

d) Confirmation of the client's home address (often a recent utilities bill or a driving licence will be sufficient although some service providers carry out further checks, such as at the voters' register or making an enquiry with a credit reference agency).

e) Details (usually proof) of the source of the funds to be transferred to the provider.

f) A summary of the client's business activities with particular emphasis on the intended use of the offshore services required.

g) Possibly a copy of taxation and/or legal advice received or requested by the client on the suitability of the intended services required.

Remember, do not just ask questions of potential clients as if you were working your way through a check list. Exercise some thought and common sense and make sure that the answers and information which you receive seem reasonable and can be substantiated.

Corporate clients

6.8 a) Proof of the identity (e.g. references, copy passport etc.) of all beneficial owner(s) as well as of all the directors and authorised signatories of the company (although this would usually be waived if the company concerned was publicly quoted).

b) Copies (possibly certified copies) of the certificate of incorporation, memorandum and articles of association (if the company is already in existence).

c) Details of the activities (or intended activities) of the company.

d) Proof of source of funds.

e) Possibly a copy of any taxation and/or legal advice obtained relating to the company's activities or intended activities.

Trust clients

6.9 a) Proof of the identity (e.g. references, copy passport etc.) of the settlor or the client on whose instructions the trust is to be created).

b) Full details required to confirm the identity of the trustees and the type of trust (if it is an existing trust).

c)   The purpose of the trust (i.e. for the benefit of the client's family etc.).

d)   Details of the source of the funds settled into the trust.

e)   Possibly a copy of any taxation or legal advice obtained prior to the creation of the trust.

6.10   A copy of the trust deed (or deeds) would not usually be requested as part of the account opening formalities, unless the service provider was to act as trustee. This is because of the danger that the service provider might be deemed to be a constructive trustee in the event of a dispute or breach of trust, on the basis that the provider had sufficient information (i.e. the trust deed) available to them which should have alerted them to an actual or possible problem.

Professional intermediaries

6.11   Much of the business which is opened in offshore centres is business which has been referred by professional intermediaries, such as lawyers and accountants, who are based in onshore jurisdictions. Usually, the initial approach to a particular offshore service provider will be the result of a word of mouth referral or perhaps a suitably impressive advertisement or article in a financial journal. Once a business relationship has been successfully established, the intermediary and service provider will develop closer ties and repeat referrals usually follow.

6.12   The service provider should have notified the intermediary of its particular account opening requirements at the time of the first referral of possible new business. However, as the introductions increase, the intermediary may ask the service provider to review its policy on the information which it requires to establish an offshore structure and might suggest that certain requirements be dispensed with on the basis that the intermediary would have conducted its own due diligence checks on the mutual client.

6.13   This might include a request that only one reference be obtained and that the intermediary provides this, or perhaps a suggestion that the name of the client be withheld on the basis that he requires complete confidentiality and does not want his details released to anyone except the intermediary.

6.14   Faced with this situation many service providers agree to modify their 'know your client' requirements and accept such information as the intermediary decides to pass to them. However, the result of this might be that the service provider is in direct contravention of his local anti-money laundering laws and before agreeing to alter his new business acceptance policies he must first make sure that what is proposed is not compromising his position, nor indeed against the law in his home country.

6.15   The laws in some centres recognise the role of the intermediary and state that if a bank, law firm or firm of accountants from a designated onshore centre (usually one which is a GAFI country) introduce clients to their centre, due diligence on the client has been deemed to have been performed on the basis that it is a requirement and duty of the intermediary in his home country. In such situations, the service provider may decide not to request references and passport copies and perhaps instead only request the name and address of the client. Usually, the intermediary would be asked to complete an undertaking that full due diligence had been performed and that the supporting documentation would be released to the service provider if required.

6.16 However, an argument may arise in such instances that the service provider should still hold at least basic 'know your client' information in their own centre. This is because they may need to produce information on the client to the local authorities under a local Court Order so if they do not hold certain personal details locally they could be criticised for failing to hold details which a 'reasonable man' would expect them to have on their clients.

6.17 Once again, students should be familiar with the laws in their local centre or in the centre with which they have closest involvement to determine what information should be requested from an introducer of business. What the service provider feels comfortable with is often the greatest test and many prefer to conduct their own due diligence (and request the information covered earlier) and not rely on details which are held by the intermediary.

Other offices of an organisation

6.18 This can be another area of concern for the service provider who is located in an offshore centre as quite often existing clients of other offices will be referred to him for the creation of an offshore account or structure.

6.19 One would hope that the other office has already performed adequate due diligence on the client and that this would have been handled at the time the original relationship was opened. However, the client might have come on board 15 years ago when there was no universal anti-money laundering guideline and 'knowing your client' did not necessarily involve asking for two references and details of the source of funds.

6.20 Nevertheless, the service provider should check that due diligence has been performed by the other office and ideally should request copies of the papers which the other office holds. If any items are missing (such as a copy of the client's passport), this would be an ideal time to ask him for it.

6.21 If the other office is reluctant to provide copies of the papers which they hold, perhaps because the client is concerned at the confidentiality aspect of his personal records being held in different jurisdictions, the service provider who is asked to take on the new business should ask his colleagues in the other office to confirm in writing that they hold at least the minimum information as laid down in the organisation's new business acceptance policy and that if necessary (perhaps in a dispute) this information could be released at a later date.

The importance of common sense

6.22 Before we move on let us stop and consider the situation where a potential client comes to you wanting to open an offshore company. He has glowing references from a bank in the USA and a law firm in England and he tells you that the US$20 million which he wishes to place with you came from the sale of real estate. You have a copy of his passport and the usual bank account opening forms have been signed. There is also a letter from his accountant explaining how the new company offers tax planning opportunities.

6.23 All of the due diligence requirements as set out in your organisation's policy on new business acceptance have been met. However, there is something about the client which makes you suspicious. Perhaps it is the fact that the bank reference is from a bank which you have not heard of and is unsigned, or the US$20 million is coming from ten different bank accounts with no indication that the proceeds were derived from real estate sales.

6.24   Common sense tells you to conduct more research and when you do, you discover that the bank reference is from a bank which does not exist and the cash was not received from land deals.

6.25   At the end of the day, the acceptance of all business is a judgement call and practitioners, especially those in offshore centres, must always remember that fact. Information which is collated should be verified which means, but is not necessarily restricted to, contacting the named referees and checking on the validity of the explanation given for the proof of source of funds.

6.26   Guidelines and policies, whether they are issued by governments or organisations, are an essential part of the fight to combat money laundering but they are no substitute for the application of common sense.

6.27   Never be affraid to reject potential new business if you cannot get satisfactory answers to your questions or if you feel it possibly involves illegal activities. It is much easier to turn a potential client down than it is to explain to a jury why you accepted business (which has since been shown to be bad) which did not meet your organisation's (or the centre's) due dilligence requirements!

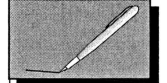

Student Activity 3

Obtain a copy of your organisation's new business acceptance policy. How do you feel potential clients view the policy which your organisation has in place and are there any areas which you believe could be improved/relaxed?

Proof of Source of Funds

6.28   Money laundering is transaction based. You must always enquire as to the source of funds which are paid into a bank account or transferred into a trust, company or other vehicle.

6.29   Be careful of vague statements such as 'I received the cash from real estate' or 'I inherited it'. Ask for proof to support these statements, such as bank statements, copies of any supporting contracts or estate accounts.

6.30   Also be on your guard against clients who wish to deposit drafts or travellers cheques. It is possible to buy such instruments from banks or other financial institutions without the need to be a customer of that institution. As a result you might be asked to deposit funds by way of a draft which has been drawn on an internationally known and well respected bank. You may therefore think that the person making the deposit is a customer of that bank. Of course he might be, but there is a also a possibility that he only walked in off the street, bought the draft with cash derived from illegal activities and has now come to you to assist in the integration process.

Record Keeping

6.31   The anti-money laundering laws generally concentrate on the proceeds of criminal activities. This is why service providers are expected to maintain full records of the transactions which they undertake for all their clients, whether they be individuals, trust clients or corporate entities. The records will, of course, include the details which we covered in the Section 'Identification of Clients', above.

6.32   There will often be requirements that the records be retained for at least a minimum period of time (e.g. for at least 6 years from the date the relationship with the client was ended).

6.33   Record keeping is a form of protection for service providers and should not be taken lightly. Often problems are encountered by service providers if they failed to make reasonable enquiries and also if they failed to record the answers or the transactions themselves.

Reporting

6.34   If a service provider, or an employee of a service provider, suspects that a client is laundering money or is involved in any other form of serious crime as determined by local law, the service provider or employee will usually have a duty to report their suspicions to the appropriate authority in the centre concerned. Normally, this would involve reporting the matter to the police, the local customs and excise department or to a particular regulatory authority (e.g. the centre's Financial Supervision Commission, Banking Supervisor or equivalent).

6.35   Service providers will usually have an internal reporting procedure and in most cases a senior officer will have the ultimate responsibility for reporting a suspicious transaction or a request which appears suspicious to the authorities. However, in some cases, the duty to report to the authorities may rest with the employee who has the suspicion, and in those instances the employee's responsibility under the local law may not be fulfilled if he only reports the matter internally and not directly to the designated authority.

6.36   Any report which is made will usually be received and handled by the authority concerned in the strictest confidence and should not breach any of the confidentiality provisions which exist either under statute or under the terms of the contract with the client. These are often referred to as 'safe harbour' provisions. Often, details of a report which is made will be passed to onshore law enforcement agencies and a combined effort made to try and achieve a conviction against those involved in the laundering process.

6.37   How to determine what is, and what is not, a suspicious transaction is a difficult area and the laws in the various centres rely to a great extent on the 'reasonable' man test. If a reasonable man would be expected to consider a transaction to be suspicious, given the history of the relationship with the client and the nature of the transaction under review, the service provider should submit the appropriate report. If they fail to act, they could be guilty of an offence as we shall see in the next section.

6.38 Perhaps a simple test as to whether or not a transaction is suspicious is to ask yourself whether the transaction or arrangement had a business purpose. If there was no apparent business purpose, in all likelihood the transaction should be reported.

There is also an interesting issue which relates to the conduct of the account or vehicle after a report has been made and we return to this later in this Unit.

Student Activity 4

Find out what the reporting requirements are in the centre where you work/live (it does not matter if this is an onshore location) and compare them with the provisions which are in place in another centre of your choice.

The Penalties

6.39 Usually there will be serious consequences for the service provider and possibly for the employee concerned if any of the following occur:

i) Assistance with the concealment or transfer of drug money or the proceeds derived from any other type of serious crime;

ii) Failure to report a suspicion or suspicious transaction;

iii) Evidence that the client has been notified that he is under investigation for money laundering (known as 'tipping off').

6.40 The penalties for non-compliance will generally be severe. For service providers this could involve financial penalties, fines and possibly the loss of their licence to conduct business. Employees found guilty could be fined and also have a prison sentence imposed.

6.41 At this point it would be appropriate to mention the case of *Agip (Africa)* v. *Jackson and Others* (1992). We cover this again in a later Unit when we look at the duties and responsibilities of directors of managed companies, but the findings also apply to the responsibility to investigate and report suspicious transactions.

6.42 In the *Agip Case* the directors of a company knew that certain transactions were suspicious but failed to investigate them fully and also failed to report their suspicions to the authorities in the offshore centre where they were based (the Isle of Man). As it turned out, the company was involved in fraudulent activities and the directors were considered to have assisted in the fraud through their lack of action. They were also considered to be constructive trustees over the funds which they received through the fraudulent transactions and were liable to repay them as part of the settlement.

Post Reporting Activities

6.43 Assuming an offshore service provider suspects one of his clients is laundering money and makes a report to the authorities in his local centre, how then should he proceed with the future operation of the client's affairs?

6.44 Making the report would offer the service provider protection against criminal prosecution should the client be found to have laundered funds. The service provider should, however, remember that if suspicious funds are subsequently received and then paid away, or previously received funds are distributed, they may still be considered to have assisted in the laundering process on the basis they continued to operate an account which they believed to be used for illegal purposes.

6.45 The service provider would, in all probability, be held to be constructive trustees over the funds which it held and subsequently distributed (refer to the *Agip Case* mentioned earlier).

6.46 Following a report of a suspicious transaction, the service provider must notify the authorities of subsequent activities on the account which are also of a suspicious nature and seek specific directions in relation to requests received for distributions from funds which they hold. Chances are the authorities will want the account to be kept activated as it will assist them in tracing the flow of funds to other parties who may also be involved in the laundering process. The service provider would be well advised to seek specific legal advice on how to proceed in this situation (and possibly obtain the advice of the Court) and also bear in mind the danger of alerting the client to a possible problem with a particular transaction which might amount to tipping off (which we have already seen is also a criminal offence).

Staff Training

6.47 Local legislation usually requires that adequate training in money laundering prevention and reporting be given to all staff involved in the finance sector of the offshore centre concerned. Failure to provide such training could also be an offence.

7 The Moving Target

7.1 Those of us who are involved in offshore finance should remember that by the very nature of our industry, we have to deal with the affairs of a large number of clients from different countries. Although we cannot be expected to have a detailed knowledge of the laws and tax provisions of all the countries in the world, it is important to understand that those laws and provisions are subject to change and what might be a legitimate transfer one day, could become a criminal offence the next and therefore subject to anti-money laundering provisions.

7.2 Perhaps the recent change in the tax laws in Mexico and the investigation into the source of the funds held by certain banks in Venezuela are two cases in point.

Summary

Now that you have read this Unit you should be able to:

● **Describe the usual stages involved in the money laundering process**

● **Provide an example of how banking services might be used in the laundering process**

● **Provide an example of how corporate services might be used in the money laundering process**

● **List five investment transactions which might give rise to a suspicion that a client is laundering money**

● **Outline the proposals of the Basle Committee in 1988**

● **Outline the objectives of FATF and the Caribbean Financial Action Task Force**

● **List the usual information required on an individual who wishes to open an offshore account**

● **List the usual information required to open an offshore trust**

● **Describe the usual money laundering reporting requirements**

● **Understand the extent of the usual penalties if convicted for money laundering activities**

Self-assessment Questions

1. Describe what is meant by the terms 'placement', 'layering' and 'integration' as they relate to money laundering.

2. Provide examples of how offshore banking services could be used to launder money.

3. Apart from the provision of banking services, describe how two other types of offshore services could also be used in the laundering process.

4. Prepare a list of ten potentially suspicious banking transactions which might be connected with money laundering activities.

5. Prepare a list of five investment-related transactions which might also give rise to suspicions that a client might be laundering funds.

6. What is the objective of the various Mutual Assistance Treaties which have been executed in recent years? Name one such Treaty which has been created.

7. Briefly explain why customer identification is such an important area of the process in the acceptance of new business.

8. Describe the 'new business' information which you would request from a client who wanted to establish an offshore company with your organisation.

9. Describe the 'new business' information which you would request from the trustees of an existing trust who wanted to open a bank account with your organisation.

10. Briefly outline the money laundering reporting requirements in an offshore centre of your choice.

Unit 6

Offshore Company Administration
Part One – The Basic Principles

Objectives

At the end of this Unit you should be able to:

● List the usual features of a company

● Outline at least five possible uses of a company

● Describe the usual procedure to incorporate an offshore company

● Describe the purpose of the memorandum and the articles of association

● List the usual matters covered in the articles of association

● Explain the difference between voluntary liquidation and strike off

● Highlight the usual duties expected of a director

● List the usual powers given to directors of a company

● Comment on the term 'nominee director'

● List five of the rights usually given to the members of a company

The provision of company services in offshore jurisdictions is an extremely important part of the syllabus and one which students should be fully familiar with if they are to succeed in the examination.

The Scheme of Work which is reproduced in the Introduction to this study text contains a number of objectives which the syllabus suggests students should set themselves in relation to this area. If you refer back to this section of the Introduction for a moment you will see that most of the topics which are to be covered on companies are very wide in nature. You may even think that many of them could be the subject of a study text in themselves. It may come as no consolation to learn that you would in fact be right as there are many texts which are available which specialise in specific aspects of company law as well as specific areas of company practice.

Having said that, much of what has been written on companies really concerns those who are involved with the legal aspects and the administration of onshore companies (notably those in the UK). Many of these basic principles will, however, still apply to those who are involved with offshore companies and because of this we shall go over them in this Unit. We shall also look at specific practical issues of particular relevance to offshore practitioners in the following two Units.

Finally, students should note that the information which we cover on companies relates solely to the use and administration of private companies. This is on the basis that they generally offer the greatest financial planning opportunities. The syllabus does not require us to cover publicly quoted companies (or their equivalent) and so this type of company will be disregarded in this study text.

If what follows in this Unit is familiar to you, please work through it anyway and view it as useful revision. If the areas are new to you, please take the time to understand them. The points which are covered in this Unit are important as if you do not fully appreciate the features and characteristics of a company you may have difficulty in fully appreciating just what useful planning opportunities companies can provide.

1 What is a Company?

1.1 Basically, a company is an entity which has been created to undertake a particular venture or to perform a series of business activities. It might have been possible for the venture or activities to be carried out by the means of a partnership although as we shall now see, the particular features of a company might have created certain advantages which a partnership could not offer.

2 Features of a Company

Separate Legal Entity

2.1 A company exists as a separate legal entity and has its own legal personality which is distinct from its members. It can sue and be sued in its own capacity. It can for example open a bank account, purchase property or execute a contract.

2.2 The distinction between the company and its members is sometimes referred to as the 'veil of incorporation' and only in certain circumstances can the law go behind the 'veil' which is considered to separate the company's legal identity from the identity of its members.

Unlimited Liability of the Company/Limited Liability of its Members

2.3 A company is liable without limits for its own debts. However, it is usual for a company to confer limited liability on its members which means that they will only be required to contribute the amount outstanding on their shares, or if it is a guarantee company, the amount of their guarantee, in the event of the company becoming insolvent or being wound up.

2.4 If the members do not have limited liability, the company will be known as an unlimited company. However, the vast majority of offshore companies are limited liability companies.

Ownership

2.5 A company will be owned by its members. If the company has issued shares, the members will usually be referred to as shareholders. If the company has no shares, only an undertaking from its members that they will contribute to the assets of the company on liquidation, the company will generally be called a guarantee company. Those companies which have both shareholders and guarantee members are often referred to as hybrid companies (a vehicle which we cover in more detail later in this study text).

2.6   The extent of a shareholder's ownership in a particular company will be determined by the number of shares which have been issued in their favour (e.g. 100 Ordinary Shares of £1.00 each). The sums which have been paid by the members to the company will be referred to as the company's capital.

2.7   The nominal amount of the shares which have been issued to members is termed the issued share capital, whereas the maximum amount of shares which could be issued (which will be specified in the memorandum of association or equivalent document) will be termed the authorised capital.

2.8   Those shareholders who have been issued with share certificates in their own names will often be referred to as registered shareholders as their personal details will be recorded in the records of the company (in the register of members). Those shares which have been issued, not in a person's name but instead in favour of the bearer of the certificate, are called bearer shares.

Management and Control

2.9   A company cannot manage itself and will therefore rely on its directors to perform this function. As we have already seen in the Unit on general taxation issues, it is usually the residence of the directors which will determine where the company will be considered to be resident for tax purposes.

2.10   Some companies (e.g. certain types of limited duration or limited life companies) will not, in fact, have directors and the management and control lies with the members. We shall return to this in a later Unit.

Governing Documents

2.11   A company must have a written constitution which sets out its internal rules and regulations. Such a document is commonly referred to as the company's articles of association (or by-laws).

2.12   There will also be a document which sets out information relating to the company which outside parties who may wish to deal with the company might be interested in. This is commonly known as the memorandum of association.

We shall return to both later in this Unit.

Creation

2.13   A company can only be created by a legal process which is commonly referred to as incorporation. The persons who create a company are sometimes referred to as the subscribers (who become the first members on incorporation).

Perpetual Succession

2.14   A company has what is known as perpetual succession which means that a change of ownership, such as the death of a member or shareholder, will not usually affect the continuance of the company. A company can only be terminated by legal process, such as voluntary liquidation or dissolution.

Ownership of the Assets

2.15 The assets of a company are owned by the company itself and not by the directors or the members of the company. All assets which the company owns should therefore be registered in the name of the company.

Supervision and Controls

2.16 A company will generally be supervised and regulated by the Registrar of Companies in the centre where the company was incorporated. It will also be governed by the company laws which the particular centre has enacted.

2.17 A company will be registered in the centre where it has been incorporated (as it will appear on the register of companies in that location). In addition, some companies may decide to apply for registration in another centre as well (perhaps because they want to establish a place of business in that second centre and they can only do this on application to the local registrar of companies).

3 Possible uses of a Company

3.1 The features of an offshore company will generally be similar in nature to those of an onshore company. In addition, the possible uses of a company will also be similar regardless of where the company has been incorporated or where the management and control is performed. Let us now look at some of the common uses which companies are put to and at the same time highlight some of the attractions which an offshore company as opposed to a company in an onshore centre can offer.

Student Activity 1

Before reading the following section, make a list of the possible uses of a company based on the features which we covered earlier.

Taxation Planning

3.2 The residence of a company may, in certain circumstances, be determined by where it was incorporated although usually it will be decided by where the company is managed and controlled. There could, therefore, be possible taxation benefits in a client incorporating a company in an offshore centre which has low or no corporate taxation (which is the situation in most offshore centres), for that company to be managed and controlled from that centre (which could be achieved by appointing local directors) and for the client to transfer the ownership of his assets to that company.

3.3 The income which the company receives and the realised gains which it makes will, in theory, only be subject to the tax rates which apply in the offshore centre where it is based with no other tax being payable by the company. There might, however, be withholding tax deducted from foreign dividends as we discussed in Unit 2.

3.4   As the client is no longer the owner of the assets he should not, in theory, be assessed to tax on those assets. That is not to say, however, that the assets distributed back to the client will not attract a possible tax liability as was outlined in Unit 2.

Succession Planning

3.5   A company can be used as a succession planning vehicle and could enable the client to make provisions for himself, his spouse, his family or indeed others during his lifetime. This could be achieved by the client and his family being made members of the company and from time to time receiving either dividend or loan payments. As new family members come along additional shares could be issued to them. As a company has perpetual succession, this planning process could continue long after the original client's death.

Avoid Probate Problems

3.6   After transferring his assets to a company the client would no longer be the legal owner of those assets. On his death, those assets would not (in theory at least) form part of his estate and would not be involved in the probate formalities to which those assets still registered in the name of the deceased would be subject.

3.7   Some of you may be familiar with the probate formalities imposed by certain onshore countries and if so, you would probably have realised that in some cases there can be considerable delays before a deceased's assets can be distributed to the beneficiaries. This delay can, in some circumstances, create considerable hardship and inconvenience for the family members.

3.8   There is also the added factor that once a grant of probate has been issued by the probate court, the terms of the deceased's will or the succession of the property based on the intestacy laws will become public knowledge as details can be obtained by the general public for a nominal charge. This can cause many problems, not least if the deceased had wanted to keep his financial affairs a secret.

Transferring assets into a company can avoid these problems.

Asset Holding

3.9   Companies can be used to act as the legal and registered owners of various types of assets such as investments, land, property, cash, securities, antiques, ships, copyrights and royalty contracts. In addition to holding assets, a company can also be used to receive payments such as dividends, commissions or royalty receipts.

3.10   At this point we should return to the possibility of using a company to hold real estate as in some onshore countries, such as Spain and France, local tax will be levied on local property which is registered in the name of an offshore company. Care should be exercised in such instances because the tax which might be payable could outweigh the advantages which were originally envisaged in holding the asset through the offshore company.

We shall expand upon the potential problems of holding immovable property through an offshore company (and also an offshore trust) in a later Unit.

Trading Activities

3.11   Companies are often used to trade and the activities could include the buying and

OFFSHORE PRACTICE AND ADMINISTRATION

selling of raw materials or finished goods and could also include invoicing and re-invoicing for the provision of services.

3.12 Companies which have limited liability are favoured as they provide an element of protection to the members as their potential liabilities, in the event of the company making a loss, will be limited to the extent of the cash still to be paid (if any) for their shares. The company will of course have unlimited liability but at least if the company has insufficient funds to cover its debts the members will not be expected or required to make up any shortfall.

We return to the issue of the provision of trading company services in the next Unit.

Confidentiality

3.13 All companies will have to register with their local Registrar of Companies as part of the incorporation process and most registrars will require details of the directors, secretary, other offices, members, share capital (authorised and issued) and the registered office of the company. They will also usually require a copy of the current memorandum and articles of association, as well as details of any changes which have been made to the information which has been filed with them.

3.14 This information is often available for public inspection but confidentiality is still possible if an offshore agent is used to provide the directors, the secretary and members of the company as the client's details would not, therefore, be recorded on any public records.

3.15 The true owner of a company is commonly referred to as the beneficial owner and most centres do not require his details to be divulged to an outside party. However, in some centres, such as Bermuda and Guernsey, there is a requirement that the beneficial ownership details are provided to the Registrar prior to incorporation, although this information is not then divulged to other parties.

4 Incorporation of an Offshore Company

4.1 Each centre will have its own local requirements and procedures for the incorporation of a company. It would of course be impractical to cover them all here but you should take the time to familiarise yourself with the procedures which are in place in at least one, and preferably two, offshore centres of your choosing.

4.2 If you already work in an offshore centre it will be fairly easy to obtain this information by contacting your local Registrar of Companies (or equivalent) for the details. If you do not currently work offshore, you should choose an offshore location (perhaps one which has close ties with your country or one which you have a particular interest in) and contact the Registrar in that centre for the incorporation details.

There are certain common steps which are usually followed when incorporating an offshore company and the following is a summary of those common areas.

Step 1 – Obtain the Approval of the Intended Name of the Company

4.3 Although there is not usually a legal requirement to have the proposed name of a company approved by the Registrar of Companies prior to submission of the incorporation papers, it is advisable to do so. This is because the name which is chosen might not be acceptable or available.

4.4 Most centres prohibit the use of certain words in the name of a company. Such words usually include 'Trust', 'Assets', 'Investments' and 'Finance'. These and other prohibited words can be used in certain circumstances but this would usually require the company to meet a certain capital requirement or perhaps the approval of the centre's regulatory authority.

Step 2 – Completion of the Application Form to be filed with the Registrar

4.5 There will usually be a standard application form which contains information such as the names and addresses of the directors and any officers to be appointed. The directors and officers would usually have to sign the form to confirm their willingness to act in these positions.

4.6 The names and addresses of the subscribers would usually be included on the form together with a note of the intended address of the registered office of the company.

Step 3 – Preparation and Submission of the Memorandum and Articles of Association

4.7 The memorandum and articles (or equivalent) would usually have to be submitted to the Registrar of Companies for approval. We look at the usual contents of these in the next Section.

Step 4 – Filing the Documents with the Registrar of Companies

4.8 The application form, the memorandum of association and the articles of association will usually be filed with the local Registrar together with a fee to cover the processing of the paperwork. There might also be local duty to pay which would usually be calculated based on the value of the authorised capital.

Step 5 – The Certificate of Incorporation

4.9 The registrar will check the documentation and if all is in order he will issue a certificate confirming that the incorporation process has been completed in accordance with the local requirements and that the company has been formed. This certificate is usually referred to as the certificate of incorporation and once issued the company can commence its activities.

Student Activity 2

Select two offshore centres and make notes on the incorporation procedures in both jurisdictions. Highlight any particular requirements which might make it easier to incorporate a company in one centre rather than the other.

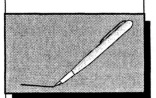

5 Registration of a Foreign Company

5.1 Some companies may wish to conduct business activities in another country and often this will involve them having to establish a place of business in that other location.

5.2 Many offshore centres permit foreign companies (i.e. companies which have been incorporated in another country) to open a place of business or trade locally provided that they register in that centre.

5.3 Registration would usually involve a process similar to incorporation as certain information would have to be produced to the Registrar of Companies. This would usually comprise a copy of the certificate of incorporation, copies of the memorandum and articles of association, details of the directors and officers, plus the intended location of the business address in the centre concerned. It would also be advisable to check whether the company could be registered under its current name as there may already be a company registered under the same or very similar title. If there is a problem with the name often a business name can be used instead for registration and business purposes in that centre.

6 The Memorandum and Articles of Association

6.1 We have already mentioned these documents earlier in this Unit and we shall now cover in detail what they are and also review their importance in relation to the management and administration of a company.

The Memorandum of Association

6.2 This document regulates a company's external affairs and provides outside parties with the sort of basic information which they should be aware of if they wish to undertake business with that company.

6.3 The following is a list of the information which would usually be contained in the memorandum of association:

a) The name of the company;

b) If the company is a limited company, a statement that the liability of the members is limited;

c) If it is to be a private company, a statement to this effect;

d) Confirmation that the company has met the local incorporation requirements of the centre concerned and that the subscribers wish to form the company;

e) If it has a share capital, the amount of the authorised capital and how much is to be issued on incorporation;

f) Possibly an objects clause setting out the intended activities of the company.

The Articles of Association

6.4   This document sets out the internal rules of the company and will provide the basis for the future administration and management of the company.

6.5   Usually the articles of association would contain the following:

a)   The name of the company;

b)   Matters relating to the share capital, such as the requirements which are to be met to allot and transfer shares;

c)   The procedures required to call members' and directors' meetings, as well as an indication of the type of business which can be conducted as such meetings;

d)   The requirements relating to the appointment and removal of the directors and other officers;

e)   Details of the powers which have been given to the directors;

f)   The rights and powers of the members;

g)   The procedures required to execute documents on behalf of the company (i.e. the affixation of the company seal);

h)   Accounting requirements (which might include in some centres the provisions to enable the company to dispense with the audit of the financial statements);

i)   How to alter the memorandum or articles of association;

j)   Circumstances which might give rise to the termination of the company.

The Importance of these Documents

6.6   The importance of both cannot be overestimated. The memorandum sets out key information which those having dealings with the company will want to be aware of, and if an objects clause has been included the directors must make sure that the company only conducts activities which are covered in those objects.

6.7   The contents of the articles will determine just how the company is to conduct its activities and in particular how certain decisions can be made. Once again, the directors must make sure that their actions, and those of the company, conform with the terms and restraints which are detailed in the articles.

Interaction with Local Company Laws

6.8   The company laws which will be in place in a particular centre will refer to the memorandum and articles and will set out what information should (or would usually) be contained in these documents. Companies which are incorporated in that centre must ensure that they follow these guidelines and that they do not include less information than that which the legislation demands.

Alteration of Terms

6.9   There will no doubt come a time in the life of most companies when the memorandum or articles require updating, perhaps because the authorised share capital is to be increased, or the directors require additional powers which are not currently covered under the articles.

6.10 It will be possible to make alterations to these documents and the first point of reference should be the articles themselves as they will (or should) cover the procedure or the consents which will be required. Usually, the memorandum and articles can only be altered by the members passing a special resolution, and any changes which are made must then be notified to the Registrar of Companies. Once again, local company laws should be checked to make sure that any planned alteration does not contravene the minimum requirements for the contents and effect of these documents.

We shall look at resolutions and company meetings generally in the next Unit.

7 Termination of a Company

7.1 It has already been mentioned that a company can continue indefinitely. However, there will be occasions where a client will want his company to be terminated and the assets returned to him. It is, therefore, important that those who administer offshore planning structures be aware of the most common methods by which an offshore company could be brought to an end. These are summarised below.

Voluntary Liquidation
7.2 This is the formal process of terminating a company and involves the retirement of the directors and the appointment of a liquidator who will handle the liquidation of the assets, payment of the creditors and distributions to the members. Notices will be required to be placed in local newspapers advising creditors of the intended actions and the Registrar will be sent copies of the relevant paperwork.

7.3 This process is only used when the company is solvent and can be expected to meet all of its debts. It is usually possible for the creditors to instigate a creditors' liquidation but this process is not common with offshore companies.

7.4 At the end of this process a certificate will usually be issued confirming that the company has been wound up and is no longer recorded on the register of companies.

This is the most expensive and time consuming method of termination but it is also the most permanent and effective.

Dissolution
7.5 This is a less formal process, the directors retain their positions and a liquidator is not required. The company would still have to be solvent and capable of discharging its debts and notice of the intended action would have to be given.

7.6 A director could usually instigate this procedure and once all the formalities had been met the registrar would issue a certificate of dissolution. However, unlike a company which has been liquidated, a company which has been dissolved can apply to the Registrar to be re-instated to the register. In view of this anomaly, the liabilities of the directors and officers will usually continue for a certain period of time.

Strike Off

7.7   This is the cheapest option as it does not require any additional work. In fact strike off is achieved by failing to perform work, as it is the end result of failing to submit the required returns to the local registrar. After a certain period of time, which varies between centres, the registrar will remove the company from the register for non-compliance with local filing requirements. However, a company which has been struck off can apply for re-instatement and as such, the liabilities of the directors will continue until such time as the possible re-instatement period comes to an end.

8   Directors

8.1   It has already been noted in an earlier Section that the powers of the directors are set out in a company's articles of association. Before we look at some of the powers which would usually be conferred we should first of all familiarise ourselves with the usual duties which are expected of a director of a company.

8.2   There have been a great number of cases which have centred on the duties and powers of directors (particularly of onshore companies). The syllabus does not require a detailed knowledge of these cases (nor are examination candidates expected to quote them) although students are expected to be aware of the general issues which have been highlighted by the courts over the years and which offshore service providers of company services should be aware of.

Those of you who act as directors of managed companies (which are sometimes referred to as client companies) might want to take particular note of the following Sections!

Usual Duties Expected of Directors

8.3   The following are the main duties which are usually expected of company directors. They will apply regardless of whether the company is publicly quoted (such as Marks & Spencer Plc) or a private limited company which has been created in an offshore centre on behalf of client as a vehicle to hold his investments.

Fiduciary duty

8.4   A director owes a fiduciary duty to the company and must exercise his powers in the best interests of that company.

Duty to avoid a conflict of interest

8.5   A director has a duty to avoid conflicts of interest and should avoid representing the company or trying to involve the company in a situation where he has, or may have, a personal interest.

Duty not to make a personal profit

8.6   A director should not profit personally from his position unless he is authorised by the company to do so. Any unauthorised profit will usually belong to the company and not to the director.

General duty of care

8.7   Directors have a common law duty of care and must be able to show that they are reasonably competent. The most commonly quoted case on this subject is the UK case of *Re City Equitable Fire Insurance Co Ltd* (1925) which established the following principles:

i)   A director is expected to show the degree of skill which should reasonably be expected from a person of his knowledge and experience;

ii) A director is expected to attend board meetings when able but has no duty to concern himself with the operation of the company at other times;

iii) A director can usually be expected to leave the normal day-to-day business of the company to the management team of that company.

Statutory duties
8.8   There may be duties which are imposed by local statutes which a director would be expected to obey, such as the duty to declare personal interests in a proposed contract.

Additional duties
8.9   The articles of association might impose further duties on the directors of a company and in view of this, it is important that the directors be fully aware of all of the terms and conditions which are contained in the articles.

Directors' Powers
8.10 As we have already mentioned, the directors' powers will be contained in the articles of association and will usually be sufficient to enable them to manage the business of the company to the best of their ability.

8.11 Some articles of association will contain a full list of the powers granted to the directors although it is common for a general clause to be inserted. This basically attempts to cover all eventualities by enabling the directors to perform any tasks or business, provided that whatever is conducted is considered by the board to be in the best interests of the company.

8.12 Examples of some of the powers which the directors would usually exercise are:

a)   To borrow or to charge assets of the company;

b)   To open bank accounts or execute documentation required to open other types of accounts (such as investment management or custody accounts);

c)   To allot shares;

d)   To remove a director from the board and/or appoint a replacement or additional director;

e)   To bind the company in respect of executing contracts, deals or arrangements;

f)   To appoint agents or other officers;

g)   To declare dividends to the members;

h) To call meetings of the members to discuss particular business matters which require the approval of the members.

8.13 The directors should only exercise their powers in the best interests of the company and their decisions should only be taken after the matter in hand has been discussed at a meeting of the directors. We look at directors' meetings in the next Unit.

Different Types of Director

8.14 In addition to the common type of board members which most companies will have there are other types of director which might be encountered. The first two mentioned below will, however, seldom be found in offshore private limited companies although it is common to see such directors appointed in the companies which provide corporate services.

Associate director

8.15 An employee of a company might be appointed as an associate director to reward him for his efforts although the position would not normally be intended to carry with it the usual powers given to board members. Associate directors would not usually be entitled to receive notices of board meetings and would not be involved in the decision making process.

Non-executive director

8.16 A non-executive director will not play a part in the day-to-day administration of the company. It is common for a well known member of the local business community to be appointed to such a position, usually with the objective of trying to project a better image locally for the company.

Shadow director

8.17 This term is often applied to a person on whose instructions the directors of a company usually act. We shall return to this when we look at the role of the client in the next Unit.

Alternate director

8.18 This is a person who is appointed by a director to act in his absence at board meetings. An alternate director is usually considered to be a full member of the board and will have the same duties and powers of other directors.

Nominee Directors

8.19 A number of service providers state in their marketing literature that they will provide 'nominee directors' to act on the boards of those companies for which they provide corporate services. Indeed, some of the individuals who have been appointed to act as directors of their clients' companies also view themselves as nominees on the basis that they only ever act on the instructions of their clients.

8.20 Make no mistake. There is no such thing or person as a 'nominee director' either in the eyes of the law or in the eyes of the authorities. Whoever accepts the post as director must expect to be bound by the usual duties expected of a director and it is no defence in law to say that he was only acting on the instructions of another! He will be responsible for his actions as director and may be liable for any inactions.

Method of Appointment, Removal and Retirement

8.21 Students, and indeed those who administer companies, should be aware of the specific requirements in their local centre although the following provides a summary of the usual methods by which directors can be appointed, removed or retire.

Appointment

8.22 Often, the person who has consented to act as a first director of a company will be deemed to be appointed on the incorporation of the company. However, in some centres there is a requirement that only the subscribers are authorised to appoint the first directors. The articles of association would usually have to be checked to discover just who can appoint the first directors on incorporation.

8.23 After the first directors have been appointed, the directors themselves will usually have the power to appoint additional directors. The members will also usually have the power to appoint directors.

8.24 Prior to making any appointment of new or additional directors, the articles should be reviewed to check whether there are any special requirements which must be fulfilled, such as the director having to be a member of the company or whether a maximum number of board members has been fixed. The articles might also specify that persons of a particular nationality are excluded from acting.

8.25 In addition, the board members should satisfy themselves that the intended director is fit and proper to act alongside them and that he appears competent and able to fulfil the role expected of him.

Removal

8.26 A director could usually be removed by the other directors or by the members (which would probably require a special resolution). The articles might specify under what circumstances a director would be removed, such as failing to attend a certain number of board meetings or suffering from an incapacity which would prevent him from continuing in office. There would, of course, be the opportunity to remove a director who was not considered to be acting in the interests of the company.

Retirement

8.27 Directors will also have the right to retire from the board and once again the articles will cover the requirements which must be met to enable the resignation to be effective. Usually a director who wishes to retire must send a letter to the company at its registered office confirming his wish to retire. The articles would then cover whether the resignation would be effective from the date the notice was received by the company or after the board has met to approve it.

8.28 Clearly, there will be situations where a new director has to be appointed to replace an outgoing director (whether through removal or retirement) as there must always be at least the minimum number of directors in office as specified in the articles.

Action required following changes to the directors

8.29 It would be usual for a meeting of the directors to be held to confirm the changes and record them in the company's records. The register of directors will have to be updated (assuming that such a register will be required in the offshore centre concerned) and possibly the company's bankers will also have to be notified on the basis that the bank mandate may have to be updated.

8.30   Most centres also require changes in the directors of a local company to be notified to the Registrar of Companies. The company's stationery may also have to be altered to reflect the changes which have taken place.

There may also be other contacts or business associates who should be notified of the changes.

We shall look at the additional actions which may be required following the appointment or retirement of a director who is provided by a service provider in a later Unit.

Student Activity 3

Select a client company which your organisation manages and have a look at the articles of association (or equivalent). Summarise the provisions of the sections which cover the appointment, retirement and removal of the directors and also the powers of the directors. Do the members figure in any of these provisions and if so, to what extent?

Directors of Managed Offshore Companies

8.31   Whilst on the subject of directors it would be useful to spend a little time considering the pressures which are sometimes put to bear on directors of offshore companies which are managed by agents (i.e. managed companies). Those of you who already act as directors of such companies may be familiar with these influences, or perhaps worse still, have experienced them first hand.

8.32   Clearly, the biggest influence which is usually brought to bear will be from the beneficial owner of a company who will often want, what he may term, 'his' directors to act in a particular manner or to conduct a particular business transaction on his authority.

8.33   In fairness to the client, he will be paying the invoices for the director services and may see no harm in demanding that the agents perform as he instructs. It can be difficult to impress upon such clients the concept of management and control and the need for this to rest with the directors.

8.34   Many of the activities or actions which a director of a managed company will be asked to perform will be reasonable and could be considered to be in the best interests of the company. However, the difficulty arises when the director believes that he is being asked to do something which is clearly not in the interests of the company or perhaps which is not in the interests of his organisation. There are three choices available. One would be to resign from the board (and probably at the same time sever the provision of all other corporate services for that client). The second option is to refuse to act as instructed. The third option is to carry out the actions despite the director's reservations.

8.35   The first option may perhaps be the best solution although some service providers may prefer to try the second or even third options before arriving at the situation where the business will be lost. Let us now consider the possible problems which the director and indeed service provider might encounter with options two and three.

The directors refuse to act in a particular manner

8.36   This would be the correct thing to do as the directors have a fiduciary responsibility and must always act in the best interests of the company as they are personally responsible for their actions.

8.37   The client may then decide to remove the directors or insist that they retire in favour of another service provider. The articles of association would determine who had the power to remove and appoint directors although usually this would rest with the directors themselves or the members. Alternatively, the directors might decide to retire in any event and therefore be willing to be replaced.

8.38   However, both of these possibilities could create problems for the directors. If they believe that the actions which they have been asked to perform are detrimental to the affairs or interests of the company, they should not accept removal or retire without seeking legal advice. It is possible that by retiring or accepting removal with the knowledge that another, more amenable agent is to be appointed who will carry out the required actions, the directors might still be implicated in any future actions or claims arising from those actions on the basis that they failed to attempt to prevent them from happening.

In some situations, the directors might be wise to obtain the directions of the court.

The directors agree to act despite their concerns

8.39   This is perhaps the worst thing that a director can do personally, and one of the main actions which service providers should prevent (and protect) their employees from doing.

8.40   If the directors do not approve of a proposed transaction or suggested action they should not perform it. To act despite having concerns, can lead to serious consequences for the directors concerned and possibly for the service provider as well.

Agip (Africa) Ltd. v. Jackson and Others (1989)

8.41   The findings of this case leads on from the previous Section as it concerns the situation where directors of a managed company fail to make adequate enquiries of the business which they are undertaking on behalf the client.

8.42   A detailed discussion of the arguments which were raised in this case is outside the scope of this study text but the conclusion will be of interest to students. Basically, it was found that where an agent provides managed company services (which includes the provision of directors) they are under an obligation to make reasonable enquiries into the nature of the business which they are conducting. In the *Agip Case*, the defendants to the action (who were a firm of accountants in an offshore centre) failed to take action when it was reasonably clear that money which was passing through one of their managed companies (for which they provided directors) was from fraudulent activities. They were held to be constructive trustees in respect of the monies illegally obtained and were found to have 'knowingly assisted' in the fraud.

8.43 The circumstances of this case were such that a reasonable and honest man should have realised, or at least suspected, that a fraud or similar crime was being committed. It therefore follows that a similar test of 'reasonableness' will no doubt be applied in future cases should this type of situation arise.

8.44 The lesson to be learned by service providers (and of course the directors) of managed companies is to make reasonable enquiries as to the conduct of the business which they have taken on, as failure to do so could make them liable and party to crimes which the dishonest client may be committing.

9 The Rights and Powers of the Members

9.1 This is another area which over the years has been the subject of much debate but, as with the role of the director, a detailed discussion is outside the scope of the syllabus.

9.2 However, it is important that students are aware of how a person can become a member of a company, how they cease to become members, and the general rights and powers which they will usually have. The general points which follow in this Section can apply to both onshore as well as offshore companies.

Becoming a Member

9.3 There are a number of ways in which a person might become a member of a company. These include subscribing to the memorandum of association on incorporation, applying for shares on the allotment of additional shares by the company, as a result of a transfer or gift from an existing member, or by purchasing the shares.

Ceasing to be a Member

9.4 The ways in which a person may cease to be a member of a company include transferring the shares, selling the shares, the transmission of ownership on the death or bankruptcy of a member and on the liquidation of the company.

Powers of the Members

9.5 The members are the owners of the company and have certain rights and powers which can impact on the directors. They also have rights and powers which the directors themselves would not usually have. Usually, the members will have the power to appoint and remove directors, the power to alter the memorandum and articles of association and the power to pass special resolutions at members' meetings which are used to authorise business such as the change of name of the company or placing the company into voluntary liquidation.

Rights of the Members

9.6 The articles of association will usually set out the members' rights. Some companies have different classes of membership and the rights of those different classes will vary. However, the following is a list of the most common rights a member of a company will have:

Dividends

9.7 The members will usually have the right to receive a dividend if one is declared by the directors.

Notice and voting

9.8　A member is entitled to receive notice of all members' meetings which are convened by the directors and will have the right to attend and vote at such meetings. If he cannot attend a meeting he has the right to appoint someone to represent him, commonly known as a proxy.

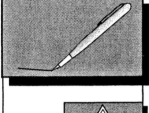

Student Activity 4

Refer again to the articles of association (or equivalent) which you used for Student Activity 3 and summarise the provisions relating to the holding and conduct of members' meetings.

Profits

9.9　On winding up, the members usually have the right to receive any surplus of assets.

Share certificate and transfers

9.10　Members have the right to have their ownership recorded in the company' s records and to receive a share certificate noting or reflecting their ownership. This is certainly the case for those companies which issue registered as opposed to bearer shares.

Accounts

9.11　Members usually have the right to receive a copy of the financial accounts of the company.

Meetings

9.12　The members have the right to call or request members' meetings. As already mentioned, we shall look at members' meetings in the next Unit.

Summary

Now that you have read this Unit you should be able to

● Describe the usual features of a company

● Provide five possible uses of a company

● Outline the usual procedure to incorporate an offshore company

● Explain the importance of the memorandum and articles of association

● Describe the usual matters covered in the articles of association

● Explain the difference between voluntary liquidation and strike off

● List the usual duties expected of a director

● Describe the usual powers given to directors of a company

● Comment on the term 'nominee director'

● Describe the rights usually given to the members of a company

Self-assessment Questions

1. Write brief notes on the following features of a company and highlight how they can create possible financial planning opportunities:

    i)   Separate legal entity;

    ii) Perpetual succession.

2. Briefly explain how an offshore company can create possible taxation planning opportunities.

3. Using an offshore centre of your choice, list the steps required to incorporate a local private limited company.

4. Explain what registration of a foreign company would usually involve and provide an example of a situation where a company might want to be registered in this manner.

5. Comment on the importance of the terms of the memorandum and articles of association for company administrators.

6. A client has asked you to terminate his offshore company as he requires the funds which are held for another business venture. What would be the usual options open to you if you decided the company should be ended?

7. Prepare a list of the usual duties which are expected of the directors of an offshore company.

8. Similarly, provide a list of the usual powers which you would expect the directors of an offshore company to be given.

9. One of your colleagues has mentioned to you that you have been appointed to the board of directors of a company which your organisation manages on behalf of one of your clients. Your colleague says that he has only mentioning this out of courtesy as you are only acting as a nominee director because the client wants to maintain full control over the affairs of the company. How would you respond?

10. Outline the powers which the members will usually have which will not be extended to the directors.

Unit 7

Offshore Company Administration Part Two – The Taxation, Regulation and General Provision of Offshore Company Services

Objectives

At the end of this Unit you should be able to:

- Describe the usual taxation treatment of a resident company

- Outline the differences between tax-exempt and international companies in low tax centres

- Describe the usual method of applying for exempt status

- List the information which the Registrar of Companies might require from a locally incorporated offshore company

- Comment on the advantages of an offshore centre requiring information on the beneficial owner of a local company

- List the usual services which are offered by corporate agents in offshore centres

- Explain why a client might want to instruct an agent to provide directors and members of his offshore company

- Outline the circumstances where a registered agent might be required and the role which they will usually provide

- Explain the type of documentation which a service provider would usually request from a client

- Summarise the actions a corporate agent should take following the resignation of one of its employees who is a director of client companies

1   Taxation Status of Companies in Offshore Centres

1.1   In this Section we shall concentrate on how companies are taxed, or treated for taxation purposes, in offshore centres. Once again, each centre will have its own legislation and procedures in place, and in view of the number of centres which offer corporate services, it would be unreasonable to expect students to be familiar with the requirements in place in every centre.

1.2   However, students should have a general understanding of the basic principles as well as the corporate options which are available offshore and this Section is designed to provide that knowledge.

1.3   After studying this Section and before moving on to the next, please find out what tax options are available to companies in your particular offshore centre (or in a centre with which you have a particular connection or specific interest in). Those of you who are involved in the administration of companies from different centres should be familiar with the taxation treatment in all the centres where you have companies under management.

Recap on the Tax Treatment of Companies

1.4   As mentioned in Unit 2, Section 1, points 1.25 to 1.27, a company will usually be considered to be resident for tax purposes where it is managed and controlled. As the management and control should be with the directors, it is usual for the residence of the company to be decided by the location of the directors.

1.5   We also mentioned that one director being resident in a particular country might be enough to decide that the company will be deemed to be resident in that country, although in some countries it will be where the majority of directors reside (or where directors' meetings are held) which will be the deciding factor.

1.6   In Unit 6, Section 3, points 3.2 to 3.4, we then touched upon the fact that offshore companies provide potential tax planning opportunities on the basis that offshore centres are generally low or no tax centres. What we now need to concentrate on is how these opportunities are presented in practice and also look at how tax savings could be possible even though some offshore centres have a local system of corporation tax which would, on the face of it, create a tax liability on the operations of locally incorporated companies.

Resident Offshore Companies

1.7   Generally speaking, a company's place of residence will be the country where it was incorporated. For example, a company which has been incorporated in Jersey will be deemed to be resident in Jersey. The place where the management and control lies may be a determining factor.

1.8   Some offshore centres impose a system of corporation tax and in those locations resident companies would come within the corporation tax regime. This could mean that it would be liable to tax locally (and using Jersey again as an example this would be 20%) on its world-wide income and gains.

1.9   A number of offshore centres do not impose corporation tax and therefore resident companies in those centres will not be subject to local taxation, although they will not be able to conduct the types of trade or activities which would generally be required by international clients. In no tax centres, this type of company is sometimes referred to as an ordinary company (such as in the Bahamas).

1.10   In practice, very few offshore companies which have been created for international clients will be incorporated as, or remain resident (or ordinary) companies. This is particularly the case in those centres which have corporation tax. The vast majority of offshore companies which are used as planning devices have a 'special' status which will either offer a reduced rate of tax (in low tax centres) or favourable administration features (in no tax centres). There will be a fee or duty payable to the local authorities in the centres concerned in return for this 'special' status.

1.11 There are occasions when it would be advisable for a company created for an international client to retain its resident status in a low tax centre. For example, a company might not trade or receive any income and as such would not have a local tax liability so an application for a special tax status would not be cost effective as the duty or fee would be more than the tax saved. However, it would generally be safe to assume that a resident company in a low tax centre would not be desirable for the majority of international clients.

1.12 It is also important to remember that foreign companies which set up a place of business in an offshore centre (e.g. they appoint local directors) or register in that centre may also be considered to be resident in that centre. This could have taxation implications if the centre where the company has taken up residence is a low tax centre as the company would be liable for local corporation tax in that offshore centre. We shall return to this possible problem area later in this Unit.

1.13 Before we move on to cover the alternatives other than resident status which are available, it is also worth noting that resident companies are generally required to comply with more stringent company law regulations than companies which are not considered to be resident.

Non-Resident Companies

1.14 Some centres provide an opportunity for a company which has been incorporated locally to apply to the local authorities for non-resident status.

1.15 If non-resident status is granted and the company is based in a low tax centre (perhaps the Isle of Man is the most regularly quoted example) it would only be assessed to tax locally on its income and gains from local activities, of which there would usually be none. Any income or gains which are made or received from its overseas activities would not suffer any local taxation in the offshore centre.

1.16 Non-resident companies in low tax centres would usually have to pay an annual fee or duty for the privilege of being assessed to tax in this manner, although the amount payable would only be a nominal sum (e.g. in the Isle of Man the cost of the non-resident duty was, at the time of writing, £600.00 per annum and is payable on the filing of the company's annual return).

1.17 There may be a requirement that the directors of a non-resident company would have to be resident outside the offshore centre concerned and the management and control would also have to be exercised off the island. Usually, this could be achieved by holding all board meetings outside the centre concerned. The company would not be able to conduct certain business activities within the offshore centre and the list of prohibited activities would usually include such things as manufacturing and mining.

1.18 In no tax centres a non-resident company would not create any local tax benefits as such companies would not be subject to tax in that centre. The benefits would usually be lower annual government duties (e.g. a non resident company in the Cayman

Islands pays lower duty than an exempted company) and the fact that directors can be resident either on or off the island concerned.

1.19   A non-resident company can provide clients with the opportunity of owning a company which can take advantage of favourable offshore tax rates and yet they can still control the operation and activities of that entity. However, with this flexibility comes risk for the offshore centre as there could be little, if any, control exercised locally over the activities of such companies. This can lead to misuse on the part of the client, who might fail to meet local company law regulations or perhaps of greater concern, use the company to conduct business which is not in the interests of the centre concerned with no-one left accountable in the centre where the company has been incorporated.

Tax-exempt Companies in Low Tax Centres

1.20   Tax-exempt companies offer another option for companies in some offshore centres to relinquish their resident status in return for a more favourable taxation position.

1.21   This option is, however, only usually available in the European offshore centres such as Alderney, Guernsey, Jersey and the Isle of Man where there is a system of corporate taxation. Such companies would usually be incorporated in the offshore centre concerned although it is possible for foreign companies who have registered locally to also apply to receive tax-exempt treatment.

1.22   If a company is granted tax-exempt status it would only be assessed to local tax on a similar basis to that which applies to the non-resident companies described above, i.e. the company would only be liable to tax on its income and realised capital gains which arise from local sources. Any profits made from trading or activities outside the centre would not be subject to local tax.

1.23   There would usually be a nominal annual fee or duty which should be paid to the local tax department but this would often be less than the duty which would otherwise be payable by a non-resident company (e.g. at the time of writing the amount payable on tax-exempt companies in Guernsey and Jersey is £500.00 per fiscal year whilst in the Isle of Man the cost is £300.00 per fiscal year).

1.24   Tax-exempt companies are not generally permitted to trade or perform business activities in the offshore centre concerned but the management and control would usually have to be conducted locally, or at the very least, there must be a minimum of one member on the board of directors resident in the offshore centre. Tax-exempt companies must not usually be beneficially owned by a local resident or a local trust, unless the trust has a clause which specifically excludes local residents from benefiting.

1.25   The requirement for a local director has been introduced into the regulations in the various centres as it enables the authorities in those jurisdictions to have someone local who they can hold accountable and also rely on in respect of the activities of tax-exempt companies. As we have already seen, there is no such comfort available with non-resident companies as no local directors would usually be appointed. This is perhaps one of the main reasons why the duty for exempt companies is less as this is the type of company which the centres would generally prefer to attract and develop.

1.26 Companies wishing to apply for tax-exempt status would usually have to submit an application form within a certain period of time (which often starts running after the company first acquires an asset or a liability and would usually be a month). The application form would have to contain certain information about the company, such as its registered office, details of its directors and other officers and a note of the date on which the company commenced its operations (or trade). There would also usually be a declaration required which a director must sign confirming that the company will not trade locally and that it is not beneficially owned by a local resident.

1.27 Although the same form would not usually be required when subsequent applications are made for future fiscal years, a declaration or similar undertaking would still be required to confirm that the company did not trade locally in the previous tax year and that it does not intend to in the year for which exemption is now being applied for. There will also usually be a time limit within which a company must apply for exemption for later years.

1.28 If a company fails to apply for exemption within the time frames set down by the local authorities, the company will not be considered to be exempt but will instead revert to being resident for tax purposes. It is therefore important that administrators be aware of the deadlines in their respective centres as a delay could be very costly!

1.29 We mentioned earlier that foreign companies can also usually apply for tax-exempt status. This may be necessary after the company becomes registered locally or after it appoints local directors to its board. Failure to apply for tax-exempt status after registration could mean the company will have a local tax liability on its world-wide operations.

International Companies in Low Tax Centres

1.30 These are the European equivalent of the International Business Companies and are available in Alderney, Gibraltar, Guernsey, Jersey and the Isle of Man. They are very similar in nature to the tax-exempt companies of those jurisdictions but international companies can elect to pay tax locally at a fixed rate, usually up to 30% or 35%, instead of paying a nominal amount of tax.

1.31 International companies can elect to pay a nominal fee or duty instead of a certain percentage rate. This sum would usually be the same amount that is paid by local tax-exempt companies.

1.32 The criteria for an application for this status is generally similar to that which applies to companies wishing to apply for tax-exemption although often an application can be made throughout the year rather than within a certain period.

1.33 International companies are not widely used by individuals but they can provide tax planning opportunities for parent companies who may wish to reduce the effects of controlled foreign company legislation (which we touched upon in Unit 2).

International Business Companies and Exempted Companies in No Tax Centres

1.34 International Business Comanies (or IBCs as they are commonly known) are offered by many of the centres in the Caribbean, such as the Bahamas, Barbados, Belize, and the Turks and Caicos Islands. However, the centre which is most widely used for the establishment and management of IBCs is the British Virgin Islands, perhaps a reflection of the minimal reporting which is required of IBCs in that centre.

1.35   Usually there are no requirements to have a local resident director (making them similar in that respect to the non-resident company) and the filing requirements are less onerous. Corporate directors are usually permissible (which is not often the case with exempt companies) and often sole directors are permissible.

1.36   Exempted companies are similar in nature to the IBCs and are found in centres such as Bermuda and the Cayman Islands.

Student Activity 1

Select one offshore centre from Europe, one from the Caribbean and another centre from the Pacific. Outline the types of companies which each centre can offer and in particular, highlight the tax treatment of each type mentioned.

2   The Regulation of Offshore Companies

2.1   The regulation of offshore companies, and in particular those agents who provide administration services, has been the subject of considerable debate in recent years although at the time of writing very few offshore centres have implemented specific controls or regulations.

2.2   However, offshore companies may be the subject of certain controls and might have to fulfill certain regulatory requirements in the centre where they have been incorporated or registered.

2.3   Obviously each centre will have its own regulations and requirements relating to locally incorporated or registered companies and students should be familiar with the rules which apply in their centre (or a centre of their choice). In this Section we look at some of the regulatory requirements which are commonly applied in many offshore centres.

Local Record Keeping and Reporting Requirements
Incorporation and registration
2.4   As we have already seen in Unit 6 anyone wishing to form or register a company must supply certain information to the Registrar of Companies before the company can be incorporated or added to the register of companies.

The registered office
2.5   There is always a requirement that a company must have a registered office which will be the address at which the company can be contacted by the local Registrar or any other parties who need or want to correspond with a particular company.

2.6   The registered office is the place where any court summons, writs or other such legal documents and actions can be served on the company or its directors. This allows creditors and others with an action against the company to have an address where they can try to progress their particular dispute or grievance.

2.7 The registered office will also usually be the place where the company will keep its registers (of directors etc.) and it would be usual to find the common seal of the company kept there (if the company wanted to keep a seal) together with accounting information.

2.8 The minute books recording the meetings of the directors and members would usually be retained at the registered office, as too would the accounting records.

2.9 The name of the company would also have to be recorded in a prominent place, where it can be viewed by the general public, at its registered office. Often there will be a name board or plaque either outside the building or in the reception area recording the name of the company, plus the names of any other companies which use that address as their registered office.

2.10 If your organisation provides corporate services it is likely that it will have a name board on display listing all those companies which use your organisation's address as their registered office.

2.11 In some centres, such as the Cook Islands and Aruba, registered office facilities can only be provided by licenced trust companies.

Company registers

2.12 Most Registrars of Companies will require that local companies maintain registers setting out the details of the directors, secretaries and members of those companies and that such details are also provided to the Registrar. Some centres also require companies to keep a register of any charges which have been taken over the assets of local companies.

2.13 Such information would usually have to be held at the registered office and might be available for general inspection by the public. Similarly, the information filed with the Registrar of Companies might also be subject to general disclosure.

Annual returns

2.14 Most offshore centres require locally incorporated companies to submit a return to the Registrar of Companies on an annual basis. The return would usually set out such information as the name and registered number of the company, its registered office, details of the directors and secretary, details of the authorised and issued capital and details of the current members, as well as any transfer of membership since the last return was lodged.

2.15 Filing an annual return is an important task for administrators to remember because failure to lodge it on time will result in penalties, and continual failure to lodge might lead to the Registrar commencing proceedings to strike the company off the register.

Financial statements

2.16 Although very few centres still require companies to file audited financial statements some centres, such as Ireland, will not process the submission of an annual return unless it is accompanied by the audited financial statements of that company.

2.17   It should be remembered that statutory requirements may dictate that a locally incorporated company must keep its accounting records in the country where it was incorporated, usually at its registered office.

2.18   It may be a statutory requirement that every local company must prepare accounts and present them to the members at least on an annual basis. However, an increasing number of centres are now dispensing this the requirement that although once again the company's articles should be checked in case there is a particular accounting requirement which has to be fulfilled.

Additional information required by the registrar of companies

2.19   In those centres which require companies to submit an annual return, it is also usually a requirement that they must notify the Registrar of Companies of any material changes to the information which was lodged, either at the time the company was incorporated, or at the time the previous annual return was submitted, whichever occurred last.

2.20   Changes to the directors or officers of the company must be submitted, also details of any alterations to the name of the company, its memorandum or articles of association. Any alteration of the authorised capital or any allotment of shares would also usually be reportable, as might the creation of any charges or change in the registered office address.

2.21   Once again there will often be a time limit (usually one month) for the change(s) to be notified and late filing of this information could incur a penalty.

Beneficial owner details

2.22   Some centres, such as Bermuda, Jersey and Guernsey, require those who wish to incorporate a company to submit details of the proposed beneficial owner of the company to the local regulatory authorities, who will then ensure that the proposed owner is a desirable client for their centre.

2.23   The information which is provided remains confidential and would not be passed to any other regulatory or fiscal authorities, unless of course the client is suspected of, or known, to launder money or be associated with other forms of serious crime.

2.24   Some clients are not keen for their details to be provided to any regulatory authorities (some in fact are reluctant to give this information to their service providers) which may mean that they would not choose a centre which had this disclosure requirement.

2.25   However, there is an argument to support a centre requesting beneficial owner details and why a client may want his details provided. This concerns the perceptions of respectability and reputation, not only of the centre but also of the client and the activities which the client's company are to perform.

2.26   Many onshore regulators and organisations are skeptical of the legitimacy of companies which have been created or administered in offshore centres which have minimal (or in some cases no) reporting requirements. They view these corporations as if they have something to hide and will often view the owners of such companies with the same skepticism. Indeed, some onshore companies refuse to trade or have any activities with companies from centres which have minimal reporting on the basis that they are poorly regulated and can create higher risk. Also, because a search at the Registry will either reveal little or no information on the ownership, activities or general good standing of such a company.

2.27   Often, however, these same regulators and organisations are much more comfortable to conduct business with companies which have been incorporated in offshore centres which insist on the disclosure of beneficial owner details.

Registered agent
2.28   Some centres, such as the British Virgin Islands, require companies to appoint a local registered agent which would act as the local point of contact for the Registrar of Companies (or equivalent). This person would be the person on whom notices of actions (if any) against the company would be served.

Usually, the registered agent would be a local service provider in the offshore centre.

2.29   A registered agent may also be required in those cases where a company which has been incorporated in another location is registered as a foreign company in that centre.

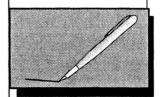

Student Activity 2

Using the three offshore centres which you chose in Student Activity 1, outline the information which is required by the Registrar of Companies in those jurisdictions. Are the regulations similar or is one centre regulated to a greater (or perhaps lesser) extent than the others?

Management and Control
2.30   As we have seen, some centres require that particular types of companies must have at least one director resident in that centre. Usually this is a requirement for the company to receive favourable tax treatment (as in low tax centres) or as part of the general statutory requirements for a local company.

Local Meetings
2.31   Another area in which some centres attempt to regulate local companies is in respect of members' and directors' meetings. Some centres, such as the Netherlands Antilles, insist that a members' meeting must be held locally at least once every year, although the majority of centres which insist that an AGM be held allow them to be conducted outside the centre.

2.32   Some centres also insist that an annual directors' meeting must be held for certain types of companies (e.g. exempted companies in the Cayman Islands).

2.33   It is worth mentioning at this point that the articles of association should be reviewed to check whether there are any additional requirements, outside the statutory ones, which cover where and how regularly certain meetings must be held.

3 The Provision of Corporate Services in Offshore Centres

3.1 Many of you may already be involved with, or perhaps even work for, organisations which provide corporate services in an offshore centre. If so, you may be familiar with many of the areas which we will be covering in this Section particularly in relation to the types of service which are often provided by offshore agents.

3.2 However, in addition to looking at the types of service which are offered we shall also be considering how a service provider might decide to structure their operation and what paperwork they would usually require their clients to complete. Some of the practical issues which face corporate agents will also be reviewed, as will the factors which a client might consider when selecting an agent to provide corporate services.

We shall start by looking at the different types of corporate services which are usually offered by offshore agents. When referring to the companies for which the agent provides services we shall use the term 'managed companies' from time to time.

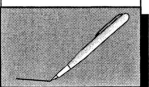

Student Activity 3

Before proceeding, list the corporate services which you have had dealings with and compare your list with the one which follows. Are there any services which you have not yet used which you feel might be of benefit to your clients?

Offshore Corporate Services
Most corporate agents will provide many of the following services from an offshore base:

Incorporation and registration
3.3 Often an agent based in a particular centre will provide services to incorporate companies in that centre. In addition, they may also offer to incorporate companies in other centres, which they will achieve by appointing agents in the required centre to act on their behalf.

Provision of the registered office
3.4 As part of the package of services on offer will be the use of the agent's premises as the registered office for the companies under management.

Provision of directors
3.5 This is the service which not only produces the highest fees for the service providers (or at least it should) but it is also the area which can pose the greatest problems and risks.

3.6 There are a few points which we need to cover in relation to the provision of director services.

a) Management and Control
Clients will not usually want to be appointed director of their company as it could

create a management and control problem, a factor which we shall consider in more detail in the next Unit.

b)   Confidentiality

Details of the directors would usually have to be provided to the Registrar of Companies and also recorded in the register of directors. Such information would, therefore, usually be available to the general public and many clients would not be prepared to be appointed to the board of their company on the basis that it would not be a confidential appointment.

c)   Duties of an Agent Acting as Director

We have already mentioned in Unit 6 that the duties of a director will essentially be the same whether the director is on the board of a publicly quoted company or acting in an offshore private limited company which has been created on the instructions of a client.

There is no such thing in law as a 'nominee' director, and whoever takes on the responsibility to act on the board of a company must appreciate that he will be fully accountable for his actions and also for his inactions. It is no defence to say that he was only appointed because a client of his employer did not want to be appointed personally.

d)   Trading Companies

Not all agents are prepared to provide directors for trading companies because of the risks and possible liabilities which this type of company can attract and indeed create. Agents who do provide directors for this type of company will often insist on a detailed indemnity from the beneficial owner of the company designed to protect the agents from possible actions against them which may arise from the trading activities undertaken.

In some instances, agents are not able to provide trading company services because their indemnity insurance will not cover them for this type of business.

It is common to find that some agents suggest that a beneficial owner be appointed to the board of his trading company in place of the agent.

Clearly, the information which an agent would require to enable it to conduct the management of a trading company would be much more detailed than that which would be requested for a passive holding company structure.

Provision of the company secretary

3.7   In many centres it is a requirement that a local company must have a company secretary. Usually, a body corporate can act in this capacity although in certain circumstances (such as for Isle of Man exempt companies) an individual must be appointed (and there may be a qualification requirement which this individual must also meet).

3.8   Service providers will usually offer to provide a company secretary for those entities which are under their management. A professionally qualified individual in the employ of the organisation may be used, or alternatively a nominee company may be appointed (and we shall look at nominee companies in more detail under a later heading).

3.9 Clients are rarely appointed to this position, often because they would usually fail to meet the residence and possibly qualification requirements which are sometimes imposed. In addition certain filing requirements apply in offshore centres (such as annual returns) and these are best dealt with locally by an officer of the company, preferably the secretary. Details of the secretary would usually have to be advised to the Registrar of Companies and also recorded in a register of officers. Most clients would not want their details recorded in this manner and would therefore wish an agent to fulfill this role.

3.10 You may find that an assistant secretary is also appointed in some companies who will have restricted signing authority. This is quite common where the secretary is to be based in the offshore centre to fulfil a local requirement, but there are documents which are prepared or have to be signed in another jurisdiction, perhaps because the administration function is handled elsewhere for cost-efficiency reasons. An assistant secretary can fulfil this role.

Provision of other officers

3.11 Some centres also require that local companies must appoint certain officers, such as a Treasurer or President. Once again, most service providers would be willing to fill these positions on behalf of their clients.

Provision of the members of a company

3.12 Those companies which are limited by shares will usually be authorised under their articles and by local statutes to issue registered shares. However, very rarely will the client want to be recorded as the registered holder of shares in his company as his details would appear on the company's register of members, which in most centres would be available for inspection by the general public.

3.13 Service providers will therefore usually offer to provide the registered shareholders for companies which issue registered shares and would become what is commonly known as a 'nominee shareholder'.

3.14 Nominee shareholders will be registered as the owners of the shares which have been recorded in their name, but they will be holding the shares as bare trustees (or nominees) for the true beneficial owner of the company, who will usually be the client, or in some cases, another offshore vehicle which has been established on the direction of the client.

3.15 Usually a corporate body is incorporated by the service provider to act as nominee shareholder for their managed companies and such companies are often referred to as nominee companies. Some service providers prefer to use their employees as the registered shareholders for their managed companies.

The next Unit covers how the beneficial ownership of shares held by nominees is recorded.

Provision of a registered agent

3.16 Service providers would usually offer to act as a local agent in the centre where they are based. As we have already seen, foreign companies usually require a registered agent and some centres (such as the BVI) insist that all local companies appoint an agent to this position.

Maintenance of the corporate records

3.17   This is a service which is very much provided on the strength of other corporate services and would include such matters as updating the registers, which are required under local company laws, and filing the forms and returns required by the local Registrar.

Preparation of financial statements

3.18   As we have already mentioned, it is usually a statutory requirement that a company must maintain accurate accounting records and sometimes that financial statements be prepared and submitted to the members on at least an annual basis.

Corporate providers would generally offer to provide accounting services.

General corporate secretarial services

3.19   This covers such matters as arranging for meetings to be held in accordance with local company laws and the preparation of the minutes which are required to record what was discussed at those meetings. Agents would usually offer to provide this service.

Documentation Required by Service Providers

3.20   Here we are concerned with the documentation which the service provider will usually require the client to execute and not the documents which would be required prior to a relationship being created (such as a copy of the client's passport, two references etc.).

There are usually three documents which the agent will ask corporate clients to complete.

A new company questionnaire

3.21   Most service providers who have been asked to incorporate a company will check with their client the particular requirements in relation to that new company. Usually, the client will be asked to complete a form which contains a number of sections and questions, sometimes referred to as a company request form.

3.22   The client would usually be asked the following:

a)   The intended name of the company, with at least one alternative in case the first choice of name is unavailable or unsuitable;

b)   The offshore centre where the company is to be incorporated;

c)   The authorised and issued capital;

d)   If the company is to be limited by shares, the nominal value, denomination, type of and currency of the shares;

e)   Whether there will be any special requirements concerning the memorandum or articles of association;

f)   What services the agent will be asked to provide;

g)   If the agent is not to provide the directors, members, registered office or other officers, details of who the client would like to be appointed;

h)   The anticipated activities of the company;

i)   The required financial year end for accounting purposes plus the currency in which the accounts will be prepared.

Company management agreement

3.23   This document would usually follow the completion of the questionnaire and would be sent to the client either before or shortly after the company had been incorporated. An agreement would also be required if the service provider has been asked to provide services for a company which has already been created.

3.24   Although the precise title of this particular document may vary between service providers, the contents would usually be similar in nature as essentially it is the document which sets out terms and conditions in respect of the services which the agent has been asked to perform. The services which are to be provided would be specified, as would the basis of the fees and expenses which will be charged.

3.25   This document may be signed by the beneficial owner of the company (who would usually be the client), although some agents also require the directors of the managed company to execute it on the basis that the agent will be acting on the company's behalf. This may be despite the fact that the agent also provides the directors of the managed company.

Indemnity in favour of the service provider

3.26   This document would be intended to provide the agent with a degree of protection should there be a problem or dispute in relation to the affairs or activities of the company.

3.27   An indemnity will be intended to protect the agent and also its employees from any liability which may arise in respect of their involvement or management of a client's company. The beneficial owner would be asked to sign the indemnity which would usually be countersigned by the service provider.

3.28   Under the terms, the client would usually be precluded from bringing any actions against the agent or its employees unless he could show that a fraud or similar serious offence had been committed by the service provider or its employees.

3.29   Some agents incorporate their standard indemnity into their management agreement and some even include similar provisions within the terms of the articles of association of their managed companies.

3.30   Despite the reliance which the service provider may place on this document, it should be remembered that an indemnity may, in practice, only offer limited protection should there be a problem which involves the agent. This would particularly be the case if the agent was, for example, a corporation which held itself out as being an expert or specialist in the area of company management (which is, after all, how most agents describe themselves) and the agent failed to manage the company in a professional manner.

3.31   The Jersey case of *West* v. *Lazard Brothers* (1993) should be of particular interest to students and practitioners as it brought into question the extent of an agent's indemnity. It was found in this case that the agent could not be indemnified against all potential liabilities, particulalry if the agent provides the directors of the company. Such wide terms in an indemnity may not be binding if they were not clearly advised to the client at the time the appointment was made.

3.32 Agents should consider the possibility that there may be statutory rules in their local centre which negate the impact and effect of any indemnities contained in a company's articles of association.

Transfer of administration function
3.33 Service providers may change during the life of a company and when this happens the agent receiving the business will require the beneficial owner to complete an indemnity and possibly a company management agreement, as discussed above.

3.34 A questionnaire, which will contain some of the information covered in the new company form, will also usually be requested by the new service provider to provide him with information to assist him in his corporate duties.

Student Activity 4
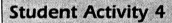

Compare the documentation covered above with that which your own organisation requires (or with that which one of your offshore agents has requested). Summarise the indemnity provisions and state whether they are included in the services agreement or in a separate deed.

Practical Administration Issues Which Affect Corporate Agents
3.35 A corporate agent will face a multitude of different administration issues during the exercise of his duties and we shall cover many of these in Unit 8. There are, however, two specific areas we shall cover in this Section which are really internal 'housekeeping' issues for agents.

Change in beneficial ownership
3.36 An agent should only provide services for those clients which have been successfully checked out and vetted in accordance with the criteria laid down in the agent's new business acceptance policy.

3.37 However, there may be occasions when a beneficial owner of a company decides that he no longer requires the company and rather than have it liquidated he decides to transfer the ownership to a friend, family member or associate. How then should the service provider proceed?

3.38 The service provider should first ascertain who the client would like the ownership to pass to and then arrange for that person (or entity) to provide information which would hopefully satisfy the agent's new business acceptance policy (e.g. satisfactory references, copy of their passport etc.).

3.39 Assuming that the proposed owner meets the necessary criteria, the agent could proceed with the transfer although he would be wise to request the following:

a) The return of the nominee declaration which may have been sent to the client;

b) The return of the share certificate(s) which may also have been sent to the owner;

c) An indemnity executed by the new beneficial owner;

d) Possibly the execution of a new management agreement.

The use of nominee declarations are covered in more detail in Unit 8.

3.40 The death of the beneficial owner will also create a similar problem for the agent and the steps which he should take would be very similar to those which we have covered above if the beneficial ownership is to pass on death.

Resignation of an employee who is an officer of managed companies

3.41 In this Section we shall concentrate on what a corporate agent should do following the resignation of one of the employees who is appointed to the boards of some (or all) of the agent's managed client companies.

3.42 The first step would be to determine how many companies the employee is on the board of, where those companies are located and how many other directors are appointed in those companies. Most service providers have their corporate records on a computer database which would make this task relatively simple to perform.

3.43 Some centres (such as the BVI, the Bahamas and the Cayman Islands) only require one director for the types of company which are usually provided for international clients and there are no restrictions on where the director can be resident. If he is the sole director, steps must be taken to replace him prior to him leaving his employ.

3.44 Alternatively, some centres (such as those in Europe) require a minimum of two directors and in many cases a local director must be on the board at all times (usually for tax status purposes). If the employee is, say, one of three on the board of such companies, and there is another local director already in place, a successor would not be as urgent as the statutory requirements would still be met.

Once again, the articles of association should be checked to see what provisions exist concerning the required number of directors.

3.45 The next step would be to arrange for the employee to sign letters of resignation for those companies where he is a director. Again, the articles should be consulted to ascertain how a director can resign, which would usually be by letter addressed to the registered office requesting to resign from the board. Many computer databases can produce such letters at the push of a button.

3.46 Assuming a replacement director has to be appointed (either because of a statutory requirement or because of the terms of the articles), the next stage would be to decide who to appoint and how this can be achieved. The articles should be the point of reference in respect of how to appoint, and the organisation's internal rules and procedures would probably contain guidance on who to appoint.

3.47 The directors can usually appoint additional directors and the members would also usually be given this power. Organisations would tend to appoint only senior officials or management to the boards of client companies in view of the duties and responsibilities expected of them. Remember that there is no such thing as a 'nominee' director!

3.48 The next step would usually be to hold a directors' meeting to accept the resignation of the employee on the various companies and to appoint his replacement. After this meeting has been held and the resolutions passed, the changes should be notified to interested parties, such as banks or other institutions who receive instructions from the company and who must know at all times who is authorised to sign on behalf of the company. In addition, the register of directors should be updated and in some centres the Registrar of Companies must also be notified of the changes. The various companies' databases should also be updated with the alterations.

3.49 The new director should receive some form of indemnity from his employer for acting in this new capacity and the outgoing director may also receive confirmation that he will be indemnified for future actions which may be brought against the company. Once again, the extent of the indemnities which may be provided must not be totally relied upon by the new director who will be personally liable and responsible for his actions.

3.50 The company's letterhead may also have to be amended and finally, the beneficial owner might also require to be notified of the changes.

Corporate directors

3.51 In some centres (mainly those in the Caribbean) it is possible for corporate directors to be appointed in managed companies instead of individual directors. Usually, a corporate director would appoint authorised personnel to act on its behalf in the performance of its corporate services. As you should appreciate, the resignation of someone on the authorised personnel list would not create the same problems and issues as the resignation of an employee who acted as a director in his personal capacity.

3.52 If you are on the board of a corporate director, remember that you will owe the same duty of care and have the same responsibilities as you would if you had been appointed to the boards of the managed companies in a personal capacity. Similarlly, if you are an authorised signatory who can execute documents on behalf of a corporate director you must aim to exercise the same duty of care as that expected of, and owed by, a director on the basis your actions could (and probably would) be enforceable on the corporate director.

Factors to Look for in a Corporate Services Agent

3.53 Finally in this Section it is worth covering some of the features which an offshore agent should posses and which a client and their advisers might be looking for in the selection process. There may be a number of factors which might lead a client or his adviser to reach a decision on which corporate agent to choose but it is likely that most of the following points will be considered:

    i)   The basis of their fee calculation;

ii) The level of experience, expertise and knowledge, not only in relation to the laws and procedures of the jurisdiction where they are based, but also in respect of other offshore centres;

iii) The nature of the services which they can offer;

iv) The extent of the paperwork which they will require (some service providers send their clients forms which are very difficult to complete);

v) Whether they have offices or representation in other centres (which could be useful if further companies are required);

vi) Their reputation and standing in the offshore market, perhaps not only in the centre where they are based, but also in the offshore world generally.

Summary

- Describe how an offshore resident company is usually treated for tax purposes

- Outline the differences between offshore tax-exempt and international companies

- Describe the requirements usually applied to tax-exempt companies

- List the information which may have to be supplied to the Registrar of Companies on a locally incorporated offshore company

- Comment on why a client might wish to choose an offshore centre which requires the disclosure of beneficial owner information

- List the services usually offered by corporate agents in offshore centres

- Explain why a client might prefer an agent to provide directors and members of his offshore company

- Outline the role of the registered agent in offshore centres

- List the documentation a service provider might request from a new client

- Summarise the actions usually required following the resignation of an employee of a corporate agent who is a director of their managed companies.

Self-assessment Questions

1. A client wants to open a company in a low tax offshore centre but is concerned that his company would have to pay corporation tax at the local rate. Comment on the options which may be available.

2. Outline the difference between an International Business Company (as offered in many of the Caribbean centres) and an International Company (as offered in some of the European centres).

3. Describe the usual restrictions which are placed on the structure and ownership of tax-exempt companies in low tax offshore centres.

4. Using an offshore centre of your choice, list the details and information which you would usually have to provide to the local Registrar of Companies in respect of a locally incorporated company.

5. List the information which an offshore company might be expected to retain at its registered office.

6. A prospective client is interested in creating a company in an offshore centre which has minimal reporting requirements. Comment on the reasons why he might request this option and suggest a centre which he could use.

7. Following on from Question 6, suggest reasons why the same client might be better advised to create a company in an offshore centre which requires greater disclosure of information.

8. An organisation is considering opening an office in an offshore centre to provide company services. List the services which the organisation might wish to provide.

9. Briefly describe the documentation which an offshore corporate agent would usually insist their clients complete before they agree to provide company services.

10. An employee of a corporate agent has resigned. Briefly outline the actions which the agent should take on the basis that the employee is a director of a number of managed companies.

Unit 8

Offshore Company Administration
Part Three – Special Offshore Company
Vehicles and the Reduction of Risk in the
Administration of Offshore Companies

Objectives

At the end of this Unit you should be able to:

- **Understand the possible benefits of a hybrid company**

- **State the main features of a limited duration company**

- **List five specific administration features and benefits which offshore companies often provide**

- **Describe the potential problems associated with bearer shares**

- **Explain the difference between an AGM and an EGM**

- **List the requirements for a valid meeting**

- **Prepare a draft outline of minutes which could be adapted and used by junior administrators**

- **Explain the potential problems of a client acting as director**

- **Outline the concerns which a service provider would have in issuing a client a general power of attorney**

- **Provide two reasons why a client might want to use more than one company in his offshore structure**

In this Unit we shall look at some of the common situations and potential problems which practitioners often face when administering offshore companies. Much of what we shall cover could equally apply to onshore and offshore companies although we shall of course concentrate on those aspects which are perhaps of greater concern to the offshore practitioner.

We shall start by looking at some of the special types of company which are on offer in some of the offshore centres.

1   Special Types of Company

Companies Limited by Guarantee

1.1   Not all offshore centres offer this type of company although the number of those which do is increasing as some of the possible benefits become more widely appreciated and recognised. At the time of writing they are currently possible in most of the Caribbean centres, Alderney and the Isle of Man.

1.2   Guarantee companies are companies which do not have a share capital. Instead, persons are elected into membership and once elected they are expected to pay an entry subscription and may be asked for further subscriptions in the future. Members will also be required to contribute to the capital should the company go into liquidation while insolvent. A member's liability will be limited to the extent of his guarantee. Usually, a nominal amount is used such as £10.

1.3   Unless provisions are included in the articles to the contrary, each member will have equal voting rights and equal rights to income or capital distributions should any be made. However, a guarantee company would often be structured so that the rights to distributions would be held by one class of members while the voting rights would be held by a second class of members.

Hybrid Companies

1.4   Those centres which allow guarantee companies will also permit this type of company, which is essentially one which is limited by both shares and by guarantee.

1.5   There are two main types of hybrid companies. Firstly, there is the type where the members contribute to the capital of the company and acquire rights pro rata to their contribution. They are then issued with shares but are also required to contribute to the capital should the company subsequently go into liquidation while insolvent. The level of contribution will usually be limited to the amount which is stipulated in the articles.

1.6   The second type is very similar to the first in that there will be members as described previously but there will also be members who are elected who would not usually be required to contribute to the capital on election. However, such persons might still be required to contribute should the company subsequently go into liquidation while insolvent.

1.7   Hybrid companies (and indeed pure guarantee companies) have in recent years been used as tax planning devices and some practitioners have also used them as a type of corporate trust.

Possible tax benefits of a guarantee/hybrid company

1.8   A detailed discussion and explanation of the possible benefits of guarantee and hybrid companies as tax planning entities is outside the scope of this study text, although the following summarises what the main thrust of the arguments are in support of using these vehicles in this manner.

1.9   Generally speaking, much of the tax legislation which is in place onshore looks to assess the interests of members who have shares in a particular company (on the basis that they are the ones who have a direct interest in the profits and income of that company). However, if the members (or perhaps a specific class of members) do not own shares but are instead only members by guarantee, there is an argument to suggest that they should not be assessed to tax on profits which are realised by the company.

1.10   There has been much debate amongst tax experts and onshore revenue authorities concerning the relative merits of the use of guarantee members as a tax saving device and students would be well advised to tell any clients who wish to create a guarantee or hybrid company for tax purposes to seek specific tax advice before proceeding.

Possible use of a guarantee/hybrid company as a 'trust'
1.11   What is required is a little creative drafting of the articles of association and from this it is possible to create a corporate vehicle which takes on many of the characteristics of a common law trust.

Hybrid companies are particularly useful in this regard and the following is one example of how such a company could be structured.

1.12   The articles could be worded so that the management and control of the company lies with the directors and also those members who have the shares. However, neither the directors nor the shareholders would be able to receive any distributions from the company. The articles would also create guarantee members who would be eligible to receive dividends and loan payments. However, they would only have restricted voting rights.

1.13   Under this arrangement, the directors and the shareholders would have a role which would be similar in nature to that of the trustees of a common law trust, whilst the guarantee members would receive an interest which would be similar to that of a discretionary beneficiary under a discretionary trust.

1.14   If required, the articles could also include provisions for the appointment of a person who would oversee the actions of the shareholders and directors and by doing so, would be similar to a protector who is sometimes appointed to act in the interests of the settlor and beneficiaries of an offshore discretionary trust.

1.15   The use of hybrid companies in this manner is increasing in popularity, particularly amongst those clients from civil law countries who are unfamiliar with the common law trust concept. Such clients are often more comfortable with placing their assets into a company rather than a trust vehicle and there is also the added bonus that a company (unlike most trusts) will have perpetual succession.

Limited Duration Companies (LDCs)
1.16   These are companies which have a limited life and at the end of the defined period (usually 30 years) the company will be wound up. In some centres they are known as limited liability companies or limited life companies. Limited duration companies are currently available in centres such as the Bahamas, the Cayman Islands and the Isle of Man.

1.17   The members of LDCs would usually be involved in the management of the company and any income which the company receives, or any realised gains which it makes, will be considered to be the income or gains of the members and not that of the company.

1.18 In view of the way in which they are structured, limited duration companies are considered to be transparent for tax purposes and as such are very similar in nature to a partnership. They present a number of possible tax planning opportunities, most notably for clients in the USA where they are a popular offshore product. Their popularity stems from the fact that it can be advantageous for profits or income to be assessed directly on the individuals behind a structure rather than on a corporate body, on the basis that additional reliefs and exemptions might be available to the individuals which would otherwise be lost.

1.19 The articles of association of LDCs should be carefully checked by corporate administrators, as such companies can be structured in a variety of ways. For example, some LDCs have directors appointed, whereas others may have 'managing members' who will have the same powers and responsibilities usually given to directors.

1.20 Some LDCs will have directors and members (although usually members will have greater powers than the directors) and in a few cases the transfer of shares will be an event which triggers the termination of an LDC.

Protected Cell Companies (PCCs)

1.21 Guernsey was one of the first offshore centres which introduced protected cell companies (PCCs). They provide the usual characteristics found in other companies (e.g. separate legal entity etc.) but their capital is divided into separate parts, known as cells, which are designed to segregate and protect the assets which are held in these different cells.

1.22 PCCs can be used to reduce risk as, in theory, creditors who attack the assets of one cell will not be able to claim against the assets of the company held in other cells. They would, however, have a claim against assets which have not been placed in a separate cell.

1.23 PCCs are a relatively new concept and there already appears to be considerable interest in their features from those involved in the mutual fund and captive insurance industries.

2 Specific Features and Benefits Offered Offshore

2.1 We have already looked at the tax treatment of offshore companies and looked at some of the special vehicles which are possible. We shall now consider some of the other benefits which companies provided from some offshore centres offer.

Sole Directors

2.2 A growing number of centres permit local companies to be incorporated and operate with only one director. Often such centres will have no restrictions on where that sole director must be resident.

2.3 Examples of the centres which allow one director are the Bahamas (IBCs), BVI (IBCs), the Cayman Islands (exempted and non-resident), Cyprus and Gibraltar.

2.4 Clearly, only having one director can make the decision making process easier.

Single Members

2.5   Similarly, as many companies require only one director, an increasing number of centres now allow single member companies to be incorporated, or for existing companies to be switched to single member status. Such an option can create administration efficiencies (e.g. only one share certificate may be required, only one entry in the register of members, resolutions might be easier to pass etc.).

Redomiciliation

2.6   A number of centres will permit a company which has been incorporated in another centre to redomicile locally. This goes much further than simply registering in another centre as it will involve relinquishing the registration which was acquired in the original centre.

2.7   Usually, redomiciliation is only possible if the company laws of the original country are similar to those of the country where the company wishes to move to. Often the Registrar of Companies will require sight of the company's memorandum and articles of association to make sure that there are no conflicts with local requirements.

2.8   In those centres which permit a change of domicile it will often only be specific types of company which can redomicile. For example, in the Cayman Islands and Bermuda only exempted companies can transfer to another jurisdiction, whilst in the BVI only an IBC can transfer in this manner. Similarly, companies wishing to transfer their domicile to one of those centres mentioned would also be expected to take on the characteristics of an exempted company or IBC, depending on the location chosen.

Audit Exemption

2.9   Only a few centres still insist that all local companies must have their annual accounts audited. Most centres now allow exempt companies or IBCs (or their equivalents) to waive the requirement for an audit. This reduces costs for the clients and also saves administration time but it would still be advisable for some types of company (especially trading companies) to have their figures audited.

2.10   The articles of association should be checked in case there is a requirement to audit accounts for a particular company.

Accounts Submission

2.11   Similarly, many centres now allow local companies to dispense with the requirement that their annual accounts must be presented to the members at the AGM. When you consider that most offshore companies are managed by agents who provide the directors as well as members, this option tends to make sense. However, it would still be advisable for accounts to be presented in some cases, especially where members are not being provided by the offshore agent.

2.12   Administrators would be wise to check the articles of association just in case the requirement to submit accounts is covered and in force.

Objects Clause

2.13   Again, a number of centres no longer require local companies to include their intended objects in their memorandum of association. This feature can be advantageous as it effectively means that such companies can conduct their business without being concerned whether they are specifically authorised to do so under its memorandum. It also means that the affairs of those companies enjoy a certain degree of confidentiality on the basis that the outside world need never know what their intended activities or purposes are.

Company Seals

2.14 Company seals are not generally required for offshore companies. Instead documents can be executed under signature of the directors or a director and secretary acting together. In practice, most companies do still have and use a company seal. The articles of association often cover whether a seal is required and if so, who is empowered to use it on behalf of the company.

2.15 The articles may also cover whether a second or additional seal can be issued. This facility would be useful in those instances where a company is registered in more than one location and a seal is needed to execute documents in different locations. Usually, the second seal would require board approval and would often have to state in its imprint that it is only for use in a particular country or jurisdiction and that it cannot be used elsewhere.

Written Resolutions

2.16 To create greater administration efficiencies you will find that many centres will allow local companies to pass written resolutions without the need for a meeting to be held. A written resolution must be circulated to all those who would be entitled to attend and/or vote at a meeting at which the proposed resolution would otherwise have to be discussed and the various parties would be asked to sign it. Once all the parties have signed it the resolution would be returned to the company and would be deemed to have been approved. Written resolutions are particularly useful when there is either a single member or a single director.

2.17 Once again, the articles of association should be checked in case written resolutions are in fact barred.

Bearer Shares

2.18 Although not all centres offer this type of share those which do have found many clients keen to take advantage of this facility.

2.19 There are two main reasons why bearer shares are popular with some clients. Firstly, they provide confidentiality as the holder's details are not recorded on the company's register of members, nor are these details held by the Registrar of Companies or required to be submitted. Secondly, the ownership of the shares passes by delivery and some clients prefer the comfort which comes with holding the share certificate which actually records and proves their ownership rights over a particular company.

2.20 There are, by the very nature of the rights of ownership of such shares, some important considerations which the agent must address if he is to provide services for a company which will or has issued bearer shares.

Security of the share certificate

2.21 As the ownership of the shares will pass by delivery it is important that the certificates be kept in a secure place. Most service providers would prefer to retain them locally rather than risk sending them to the client in case they are lost in transit (or even lost by the client). If the certificates are kept by the agent he should make sure they are retained under secure conditions, perhaps in a safe under dual control. They certainly must not be retained with the other papers in a documents file as registered share certificates are often held.

Change of ownership

2.22 This should perhaps be of more serious concern to the service provider. If he decides to send the bearer share certificates to his client there would be nothing to prevent the client from passing those shares to someone else, which would effectively transfer the ownership of the company without the service provider being aware that a transfer had taken place.

2.23 The concern here would be that the new owner might not be the type of client which the agent would want to provide services for. Nor would the agent have been able to perform his usual checks on the new owner or put in place the usual agreements and indemnities which we covered in Unit 7.

2.24 For these reasons, service providers are generally reluctant to provide services for companies which have issued bearer shares.

2.25 However, there is an option for clients who require confidentiality and security and we shall cover this when we look at the use of nominee declarations for registered shares later in this Unit.

Share premium

2.26 In many centres it is possible for shares to be issued at a premium. For example, a beneficial owner may want to contribut capital of US$1 million into his company but does not want to increase the authorised share capital beyond US$50,000 (perhaps because of the additional duty this might create).

2.27 Instead, the company could receive, for example, US$50,000 to cover the par value of 50,000 US$1.00 shares and the remaining cash could be treated as a premium on the shares of US$19 per share. The share premium would be recorded in the company's finances and could be used for certain cash requirements in the future (although there may be local restrictions on the use of such a reserve).

Student Activity 1

Select one offshore centre in Europe, one in the Caribbean and another in the Pacific. Compare and contrast the specific attractions of those centres, based on the list which you have just read under Section 2.

3 The Decision Making Process

3.1 Companies have many attractive features and can fulfil functions. But one thing that they are unable to do is make a decision. Decisions have to be taken for them and as we have already mentioned, this would usually be the responsibility of the directors on the basis that they manage the day-to-day affairs of a company.

3.2 However, in certain circumstances a company will act following a decision which has been taken by the members, who are, after all the owners of the company and therefore entitled to have a say in certain aspects of the business of their company.

3.3 In this Section we shall concentrate on how a company, or rather how the directors and members, reach their decisions and also how those decisions are then recorded. Directors' and members' meetings and resolutions are key areas of which company administrators (and of course students of this subject) should be aware. They are also areas which commonly create problems as the importance of accurate and comprehensive records detailing the actions which an offshore company has undertaken cannot be overestimated. Administrators and students should be aware that failure to conduct proper meetings or pass valid resolutions can result in the legality and effect of an offshore company being undermined which could result in disastrous consequences, not only for the client, but also the service provider and possibly the centre as a whole.

3.4 Before we look at some of the practical issues which arise from meetings and resolutions, we should first of all remind ourselves of the importance of the articles of association and the local statutory provisions in place covering these matters.

The Articles of Association

3.5 It has often been mentioned that before a particular course of action is followed, the director (or administrators) of a company should first of all refer to the articles of association to determine whether the action which is proposed is authorised under the articles. The decision making process is no exception as the articles would usually cover what formalities must be met to enable a decision to be taken. This information would often come under a heading such as 'Directors' Meetings', 'Meetings' or Resolutions.

Statutory Requirements

3.6 Of similar importance are the statutory provisions relating to the holding and conduct of meetings and the passing of resolutions in the centre concerned. Usually, the local company laws will set down the minimum requirements which a company must fulfil in relation to the decision making process for particular matters, although in practice the articles of association would usually over-ride what the statutes covered.

3.7 However, administrators should still bear in mind what the local laws specify in relation to the holding and conduct of meetings and the passing of resolutions otherwise they will not be able to confirm that the provisions included in the articles of their companies are sufficiently detailed.

We can now move on to cover some of the practical aspects of directors' and members' meetings.

Types of Meeting

We are concerned here with only two types of meeting, namely members' meetings and directors' meetings.

Members' meetings

3.8 Members' meetings are sometimes referred to as company meetings as they involve the owners of the company. However, they should more accurately be described as general meetings of the company.

3.9   Some centres require companies to hold a general meeting every calendar year. The annual meetings are commonly known as annual general meetings, or AGMs. All other general meetings are known as extraordinary general meetings, or EGMs.

3.10   It is important that the local statutory requirements are followed concerning the holding of an AGM as often the submission of an annual return will be linked to the date of this meeting. If the meeting is not held the return, too, might be delayed which would result in the company being in default with its filing obligations which could in turn lead to the company, in time, being fined and possibly struck off the register.

3.11   The local centre's company laws will specify when the first AGM must be held (which in many centres must be within 18 months of incorporation) and also the timing of subsequent meetings (which would often be within 15 months of the previous AGM but always one in every calendar year).

3.12   The nature of the business conducted at the AGM will usually be determined by the articles of association although it usually includes such business as the declaration of a dividend, considering and approving the annual accounts (which should already have been signed by the board), considering the directors' and, if applicable, the auditors' reports in the accounts and approving any alterations required to the board of directors.

3.13   The business to be conducted at an EGM will be those matters, usually of an urgent nature, which will not, or cannot wait until the next AGM (such as the removal of a director).

Directors' meetings
3.14   There is usually no statutory requirement to hold a directors' meeting although one exception is a Cayman Islands exempted company which must have an annual meeting of the directors. The directors will meet as and when required to discuss and conduct business which relates to the day-to-day affairs of the company.

Attendance at Meetings
3.15   Again, the articles should cover this but generally all members of the same class (i.e. all ordinary shareholders) would be entitled to attend and vote at a general meeting and all directors would be entitled to attend and vote at a meeting of the directors.

3.16   Those who are entitled to attend a particular type of meeting would receive notice of that meeting. The articles of association would usually stipulate the minimum length of notice which that director or member should receive to advise them that a meeting was proposed. This notice period often ranges from between seven and 28 'clear' days. Clear days in this respect would exclude the date the notice was issued as well as the proposed date of the meeting.

3.17   If the required notice period is not met the meeting will not have been convened in accordance with the requirements of the company, and as a result, any proceedings will be considered invalid. Making sure notices are sent to every interested party on time would of course prevent this problem. Another possible solution could be to include provisions in the articles allowing for meetings to be held at shorter notice, if required.

3.18 Provided the necessary agreement of the parties concerned is obtained, a meeting could then be called within this shorter notice period and any proceedings would then be valid. This facility would be useful in instances where a meeting is required to discuss an urgent item of business which could not wait for the usual notice period to expire.

3.19 If a member cannot attend a particular meeting he may appoint someone to represent him. This person is often referred to as a proxy and will be able to attend the meeting and vote on behalf of the member who was unable to attend in person. The articles would usually cover the requirements for this appointment but rarely would this require the approval of the directors.

3.20 If a director is unable to attend a board meeting (perhaps because he will be out of the country) the articles would usually allow him to appoint someone to represent him. This person would be called an alternate director but, because the powers of an alternate are usually the same as those given to full board members, such an appointment would generally require the approval of the other directors.

3.21 The articles will also usually state the minimum number of persons who will be required to be present at a meeting. This minimum number is generally referred to as the quorum. If the quorum is not met but the meeting is still held, the proceedings of that meeting would in most cases be invalid.

3.22 Finally, before we leave the subject of attendance at meetings we should mention that the articles of offshore companies now commonly include provisions which enable meetings to be held by telephone. This can save time and enable urgent matters to be discussed within the shortest time frame possible.

3.23 The articles of association of companies which allow telephone meetings should include provisions as to where a telephone meeting is deemed to be held for 'control' purposes. This would usually be where the chairman resides and to avoid possible problems, an offshore director should be elected chairman of such meetings.

Resolutions

3.24 Once the meeting has been duly convened (by notice) and constituted (by a quorum being present) proposals, usually referred to as motions, can be put to the meeting which will be discussed by those present. Following the discussions a decision will then be taken which is commonly referred to as a 'resolution'.

3.25 The members can pass different kinds of resolution. Ordinary resolutions cover 'ordinary' business such as the approval of the accounts at the AGM whereas special resolutions cover 'special' or urgent business such as altering the articles of association, removing a director or placing the company into voluntary liquidation. Usually, longer notice would be given for those meetings at which a special resolution is to be proposed. Special resolutions often require more than just a simple majority of votes in favour to be effective (the majority often required is 75% or more).

3.26 The articles will often state what type of resolution will be required for certain types of business. Care should therefore be taken to ensure what kind of resolution is required as otherwise the decision might not be valid.

Recording the Decisions

3.27 We now move on to look at minutes of meetings. The minutes provide a record of when and where a meeting was held, who was present, what was discussed and what was subsequently decided. The minutes should be agreed and approved and are usually signed by the chairman of that meeting or perhaps by the chairman of the next meeting. For those of you who are unfamiliar with this term, the chairman of a meeting is the person who has been appointed to control the conduct and proceedings of a meeting.

3.28 We have already mentioned that a company cannot make a decision for itself and that it relies on the directors and, in some cases, the members to make decisions for it. Major administrative and possible legal problems can result if a decision has been taken which the company then acts on, but there is no record of the directors or the members making that decision.

3.29 Without such a record, the validity of actions which the company takes could be brought into question. Perhaps of greater and more obvious concern should be the fact that the beneficial owner might be brought into the equation as the person who in fact instigated the action, rather than the directors or members. We shall return to this when we look at the role of the client later in this Unit.

3.30 However, having a record of a meeting in place does not mean there will never be any questions raised as to the validity of the decisions taken. Far from it, as all decisions must be taken with the benefit of the company in mind. However, without such a record it can be difficult to prove why such a decision was actioned and on whose authority the company has acted.

3.31 Students should, therefore, understand the importance of minutes of meetings and also be familiar with their preparation, which is what we shall now concentrate on.

Format of the minutes of meetings

3.32 Those of you who are involved with the preparation of minutes may be familiar with your own organisation's in-house style and wording. This may differ from the style of the minutes which other organisations use. That is not to say that your organisation's style is right or that anothers is wrong. It is just that there is no specified or stipulated format which has to be followed.

3.33 Although actual wording or specific phrases may differ, you will probably find that the basic format of company and directors' minutes will essentially be the same, often regardless of service provider and also regardless of jurisdiction. The following is a format which is commonly used:

a) Type of Meeting
The type of meeting will usually be recorded, followed by when and where the meeting was held. Often the time of the meeting would also be noted.

b) Persons Present
Who attended the meeting will be covered, together with confirmation of who (if anyone) was absent. It would be usual for a note to be made that a quorum was present and also confirmation that the required notice had been given or if not, that short notice had been agreed.

c) Chairman

The appointment of the Chairman would often be next and in some cases reference may also be made to the person who acted as secretary (usually the company secretary would perform this task and take the minutes).

d) Previous Minutes

The fact that the Chairman (or perhaps the Secretary) read the minutes of the previous meeting would then usually be recorded. The Chairman would also sign them if this has not already been done. Any matters arising from the minutes of the earlier meeting would then be covered.

e) Business Conducted

The business which was covered in the meeting, which should correspond with the business set out in the agenda dispatched with the notice, would then be mentioned.

f) Resolutions

Discussions leading up to a decision would not usually be recorded in detail although it is common to see wording to the effect that discussions did take place (i.e. 'After a brief discussion.....'). Decisions which were then reached would usually be prefixed with wording such as 'IT WAS RESOLVED'.

g) Attachments to the Minutes

If a document was presented to the meeting for discussion, a copy would usually be attached to the minutes for reference purposes and would be cross-referenced along the lines of 'The Chairman presented to the meeting a [contract, agreement, etc.], a copy of which is attached and deemed to form part of these minutes as if set out herein at length.' This would prevent the need to refer to the document in detail in the text of the minutes.

h) Termination of the Meeting

Once all the above had been covered, the Chairman would close the meeting, although before doing so he might fix the date of the next meeting.

i) Signature

Usually, the Chairman of the meeting signs the minutes although this might be deferred until the next meeting when the Chairman of that meeting might sign them.

j) Filing

Minutes are usually kept in a register or book at the registered office of the company. Often there will be a separate book for directors' and members' minutes. Some resolutions (notably special resolutions) might have to be filed with the local Registrar of Companies in the centre concerned. Students should take the time to discover what local filing requirements exist in their centre or in a centre with which they have a particular interest.

Student Activity 2

Compare the style of your organisation's minutes with those which are prepared by any of your competitors (or, failing that, the format covered earlier). Highlight any differences and try to explain why these differences might exist.

Examples of Meetings and Resolutions Required

3.34   The possibilities are of course endless and local requirements may vary between centres. However, here are a few examples of common administration situations which require a decision to be made on behalf of a company. Against each one is a note of the type of meeting (and resolution) which would usually be required.

Appointment of an additional director

3.35   Either a resolution of the directors at a directors' meeting or an ordinary resolution of the members at an EGM.

Removal of a director

3.36   Either a resolution of the directors at a directors' meeting or a special resolution of the members at an EGM.

Appointment of the company secretary

3.37   Directors' resolution at a meeting of the directors.

Allotment of shares

3.38   Directors' resolution at a meeting of the directors.

Increase in authorised capital

3.39   Special resolution of the members at an EGM.

To open a bank account

3.40   Directors' resolution at a meeting of the directors.

To appoint an investment manager

3.41   Directors' resolution at a meeting of the directors.

Change the name of the company

3.42   Special resolution of the members at an EGM.

Approval of the annual accounts

3.43   Directors' resolution at a meeting of the directors.

Consideration of the annual accounts

3.44   Ordinary resolution of the members at an AGM.

Written Resolutions

3.45   Although we have concentrated on the types of meetings which will be required to conduct certain types of business, it should not be forgotten that in many instances an offshore company can make a decision by written resolution without the need for a meeting to be held.

3.46 Often a written resolution signed by the director(s) or member(s), depending on the type of business to be decided, will be the preferred choice rather than the holding of a meeting. Indeed, if there is only a sole director or single member, a written resolution is the ideal method for their decisions and actions to be recorded.

3.47 Written resolutions may not be permitted in every offshore centre nor by every company. Students should, however, be aware that this option does exist.

Student Activity 3

Select any two of the situations from the above list and prepare draft resolutions which cover the business which is to be conducted.

4 The Role and Involvement of the Beneficial Owner

4.1 This is one of the areas which can cause the administrators of offshore companies the most problems as many beneficial owners (usually the person on whose behalf a company has been created) seem to think that they can open an offshore company and enjoy the various potential benefits which this can create, yet at the same time retain total control over the assets which they have placed into their company.

4.2 As we have already seen, it is often where the management and control of a company is exercised which determines where that company will be considered resident for tax purposes. If it can be argued that the client is managing the assets or affairs of an offshore company, it could affect the tax situation of that entity and possibly undermine, and even remove, any benefits which might have been possible by basing that company in an offshore centre in the first place.

Let us now look at some of the ways in which a beneficial owner might attempt or wish to exert some control over their company and how the service provider might want to respond.

The Client Wants to be Appointed a Director or as the Sole Director

4.3 There will be no statutory restrictions to prevent a client from being appointed as a director of their offshore company (provided he has the necessary capacity and is not precluded from acting), although some companies must have at least one director resident in the offshore centre concerned.

There are, however, a few issues which need to be addressed.

Management and control

4.4 If the client were to be appointed a director there could be a management and control problem, especially if he were to become the sole director or one of only two on the board. In such cases there would be an argument that the client was able to control the company, and this could mean that it would be deemed to be resident in the country or jurisdiction where the client was based, possibly making it liable to tax in that centre and therefore losing the potential offshore benefits.

4.5   If the client insists on being represented on the board, a possible solution might be to have three or more directors with the majority resident in the offshore centre. In addition, one of the offshore directors could be appointed Managing Director in an attempt to show to the outside world that the company is managed and controlled by the offshore board members and not by the client.

Split boards

4.6   Some service providers will refuse to provide directors if the client is also to be appointed as a director. The situation where an agent provides a director alongside the client (or perhaps his adviser) is often referred to as a split board as the agent will not provide the majority of the board members.

4.7   The concern of the service provider in such situations would usually be that the outside director(s) might carry out activities on behalf of the company without first referring to the other board members.

4.8   Those agents who do act on split boards will usually arrange for the articles to be worded in such a way that decisions cannot be taken without their approval. This would usually involve the quorum at directors' meetings being set so that at least one of the agent's representatives on the board has to be present to enable a valid decision to be made. Similarly, the usual power given to the members to remove and appoint directors would be altered so that notice of a meeting to discuss such business would have to be communicated to the full board who would have the right to attend and, if appropriate, vote.

The Client Wants to Act as an 'Agent' or Adviser

4.9   As an alternative to being appointed to the board of directors, a client might instead wish to have the power to manage the investments or arrange contracts on behalf of the company, usually as an agent.

4.10   The directors would be able to do this, but again, there is a management and control issue. The powers given to the client in his capacity as agent should not be greater than, or override, those of the directors in respect of those assets.

The Client Requests a Power of Attorney

4.11   There are essentially two types of power of attorney. Firstly, there is a special power of attorney which is restricted to activities which are expressly specified under the terms of the deed. Secondly, there is a general power of attorney which gives the person appointed much wider powers over 'general' business matters and not restricted to specific areas.

4.12   Very few service providers would be prepared to issue a general power of attorney, especially in those cases where they also provide the directors. It would not matter on whose behalf the power was issued as the wide powers which would generally be bestowed under a general power of attorney would enable the donee to conduct business on behalf of the company, and his actions would almost certainly bind the company.

4.13   Apart from the general concerns over the perceived place of the management and control which a general power of attorney would create, there is a greater danger that the donee of a general power could incur liabilities which the directors are not aware of and for which they could be liable.

4.14   A special power of attorney restricted to certain matters would be more favourably considered but once again the powers given should not be seen to be sufficiently wide so as to transfer overall management and control to the client or donee. If granted, the directors would be expected to monitor the activities of the donee of the power and to consider, from time to time, the duration of the arrangement which should not be for an indefinite period.

The Client Wants Signing Authority

4.15   The client might wish to have the power to sign on the company's bank account. Once again, there is a management and control problem if this were to be granted, as such a power means the client controls the assets of the company.

4.16   A possible solution might be to allow the client to have signing authority but with payments only being instigated if the instructions were countersigned by two directors, both provided by the offshore agent. The directors would retain control over the account, but a question could still be raised as to why the client could sign on behalf of the company in the first place and also in what capacity he was authorised to do so.

The Client Would Like a Credit Card in the Company's Name

4.17   A number of service providers are happy to issue corporate credit or debit cards in the name of a corporate entity and for those cards to be used by the beneficial owner of the company concerned.

4.18   However, this should raise concerns similar to those covered in the Section above in that if the client were able to incur debts which would be covered by the company's assets, there would be a strong argument that by doing so he controls those assets. Questions over the capacity of the client and his right to have such a card would also be raised, especially if the company was fully managed by the agent.

4.19   A solution might be to issue a credit or debit card in the name of the client and for the company to guarantee to cover any debts which are incurred under that card. Repayments could then be treated as a loan from the company to the client which would be agreed by the board from time to time.

The Client Wants to Direct the Directors

4.20   This is the most common request which is made by clients. They understand the need for management and control being offshore but still want to tell the directors what to do.

4.21   Some administrators find this a difficult area because the client has instructed the corporate agents to provide various services on his behalf, for which he is paying a fee, and will also (in most cases) be providing the funds which the company will hold and possibly manage. On the other hand, the directors are personally responsible and liable for their actions and they must only act if they feel it is in the best interests of the company to do so. They should also be comfortable that the actions are within their powers and not in contravention of the articles of association or the company laws of the offshore centre.

4.22 Before the company has been incorporated and certainly before any administration services are provided, the agent must impress upon the client the benefits which an offshore company can create and then make him understand how these benefits can be eroded if the client tries to take over the management and control.

4.23 Certainly the agent can act on requests which are received from the client, provided the agent is comfortable with the request. When they do act in this manner, the agents must of course make sure that the appropriate meeting is held or resolution passed and that the decision which is taken is properly documented (recorded in writing). This provides, one would hope, sufficient proof that the decision was taken by the directors (or members) and not of course by the client, showing that management and control is firmly offshore.

5 Nominee Declarations

5.1 It has already been mentioned that bearer shares can create administration problems and often the secrecy which they provide is outweighed by the security aspects.

5.2 The alternative to bearer shares is registered shares but as we have seen, details of the holders of registered shares are usually advised to the local Registrar of Companies and often recorded in the register of members (which is sometimes available for inspection by the general public).

5.3 Many clients are therefore concerned that their ownership of an offshore company will be recorded publicly. However, there is a solution which we have already touched upon.

5.4 Service providers will usually be willing to provide the registered shareholders of an offshore company on behalf of their clients. Usually, the agent will own a company which it has incorporated for the sole purpose of acting as the registered shareholder for managed companies. Such a company is often described as a nominee company. However, some agents use their employees as the shareholders.

5.5 Clearly, neither the agent nor his employees are the true owners of the companies for which they act as registered shareholders. They are only in that capacity as agents, or nominees. What they will (or should) therefore do is execute a document which confirms that they are merely holding the shares on behalf of another party (which would usually be the client). This document is commonly called a nominee declaration although some would prefer to use the terms shareholder declaration, declaration of trust, or nominee shareholder declaration.

5.6 Basically, the registered shareholder would declare who the true (or beneficial) owner of the shares is and state that he is only holding the shares as his nominee, or bare trustee, on trust for that person or entity. The declaration would also usually confirm that the nominee will act and vote in accordance with the instructions of the beneficial owner and often it is attached to the share certificate.

5.7 Some service providers send the declarations to the beneficial owners whilst others keep them and instead send to the client the share certificate and a signed stock transfer form with the transferee details left blank. However, this could enable the client to transfer ownership of the company without telling the service provider, a problem which we touched upon when looking at bearer shares earlier in this Unit.

5.8 Many service providers word the declarations in such a manner that they provide for future beneficial owners of the shares on the death of the original owner. Some even suggest that these documents could be worded in such a manner that they could act as a type of trust arrangement in perpetuity.

5.9 However, students should remember that a declaration is really a nominee agreement despite the fact that the word 'trust' may appear in the title or the terms of the document and as such, there is an argument that it should not be relied upon to transfer ownership on the death of the beneficial owner. Indeed, if a nominee transfers shares on the death of the owner to a person who is not entitled to the deceased's estate, he might be committing a fraud on the estate which could create serious consequences for the agent involved.

5.10 Instead of using a nominee declaration to provide for future generations of ownership on the death of the beneficial owner, the agent should perhaps suggest that a discretionary trust be created and that the shares are registered in the name of a nominee shareholder. A nominee declaration would then be issued by the shareholder in favour of the trustees of the trust.

5.11 Some clients like their companies to be owned equally with their spouse or some other party, and ask this joint ownership to be reflected in the nominee declaration. This is possible (notwithstanding the possible problem covered in 5.9) but the client should be asked to confirm whether the joint ownership is to be under a joint tenancy or as tenants in common.

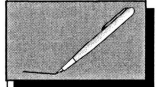

Student Activity 4

Obtain a copy of your organisation's nominee declaration (or obtain a copy of a declaration which you have received from another service provider). Summarise the terms and in particular highlight the rights of the beneficial owner of those shares.

6 Funding of Offshore Companies

6.1 Companies will generally require assets to perform their intended activities and how those assets are transferred in will be an important consideration for service providers. Often it will also determine how funds can then be distributed back to the beneficial owner.

There are a number of options which are available but perhaps the following are the most commonly used methods.

Loans

6.2   Usually, the beneficial owner of a company will introduce funds by way of a loan. Any loan which is made or eventually repaid should be approved by the directors and properly recorded. This would usually involve the completion of a loan agreement or promissory note setting out the details of the loan and for a directors' meeting to be held, at which the proposed transaction is discussed and an appropriate resolution passed.

6.3   A loan agreement, rather than a promissory note, would often be desirable which should include terms which cover, among other things, the lendee and lendor, the amount lent, the proposed duration of the loan with details of how this can be altered and also a clause which confirms the interest, if any, which is to be paid on the balance outstanding.

6.4   Ideally, there should be a commercial reason why a loan is to be made. Usually this would require a market rate of interest being payable. However, many loans, which have been created involving offshore companies, are structured as interest-free arrangements with no fixed date for repayment. The directors and administrators of companies who have entered into such an arrangement would be well advised to take note that the loan might be difficult to justify if ever questioned by an outside party.

Allotment of Shares

6.5   The owner could introduce funds in return for shares. However, it might prove difficult for the company to be able to return funds which have been introduced in this manner as it might mean having to cancel issued shares, an action which might require court approval in some centres.

Dividends

6.6   Realised gains and income could be distributed to the members by way of a dividend. As the members would usually be holding the shares as nominees on behalf of the beneficial owners, any sums distributed in this manner would pass directly to the client (in accordance with the nominee declaration which should be in place).

6.7   However, dividend payments are generally treated as income and there might be tax implications if funds were distributed in this manner. In addition, withholding tax may have to be deducted from dividends which are paid by certain types of offshore companies from low tax centres (usually resident companies) to persons who reside outside that centre.

Capital Distributions from Reserves

6.8   As an alternative to a dividend, it might be possible, under the terms of the articles of association (and provided it did not contravene local company law), to make a distribution out of the reserves of the company. This would usually be treated as a capital distribution rather than an income payment and might therefore avoid the possible taxation problems which could arise if a dividend payment was made. Often assets contributed by the beneficial owner will be treated as a capital contribution, thus making a return of capital possible if these assets are to be repaid in the future.

Salaries/Commissions

6.9   It might be possible to introduce funds into the company by way of services which the client has performed, either for or on behalf of the company. For example, the company might enter into a contract for the provision of certain services (such as advice or know-how) which the company asks the client to perform (under terms of a contract perhaps). The company would then invoice the recipient of the services and in turn the client is paid a salary or commission in recognition of their services performed.

7   Multi-Company Structures

7.1   In many cases more than one offshore company will be used in a structure to meet the needs of a particular client. In addition, offshore companies are widely used in collaboration with offshore trusts.

We shall look at the trust and company structures in detail in later Units and in this Section we shall provide a few reasons why multi-company structures might sometimes used.

Reducing Risk by Diversification

7.2   Although there are usually no restrictions on the type or number of assets which an offshore company can hold or own, it is usual practise for separate companies to be used to hold different types of assets. For example, if a client wanted to place his property, investment portfolio and works of art into an offshore structure, it would be common practice for his adviser to suggest that three companies be used, one to hold the property, one for the investments and one to hold the works of art.

7.3   If the ownership is divided in this manner, the client should enjoy a greater level of protection and security than if all the assets were held by one company. This is designed to provide protection in the situation where a dispute may arise relating to part of the client's assets, as the dispute should, in theory, be restricted to the company which is used to hold the asset under dispute. The other assets should be protected as they would be owned by a different entity which one would hope would not be party to the problem.

7.4   By the same token, if there were, for example, three freehold properties then three separate offshore companies would usually be created, with one being used to hold each property.

Lex Situs

7.5   This is perhaps an extension to the above reason. The law of the jurisdiction where the asset is held may demand that a company be used to hold that particular asset. For example, realty will usually have to be registered in the name of a company or an individual.

Confidentiality

7.6   Some clients prefer to use more than one offshore centre in which to conduct their financial affairs. They perceive that this would offer greater scope for confidentiality and secrecy. Hence, you will often find that a client will place a proportion of his assets in a company in one centre and another company would be used in another centre in which the balance of his assets are held.

In this way the protection which can be provided by a multi-company structure can be further enhanced by multi-jurisdictional protection.

8 Administration Reviews

8.1 A discussion of the administration of offshore companies would not be complete without spending some time looking at the review process which those who provide company management services should undertake on their client's companies on a regular basis.

8.2 It is sometimes surprising how much effort a corporate agent might make in establishing a client relationship and working with other intermediaries in incorporating a company for a particular client, compared with how little time they subsequently spend in the future making sure that they are servicing the business as required.

8.3 After all, it does not really matter how sophisticated an asset planning structure might be if the company at the centre of the arrangement has failed to apply for tax exemption or is in arrears with the local statutory requirements and in danger of being struck off.

8.4 We all hope that the documentation side of the companies which we administer is in good shape. The reality can be a little different. Those administrators who conduct a full review of the records and affairs of the companies for which they act will be in a better position to spot, and possibly rectify, any possible problems more easily and more efficiently than those administrators who fail to implement such a procedure.

8.5 The following is a list of areas which should form the basis of a checklist of points which an annual review of a client company's affairs should address.

Local Statutory Requirements

8.6 Clearly, the statutory requirements which must be fulfilled will depend upon the local laws in place in the centre concerned. Students should be familiar with those requirements which apply in their own centre or at least in a centre with which they have a close connection.

8.7 Examples of some of the requirements which may apply are:

a) An AGM might have to be held in each calendar year;

b) An annual directors' meeting held in the local centre might be required;

c) There might (and usually would) be a requirement that an annual return has to be prepared and lodged with the Registrar of Companies, together with the appropriate filing fee;

d) Changes in the directors or other officers of a company might have to be advised to the Registrar of Companies;

e) Changes to the capital of the company, its registered office address or alterations to its memorandum or articles of association (or equivalent) might also have to be notified to the Registrar of Companies;

f)   The annual accounts of a company may have to be presented to the members of the company for approval and indeed may also have to be audited. Some centres allow an annual audit to be waived but this may require the yearly approval of the members. Similarly, the waiving of the presentation of accounts may be possible but again approval might be needed from the members;

g)   There may be a requirement that the company must not trade locally;

h)   There might also be a requirement that a director (or the majority of directors) be resident in the offshore centre;

i)   Some centres require that certain officers have to be appointed, such as a secretary or treasurer, and that those officers must themselves meet certain criteria, such as residency in the centre and/or hold a particular qualification;

j)   The registered office might have to hold up-to-date registers of directors, officers, members and possibly charges as well as the company seal, minute books and accounting records.

8.9   The administrator who is conducting the review should make sure that all the necessary statutory requirements have been met, and if there are any breaches, that they are remedied as quickly as possible.

Minutes/Resolutions

8.10   The book or books containing the minutes of the meetings or written resolutions of the directors and members should be thoroughly reviewed. This is mainly to ensure that any actions or decisions which have been taken have been correctly recorded and that the actions or decisions so approved have been carried out.

8.11   The minutes should, in most cases, be signed and any attachments which are referred to should be affixed. Often minutes are allocated a number for filing and record purposes and the review process should show whether any are missing from the file. Some practitioners refer to the date of the previous meeting in their minutes and if this system is used, the minute book(s) should be reviewed to make sure that there are minutes on file which correspond to the previous meeting details. Similar procedures are usually applied to written resolutions.

8.12   If members' meetings have been held and proxies appointed, the appropriate form appointing the proxies should be attached to the minutes.

8.13   If an alternate director attended a meeting of the board, written confirmation of his appointment to this position should be held in the files and depending on the requirements of the articles of association, a resolution of the directors should be held approving his appointment. Similar actions would be required for a written resolution of the directors where an alternate director has signed the resolution.

8.14   In addition, copies of any notices which have been issued should also be held on file, ideally with the minute of the meeting or resolution for which the notice was required.

8.15   Finally, for recently incorporated companies, a check should be made that the necessary action has been taken to activate the company. Some articles of association require that the first directors have to be appointed by the subscribers. This might differ from the local company law which may state that those who consented to act on the application for incorporation are deemed to be appointed on incorporation. It is possible that the service provider might have forgotten to hold a subscriber's meeting after incorporation to appoint the directors, on the basis such a meeting is not required in the majority of cases.

8.16 A check of this at the annual review stage might reveal that an embarrassing omission has been made but at least such a situation can be rectified relatively quickly and a subscribers' (or members') meeting held to make amends. Without the review it might be many years before the error was spotted which could possibly create additional complications and problems.

Taxation Treatment

8.17 This is a priority on the checklist for a company which has been incorporated or registered in a low tax, as opposed to a no tax, centre. The administrator conducting the review should make sure that the company has been granted, or at least recently applied for, the required special tax status which will prevent the company from paying tax at the full rate in the offshore centre.

8.18 If the application has not been made it may be possible to make a late filing. If it is too late to make an application, it may be possible to appeal against a liability at the full corporate tax rate on the grounds that the failure to make a submission was a clerical error. There are of course no guarantees that the local tax department will view such a plea with any leniency as it is the responsibility of the company to make such an application. However, it would be advisable to bring such a mistake to the attention of the tax department concerned as soon as possible.

Documentation

8.19 The annual review process provides a suitable opportunity to look at the documentation which the company has executed or holds. It also offers the chance to put in place documentation which the company should already have in place.

8.20 Sometimes documentation which has been prepared in previous years might now be out of date. For example, the company might have executed bank account opening documentation and provided the bank with an authorised signatory list. However, subsequent changes to the directors might not have been notified to the bank and therefore the previously submitted paperwork is out of date and new documentation is required.

8.21 Usually, the review process highlights paperwork which has not been prepared, such as a loan agreement between the company and the beneficial owner following the owner introducing funds to the company.

8.22 If the administrator conducting the review notices that documentation is required, he may need to obtain legal advice on how to proceed and must not simply arrange for the missing documentation to be executed and 'backdated'. Backdating papers can be a criminal act and although it is possible for a directors' or members' meeting to be held to ratify actions, it is advisable to complete paperwork at the time of the transaction.

Accounting Information

8.23 Usually, the annual review process will coincide with the preparation of the company's financial statements. This can create efficiencies as the company's records would have to be reviewed at the time the accounts are being prepared and possibly audited.

Internal Records

8.24 Finally, an annual review provides the administrator with the opportunity to check that the service provider's internal records are correct and that internal procedures and policies have been followed. Here are a few of the more common internal matters which would be reviewed:

a) That the beneficial owner has executed an indemnity and that a management agreement is in place. This would also be a good time to check whether any other 'due diligence' procedures need to be addressed, and if necessary, additional or missing paperwork could be requested from the beneficial owner (such as a copy of their passport);

b) That the fees have been charged at the correct rate;

c) That the database of the company (which would usually be computer-based) is current;

d) Undated signed letters of resignation of the current directors and officers are on file for use in the future;

e) The required number of share certificates have been issued and executed as required, and that where nominee shareholders have been used, nominee declarations are in place which meet the requirements of the beneficial owner(s). If there is more than one beneficial owner, the declaration should be worded so as to clarify whether the shares are beneficially held on a joint tenancy or as tenants in common. Similarly, it might be advisable for the declaration to provide for what is to happen to the shares on the death of the beneficial owner (although care should be taken as this might amount to a fraud on the estate as we mentioned in an earlier section.

f) Diary cards have been established to make sure that future statutory and other filing requirements are the subject of reminder messages;

g) Items held in safe custody are reconciled against a list of items the service provider believes should be held.

Summary

Now that you have read this Unit you should be able to:

● Describe the possible benefits of a hybrid company

● Outline the main features of a limited duration company

● List five administration benefits commonly available as a result of the features usually associated with an offshore company

● Explain why a service provider might be reluctant to issue bearer shares in client companies

● Explain the difference between an AGM and an EGM

● Describe the requirements which must be met in order for a meeting to be valid

● Prepare a format of the minutes which could be used for a meeting of the directors

● Explain why a client should not usually be appointed a director of an offshore company

● Outline the concerns which a service provider would have in issuing a general power of attorney to a client

● Explain why multi-company structures are popular with some clients

Self-assessment Questions

1. Briefly explain how a hybrid company can be structured to take on some of the features of a discretionary trust.

2. Describe the usual role of the members of a limited duration company.

3. List six of the features which an offshore company might have which could be attractive to an international client.

4. A client has asked you to incorporate a company in an offshore centre which allows bearer shares. He then requests you to send the bearer certificates to him. How would you respond?

5. Describe how a company can make a decision.

6. List the usual business which is conducted at a company's AGM and compare this with the business which is usually conducted at an EGM.

7. Prepare a list which contains the main headings or areas which you would expect to see covered in the minutes of a directors' meeting.

8. One of your clients has asked to be appointed to the board of directors of his company. There are currently two offshore directors, both provided by your organisation, and he has asked that one resigns to create the vacancy required. Respond accordingly.

9. The same client then asks the company to issue a power of attorney with him as the donee of the power. How would you respond to this request?

10. Explain why some clients might wish to use more than one offshore company to hold their various assets.

Unit 9

Offshore Trusts
Part One – Basic Trust Principles

Objectives

At the end of this Unit you should be able to:

- **Provide a definition of a trust**

- **Explain the difference between an express and a resulting trust**

- **Briefly explain what is meant by the term 'three certainties'**

- **List at least five factors which might affect the validity of a trust**

- **List at least five possible uses of an offshore trust**

- **Briefly describe the differences between the two types of purpose trusts available in some offshore centres**

- **List at least five duties usually expected of a trustee**

- **List ten of the powers which a trustee would usually expect to see in a trust deed**

- **Outline the usual statutory requirements concerning who can appoint a trustee**

- **Summarise the usual rights of a beneficiary including the right to receive details of their interest.**

In the introduction to Unit 6 it was mentioned that companies were an extremely important part of the syllabus and that students should be fully familiar with this area of offshore finance. The same must now be said of offshore trusts. Many professionals in the field of finance believe that it is the potential benefits which offshore trusts can provide which has sparked the growth in offshore business as a whole and which has enabled the majority of centres to develop their finance sectors and infrastructures.

To succeed in the examination, students must be familiar with the basic principles which support the trust concept, be aware of the possible benefits which an offshore trust can create, be aware of the trust services which are commonly provided from offshore centres and, finally, understand how to avoid some of the potential administration pitfalls which can entrap the unwary trustee.

The following three Units will address all of these issues and we shall start in this Unit with a look at some of the basic trust principles which students (and of course administrators) should be aware of.

1   Definition of a Trust

1.1   A precise definition of a trust is difficult as there are so many variances but generally speaking it is the relationship which exists when a person, called the trustee, is compelled in equity to hold property, called the trust property, for the benefit of persons, called the beneficiaries.

1.2   The person who creates a trust is usually referred to as the settlor or in some countries he is called the grantor (e.g. USA). The settlor could be a beneficiary and even the trustee of his own trust. This, however, could create problems which we shall address in Unit 11.

1.3   There can be more than one trustee and in some cases a trust protector may be appointed, whose role would usually be to oversee the actions of the trustees and make sure that the settlor's intentions in establishing the trust are met.

1.4   The trustee will have a number of duties and responsibilities which he will be required to fulfil and will also be granted certain powers over the property under his control. If a trustee carries out an action which he should not have done or fails to perform a task which he should have carried out, he might be in breach of trust, a situation which all trustees must try to avoid.

1.5   The trust is a common law vehicle and the trust legislation which you will find in offshore centres will be derived from UK trust statutes and precedents. Although each centre which offers trust services will have its own trust laws, many of the main principles and concepts will be the same. Much of what is contained in this Unit (and in Units 10 and 11) will be common to and apply to all centres, although you are advised to check the trust provisions in your own centre, or in a centre with which you have a particular interest, as there are some areas which differ between jurisdictions.

2   Creation of a Trust

Trusts can be created in a variety of ways but students are only required to be familiar with the most common methods.

Express Trusts

2.1   An express trust is created as a result of a positive, intentional action on the part of the settlor, such as him executing a trust deed or other such instrument to create an intervivos trust (which is the name given to a trust created during the settlor's lifetime). Another example of an express trust is a testamentary trust, the terms of which are contained in a person's will and which only comes into force on the testator's death.

2.2   The majority of offshore trusts are intervivos express trusts. However, there are two further methods of creation which students should be familiar with.

Implied Trusts

2.3   These are created as a result of what the law infers as being a person's intention. There are two main types of implied trust, resulting and constructive:

Resulting trusts

2.4 This could arise following a transfer of property from A to B without any indication that a gift was intended or has taken place. The property would be held on a resulting trust for A, as on B's death the property would revert (be transferred back) to A. Similarly, A could transfer property to B to hold for C's lifetime. If there is no instruction as to what is to happen to that property on C's death the property would be held on a resulting trust for A, as on C's death the property would return to A (or A's estate if he too had died).

Constructive trusts

2.5 These are trusts which are imposed by the courts and occur where it would be inequitable for a person to be considered to hold property for his sole benefit. An example of this would be where a matrimonial home has been purchased in the name of the husband but both he and his wife contributed to the value. In such a case the husband would hold the property as trustee and he and his wife would be the beneficiaries.

Statutory Trusts

2.6 These are trusts which come into force as a result of the operation of a statute, such as those created under the intestacy succession rules in the UK.

Legal Entity

2.7 Students should be aware that a trust is not in itself a legal entity, unlike a company. It is the trustees who are the legal owners of the trust property and it is they who would be the party to a legal action involving the trust property.

2.8 It is because of this that certain types of trust assets, such as quoted investments and realty, are not usually registered in the name of a trust but instead are registered in the name of the trustees of the trust.

3 The Legal Requirements for a Valid Trust

3.1 For a trust to be effective and hopefully meet the objectives for which it has been created (we cover the uses of trusts in the next Section) it must meet certain legal requirements. If it fails to meet these requirements it would generally be considered to be invalid and would not take effect or be deemed to have ever existed. This could have disastrous consequences for the settlor and possibly the trustee.

3.2 The following is a summary of the requirements which must usually be fulfilled to enable a trust to be considered valid. Once again, we shall concentrate on the main areas which students should be aware of and leave some of the more 'technical' arguments and theories to other texts.

Capacity of the Settlor

3.3 Generally speaking, any person over the age of majority, which in most countries is 18 years of age, who has the capacity to manage his own affairs can create a trust.

Purpose of the Trust

3.4 A trust must not attempt to promote immorality, restrain marriage, separate a parent and child or generally be for a purpose which is considered illegal or against public policy. It is also usually improper to make an immediate gift which is subject to a permanent restriction or alienation.

The Three Certainties

3.5 The three certainties must also be present for a trust to be valid and these can be summarised as follows:

Certainty of subject matter

3.6 The property which will be transferred into and subsequently held in the trust must be clearly identified in the trust deed. Often a trust is created with only a nominal amount of trust property, such as £100, and additional assets will then be transferred to the trustees at a later date.

3.7 If there is no certainty of subject matter, a trust can not be created as a proper transfer of property has not taken place between the settlor and the trustees. The result is that any property which would otherwise have been used to create the trust will remain the property of the client.

Certainty of objects

3.8 It must be certain who is to benefit under the terms of the trust and also what the nature and extent of their benefit will be. The trust deed should therefore specify who the beneficiaries will be and also the nature of their benefit (e.g. discretionary, life interest etc.). If it is uncertain who is to benefit, the trust will fail and the property will be held by the trustees for the settlor on a resulting trust.

3.9 Charitable trusts and non-charitable purpose trusts do not have to meet this certainty as we shall see later in this study text.

Certainty of words

3.10 It must be certain from the wording of the trust instrument or deed that it was the intention of the settlor to create a trust. Expressions by the settlor which suggest he wished or desired to create a trust should be avoided. If there is uncertainty concerning the intention to create a trust, the transferee will take any property transferred to him absolutely as the owner (i.e. the 'trustee' would take the property which would otherwise have been held by him on trust).

Properly Constituted

3.11 The settlor must make sure that he completes the transfer of the intended trust property to the trustees. If he fails to complete all that is necessary to effect this transfer, such as failing to sign a stock transfer form to transfer an investment asset into the name of the trustees, then the trust is said to be incompletely constituted and will not be valid.

Trust Duration

3.12 In most centres there is a requirement (Panama and the Turks and Caicos being the notable exceptions) that trust property must vest (or be transferred to or held for a beneficiary) within what is termed the perpetuity period. If the property is not vested within that time the trust would generally fail.

3.13 The maximum period for which vesting may be postponed is usually referred to as the perpetuity period and starts from the creation of the trust. Some trust deeds refer to this period as the trust duration period.

3.14   The length of the perpetuity period of a trust will vary depending upon the offshore centre chosen. However, many centres have chosen the options available under English trust law which is either the period of a life in being plus 21 years or, as is more usually the case, a specific number of years not exceeding 80.

3.15   There has been much legal debate on what constitutes a life in being. A very simplistic definition is that the life in being will generally be a person who is alive at the creation of the trust and who is referred to under the terms of the trust deed as being the person on whose life the perpetuity period has been based. The trust property will then be distributed 21 years after the death of that person.

3.16   Most offshore trust deeds use a fixed period of years which range from 80 years (e.g. the Isle of Man) to 150 years (e.g. the Cayman Islands). If a life in being is quoted it will usually be based on 'Royal Lives'. A 'Royal Lives' clause would usually stipulate the period expiring 21 years after the death of the last surviving descendant living at the date of the trust deed of his late Majesty King George VI, would constitute the perpetuity period.

4   Possible uses of an Offshore Trust

Trusts can be used for a variety of reasons as we shall now see.

Student Activity 1

Before you read the list which follows, prepare your own, setting out what you believe to be the possible uses of an offshore trust. How many did you think of?

Possible Tax Planning Opportunities
4.1   A detailed discussion of the taxation of trusts is outside the scope of this subject but in theory the main tax planning opportunity which a trust creates is that the settlor would cease to be the owner of the trust property and therefore not subject to tax on those assets. Instead, it would be the trustees who, in theory, would be liable to pay tax on the trust's income and realised capital gains.

4.2   If the trust is located in an offshore centre (which will impose either no or low rates of tax) there can therefore be considerable tax saving opportunities available.

Please refer back to Unit 2 where this concept is covered in more detail.

Family Succession Planning
4.3   A trust can be used to enable a settlor to make financial provisions for himself, his spouse and his family (or indeed others) during his lifetime and also after his death.

Provisions for Those Who Cannot Manage Their Affairs
4.4   A trust can also be used to make provision for those who, through whatever reason or incapacity, are unable to look after their own financial affairs. The individuals

concerned would usually be included in the trust deed as beneficiaries but would only receive distributions at the discretion of the trustees.

4.5   Similarly, a trust can be used to protect family funds from spendthrift members of the family. The person concerned would usually be entitled to receive the income from the trust fund but with no entitlement to the capital.

Asset Protection

4.6   A trust can be used to protect a person's assets from local government agencies or authorities who might have the power to freeze or expropriate assets of citizens or residents of that country. If the assets are not held by a citizen or resident of that country (i.e. they are owned by offshore trustees) they could be protected from this particular line of attack.

4.7   A trust can also be used to protect property from the claims of forced heirs and in some cases from future creditors, both uses we shall return to in Unit 11.

4.8   In addition, a client might own a particular asset which he would like future generations of his family to enjoy or benefit from. Such an asset could be the family home, a valuable work of art or shares in the family business. A trust could be created to hold that asset with restrictions imposed relating to the disposal of the property.

To Avoid Probate Problems

4.9   A trust can also help solve the probate problems which we discussed when looking at the use of companies in Unit 6, although this time, the assets would be in the name of the trustees instead of the company.

Protection from Creditors

4.10   Some offshore trusts can be used to protect an individual from the claims of future, unknown creditors. We shall return to this possible use in Unit 11.

To Defeat Foreign Claimants

4.11   A trust can also be used to defeat the statutory rights which certain family members might have on the death of the settlor. Once again, we shall return to this possible use in Unit 11.

To Cover Emergencies

4.12   A trust could be used as a contingency planning vehicle to provide cover in the event of an emergency. For example, a client could put in place the paperwork and transfer of assets to create a trust which would only be activated on the happening of a particular event, such as his incapacity or perhaps kidnap!

4.13   Once activated, the client's assets would be managed by the trustees and his family would continue to be provided for.

To Provide Greater Confidentiality

4.14   A trust is a confidential arrangement between the settlor and the trustees with minimal or, in the majority of cases, no reporting requirements. Indeed, often the beneficiaries will not know of the existence of the trust under which they have been given an interest.

4.15   Some trusts are created without the settlor being party to the trust deed which increases the secrecy element. This would usually involve the trustee executing a deed under which he would declare that he was holding the specified trust property in accordance with the terms as set out in the deed. This is commonly referred to as a declaration of trust.

4.16   A variation on this theme, although not necessarily advisable, is the situation where a trust deed is executed by a person who is referred to as the settlor in the deed but who is in fact acting on the instructions of another party. The person who creates the deed is essentially a nominee or 'dummy settlor' whose purpose is to conceal the true identity of the settlor.

We return to dummy settlors and declarations of trust in Unit 11.

5   Types of Private Trust Commonly Used Offshore

5.1   Now that we have looked at some of the possible uses of an offshore trust we can turn our attention to the types of trust which are commonly created and administered in offshore centres.

5.2   In this Section we shall only concentrate on the private trusts which are widely used, as opposed to the 'corporate' or 'institutional' trusts which we cover in detail in Units 13 and 14.

Fixed Trusts

5.3   A fixed trust is one where the interests and rights of the beneficiaries have been fixed in accordance with the terms of the trust deed. For example, a named beneficiary will have a current entitlement to the net income of the trust fund (usually referred to as the life tenant) and on their death, named beneficiaries will share the capital of the fund equally (usually referred to as the reminndermen as they receive what remains on the death of the life tenant).

5.4   The rights of the life tenant (over the income) and the remaindermen (over the funds which remain after the death of the life tenant) may be enforced against the trustees.

5.5   Other terms are often used to describe this type of trust and include strict trust, interest in possession trust and life interest trust.

Discretionary Trusts

5.6   This is the most common and widely used type of trust in offshore centres.

5.7   A discretionary trust is one in which none of the beneficiaries have an absolute current right to receive funds and instead, it is left to the trustees to decide who is to benefit, when they are to benefit and by how much they are to benefit. The trustees therefore, have discretion concerning the trust property and also in respect of other administrative issues, many of which we cover in detail in Units 10 and 11.

5.8   It is the flexibility which discretionary trusts offer, compared to the features of a fixed trust, which makes this type of trust so popular.

5.9   In view of the fact that the persons who can receive funds from a discretionary can only receive a benefit if the trustees exercise discretion in their favour, it is usual to refer to them as 'discretionary objects'. However, for the sake of consistency, the term 'beneficiary' will be used in this study text to refer to those who may also benefit under a discretionary trust.

5.10   The other type of trusts, which are covered below, will either be fixed or discretionary in nature but each is usually addressed by a particular name, as we shall now see.

Protective Trusts

5.11   This is a type of fixed trust and would usually be created to protect an improvident beneficiary from himself. The settlor would have decided that the beneficiary concerned would not be able to handle the financial responsibilities associated with receiving capital from the trust (perhaps because he is a spendthrift or fond of gambling). The beneficiary would be given a life interest in the trust property (thereby becoming the life tenant) and therefore be entitled to the income as it arises.

5.12   In the event of him attempting to sell, assign or give away his life interest in the trust (usually signs that he is trying to enlarge his interest to receive a capital sum in exchange for his income entitlement), the beneficiary's interest in the income would cease and the property would instead be held on a discretionary trust under which the beneficiary, usually along with others, would have a discretionary interest.

Accumulation and Maintenance Settlements

5.13   This is a type of discretionary trust and can create certain tax planning opportunities, especially for clients in the UK.

5.14   Under UK tax legislation, certain conditions have to be met if an accumulation and maintenance trust is to receive favourable tax treatment. These can be summarised as follows:

   i)   The trust must be for the benefit of children (who would usually be the grandchildren of the settlor);

   ii)   The children must be entitled to receive trust property (usually the right to income) upon reaching a certain specified age, which must not be greater then 25;

   iii) During the period prior to the children reaching the specified age, income can either be applied for their maintenance or accumulated.

5.15   Often the trustees will divide the trust property into separate funds for each of the children and they will be deemed to have a share of the capital on the happening of the event which gives them an absolute right to the capital. Any income which is to be accumulated will also be divided between the children and added to an accumulations fund which the trustees will probably set up for each child.

5.16   When a child attains the age at which he receives the income as of right, his accumulations fund is usually frozen and no further sums are added to it. This is because the share of income for that particular child will be due to him as it arises and the income can no longer be accumulated.

5.17 On the happening of the event which means the child can receive capital as of right, he will be paid his share of the capital held in the trust fund, plus the accumulated income held in his accumulated income fund.

5.18 In most accumulation and maintenance trusts the trustees will also have the power to make capital advances or appointments of capital to the children.

The possible tax benefits are outside the scope of this syllabus.

Charitable Trusts

5.19 These are discretionary trusts which are created to benefit charitable organisations. They are usually free from tax, are not subject to the trust perpetuity rules which apply to other types of trusts and are not required to meet the certainty of objects because of the Cy-pres doctrine. Under the Cy-pres rules, a charitable trust will not fail even if it is unclear which charity is to benefit. Instead the settlor's general charitable intentions will be considered and the trustees can apply the trust property to the charity or charities which most closely meet the original intentions of the settlor.

5.20 A trust will usually be recognised as being charitable if the purposes of the trusts are:

a) For the relief of poverty;

b) For the advancement of education;

c) For the advancement of religion;

d) For any other purpose which is beneficial to the community.

Non-charitable Purpose Trusts

5.21 Until recently, the only form of purpose trust which was permitted was the charitable trust. However, a number of offshore centres, such as Bermuda, the BVI, the Cook Islands, Cyprus and the Isle of Man, have introduced legislation which allows for the creation of non-charitable purpose trusts.

5.22 These are discretionary trusts but they are not created for the benefit of persons or charities (in other words, there are no beneficiaries) but instead for a particular purpose. This purpose must be specific (clearly stated in the terms of the trust deed), reasonable and possible. In addition, the purpose must not be unlawful, immoral or contrary to public policy.

5.23 A trustee (who would usually be required to be of appropriate standing such as a trust corporation, a lawyer or an accountant) would be appointed.

5.24 There would also be an enforcer appointed under the terms of the trust deed whose role would be to enforce the terms of the trust against the trustees (if necessary) and also to oversee the actions of the trustee. The powers of the enforcer would be similar to those of a protector but his fiduciary responsibilities would be governed by the statute which allows purpose trusts. There must be an enforcer in this type of trust and the trust deed should refer to the method of appointment. As a last resort the power to appoint an enforcer would pass to the court.

5.25 The duration of a purpose trust would usually have to comply with the perpetuity rules of the local centre although in the BVI such a trust can continue indefinitely. There will usually be a provision in the trust deed to cover how the trust will terminate and also what will happen to the balance of the trust property on termination.

5.26 Some practitioners structure a purpose trust to enable funds to revert to the settlor when the purpose of the trust has been fulfilled. A detailed discussion of the possible merits and potential problems associated with this is outside the scope of the syllabus but students should remember that the essence of a purpose trust is that there must not be a beneficiary (although having said that, the Cayman Islands are in the process of drafting legislation which allows a purpose trust to benefit persons as well as non-persons). If funds could therefore be paid to the settlor, there is an argument to suggest that the structure failed to meet the necessary criteria for a purpose trust.

Purpose trusts can be used for a variety of reasons and the following is a summary of the most common ones:

To hold a particular asset

5.27 A purpose trust could be created with the sole purpose of holding the shares in a private limited company (perhaps the voting shares) which in turn holds a particular asset. Alternatively, the trust could own the asset directly and not through an underlying company.

5.28 Some practitioners are of the opinion that the purpose of holding an asset is in fact an investment power and suggest that in such cases the deed should also include substantive powers to enable the trustees to distribute capital or income.

To assist in corporate financing schemes

5.29 A purpose trust could be used to own a company which is to transact a particular contract, such as the building of a ship or the leasing of an aircraft. A parent company would create the trust and the trustees could borrow funds secured against the assets of the underlying company. This structure could provide protection for both the bank (which lent the funds) and also the parent company. This is because the ownership of the assets could not change (because of the ownership by the trustees) and the trust would also offer protection against creditors of the parent who may come along in the future.

Asset protection

5.30 Group risks could be isolated by using a purpose trust. For example, the ownership of shares in a company involved in a high risk industry (such as oil exploration) could be placed in a purpose trust and the possible risks could then be removed and separated from the other assets which the parent organisation owns.

Creditor Protection Trusts

5.31 This type of trust is perhaps more commonly known as an asset protection trust and has been very popular in recent years, particularly with clients from the USA, especially those in the medical profession.

5.32 If a person creates a trust in an onshore centre there is a possibility that it might be set aside if a creditor comes along in the future, makes a successful claim against the settlor and the settlor does not have sufficient assets outside of the trust to meet the claim. In this situation the trust would probably be set aside and the creditor paid out of the property which was previously held in the trust.

5.33   Similarly, a settlor might be declared bankrupt a few years after creating the trust and once again the trust could be set aside.

5.34   A creditor protection trust is a device which is designed to protect a settlor's assets from future claims by creditors and from claims which may arise on future bankruptcy. Such trusts are offered by a number of offshore centres, most notably the Cayman Islands, the Bahamas, the Cook Islands and Gibraltar, and the protection is provided by specific legislation which such centres have in place which protect local trusts (and the property which those trusts hold) from attacks by future creditors. Basically, the burden of proof is on the claimant and the courts in those centres are generally loathe to make a judgement against trustees. This, together with the cost involved in pursuing a claim against a settlor in an offshore jurisdiction, often leads to the creditor deciding to drop his claim before the matter proceeds to court.

5.35   The ideal type of trust for this vehicle would be discretionary. We look at some of the practical administration issues relating to creditor protection trusts in Unit 11.

Forced Heirship Protection Trusts

5.36   In Civil Law countries, such as South America, Central and Southern Europe and the Middle East, local laws are in place which require persons from those countries to leave a certain percentage of their assets on their death to certain heirs, usually their spouse and children.

5.37   This restriction on testamentary freedom can create problems for clients from those areas, but it has also created opportunities for some offshore centres who have introduced legislation which encourages clients from those countries to create local trusts which would be protected from claims by forced heirs. Basically, under the laws of such centres as the Cayman Islands, the Bahamas, Bermuda, Gibraltar and the Isle of Man, the capacity of the settlor and the legality of the trust will be governed by the laws of the offshore centre and the rights of heirs and forced heirship laws will be ignored by the local courts.

5.38   The ideal type of trust for this vehicle would also be discretionary and we shall look at some of the practical administration issues relating to forced heirship protection trusts in Unit 11.

Hybrid Trusts

5.39   This is essentially a cross between a discretionary trust and a fixed trust. The trustees will have power to appoint capital at their discretion, similar to a traditional discretionary trust, but in default of appointment, income is to be paid to a named individual (just as a life tenant is entitled to income in a fixed trust).

Trading Trusts

5.40   Although not widely used, some practitioners have used trusts as trading entities. Structures will vary but generally the trustee would be a company with limited liability which is empowered to conduct trading activities. The employees of the trustee company would then manage the business and all invoices and correspondence would be issued from, and addressed to, the trustee company.

5.41 The business would usually be held on a discretionary trust for a specified class of beneficiaries although in some cases a fixed trust might be preferred.

Revocable Trusts

5.42 Generally, revocable trusts are not advisable. Under this type of arrangement the settlor would usually retain a number of powers and rights which one would usually expect to pass to the trustees (such as the power to authorise the payment of capital, the power to appoint trustees and the power to terminate the trust). In addition, the trust would usually terminate on the death of the settlor and the funds would be distributed in accordance with the terms of the trust or of his will.

5.43 Some practitioners call this type of trust 'short form trusts' or 'simple trusts'. Although they are in essence discretionary trusts, depending on the exact wording, it is debatable whether the trustee actually has any discretions which he can exercise at all.

There are a number of areas which could cause concern with a revocable trust and these are covered in detail when we look at sham trusts in Unit 11.

Grantor Trusts

5.44 This is a term which will be familiar to those who have had dealings with clients or advisers from the USA.

5.45 A grantor is the name given to the person who creates a trust (known as the settlor in most other countries) and a grantor trust is the term which is commonly applied to a trust under which the grantor is treated as the owner of the trust property under US tax law.

5.46 At the time of writing, there is considerable debate concerning the taxation treatment and reporting requirements of foreign trusts in the USA following the amendments made by the Small Business Job Protection Act (1996) to the US Federal tax rules. A detailed discussion and appreciation of all of the issues is outside the scope of the syllabus but the main points which students should be familiar with (especially those with clients in the USA) are covered next.

The previous treatment of 'grantor' trusts in the USA

5.47 Under US Federal tax law, grantor trusts were disregarded for tax purposes on the basis that the grantor was treated as the owner of the assets (usually because he had power to revoke the trust or had a life interest) and taxed accordingly.

5.48 Where a non-US person was the grantor, distributions to US beneficiaries were also outside the scope of Federal tax.

Changes introduced

5.49 The Small Business Job Protection Act (1996) effectively limits grantor trust treatment and the benefits will generally no longer apply to those trusts which were, or are, created by non-US grantors (often referred to as 'foreign non-grantor trusts').

5.50 The main changes which came about under the 1996 Act are as follows:

a) Distributions to a US person from an offshore trust created by a non-US person will generally be taxed as income in the hands of the US beneficiary.

b) Loans received by US beneficiaries of an offshore trust could be treated as a distribution and taxed as income.

c) Distributions to a US person from an accumulated income fund could be subject to an interest charge.

d) US grantors of an offshore trust must notify the IRS and provide information relating to the trust.

e) US beneficiaries who receive a distribution from an offshore trust must provide details to the IRS.

f) Failure to provide information in d) and e) above could result in penalties being imposed.

g) If an offshore trust was created by a US grantor or there are US persons who may benefit from an offshore trust, the trustees are required to submit details to the IRS. Failure to report could lead to the grantor being penalised.

h) In addition to having to make a report in g) above, the trustees should also appoint a US Agent who the IRS can contact for additional information if required.

Those of you who administer trusts which have a US connection should obtain advice on how these new provisions will affect those cases.

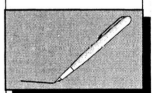

Student Activity 2

Select one offshore centre from Europe, one from the Caribbean and one from the Pacific and find out the different types of trust which are available in each of the centres chosen. Is there a particular type of trust which is found in one of the centres but not in the others?

6 The Role of the Trustee

6.1 Now we shall spend some time assessing the role of the trustees. After all, if you are unfamiliar with the usual duties and powers of trustees it will make it extremely difficult for you to spot the potential pitfalls which lie in wait for the unsuspecting trustee and trust administrator.

6.2 Once again, we shall only cover the main areas which are of direct relevance to the syllabus. For those of you who are interested, there are a variety of texts widely available which are devoted entirely to various technicalities which relate to the general powers and duties which are covered in this Unit. However, such a detailed understanding of these issues is outside the scope of this course.

Trustee's Duties

6.3 The trustee's duties are those actions which he is required to perform. They are either laid down by statute or have been formulated from case precedents. The main duties of offshore trustees are as follows.

To carry out the provisions of the trust deed

6.4 This is the primary duty of a trustee and its intention should be self-explanatory.

Prior to appointment

6.5 The trustee should read the terms of the intended trust deed and familiarize himself with the nature of the property which is to be held in trust. If he is replacing an existing trustee or acting as an additional trustee he has a duty to ensure that no prior breaches of trust have occurred (otherwise he will also be liable for any losses which could result from that breach). To do this he should request a copy of the trust deed(s) and accounts and make other enquiries which would seem reasonable to determine the status of the trust property.

To secure and control the trust property

6.6 On appointment, a trustee should make sure he has the legal ownership of the trust property and that the trust property is under his control.

To act unanimously

6.7 Where there is more than one trustee they have a duty to act personally and jointly. Unless the deed so specifies, a majority decision cannot bind the minority. We look at co-trustees in a following Section.

General duty of care

6.8 Trustees owe what is often described as a general duty of care. This means that when the trustee is managing the trust funds he must take all the precautions which an ordinary prudent man of business would take in managing similar affairs of his own.

6.9 Professional trustees, such as trust corporations and those other corporations or individuals who charge a fee for acting as trustee, owe a higher duty of care and are also expected to display expertise in every aspect of their administration of a trust.

Duty of investment

6.10 Trustees have a general duty to invest the trust assets prudently and also a specific duty to invest the assets either in accordance with the terms of the trust deed or if the deed is silent, within the provisions of local trust statutes.

Distribution of assets

6.11 Trustees must ensure that distributions are made from the correct part of the trust fund (i.e. from income or capital) and that they are only made to beneficiaries who have an interest in the trust property. Distributions must not be made to those who are not beneficiaries.

Not to profit

6.12 A trustee cannot profit from his role unless the trust deed expressly empowers him to do so. Charging a fee for the provision of trustee services is considered to be a profit and unless the trust deed authorises a fee the trustee will not be paid for his services. If the deed is silent and the trustee is a bank, in theory the bank cannot claim normal bank charges if it also provides banking services to the trust.

6.13   If the deed is silent the trustee might still be able to charge a fee if he can obtain the approval of all of the beneficiaries, although this could be difficult especially in respect of discretionary trusts where perhaps some of the beneficiaries are minors or not yet ascertained. If the trust deed allows, the terms could be changed to authorise fee charging. As a last resort the trustee could always obtain the consent of the Court to charge a fee but this option could be an expensive process and the Court may ask why the trustee consented to act in the first place without a fee clause in place.

6.14   Profit does not include disbursements and so reasonable expenses are allowable whether or not there is a specific power to charge a fee.

To keep accounts and report to beneficiaries

6.15   Trustees must keep clear and accurate accounts of the trust property and in the case of fixed trusts, inform the life tenant and remaindermen of the extent of their interests by sending them copies of the accounts.

6.16   In discretionary trusts, the trustee may have to release details of the trust property if he receives a request for this information from a discretionary beneficiary, but he is not under an obligation to release information which relates to the reasoning behind the exercise of a discretion (as confirmed in the case of *Re Londonderry's Settlement* [1965]).

To keep trust property separate

6.17   A trustee is under a duty to keep the trust property separate from his own assets. Such segregation means that trust property will not form part of the trustee's own property and will therefore be 'ring fenced' in the event of his death or his bankruptcy.

Duty to act impartially

6.18   Trustees are expected to act after taking into account the interests of all the beneficiaries. This does not mean that they must treat the beneficiaries equally (unless the trust deed tells them to).

Reducing or waiving duties under an express provision

6.19   Many offshore trust deeds contain provisions which are designed to reduce the duties expected of the trustees. Whether such provisions are valid will depend on the circumstances of the case in question and also whether any statutory provisions exist which prevent a reduction in those duties. We consider this type of clause as well as indemnities in general in Unit 11.

Usual Powers of Trustees

6.20   The powers would usually be contained in the trust deed although in some cases statutory powers may be available. The following is a summary of the usual powers which are contained in offshore trusts.

Power to sell

6.21   The trustee will usually have the power to retain the trust property or to dispose of it. This is often referred to as a trust for sale. Under a trust for sale, the trustee will be able to sell by whatever method obtains the best price which could, in the case of realty, be by auction or by private treaty.

Powers to borrow and to lend

6.22 The trustee would usually be empowered to borrow funds using the trust property as security and the power to lend would usually only extend to loans to beneficiaries.

Powers of maintenance and advancement

6.23 Trustees usually have the power to make maintenance payments and to advance capital.

6.24 Maintenance payments are generally of an income nature and are made to infant beneficiaries to cover day-to-day expenses incurred or payable on their behalf such as school fees. Often the deed will state that any income which is not applied for maintenance purposes must (and this is not a power but a directive) be accumulated, which effectively means the income is then treated as capital. Any income so accumulated should be held in a separate income accumulations account and, depending on the terms of the trust, might be payable to the infant when he attains majority. It should be noted that the laws of most offshore centres allow for income to be accumulated for the duration of the trust period but this is not the case in the UK where income can only be accumulated for a certain period of time.

6.25 An advancement is a capital payment and would usually only be made to cover the cost of substantial, non-repetitive items which the beneficiary wishes to buy such as a house for his occupancy. Statutory provisions usually restrict the amount which can be advanced to each beneficiary (e.g. one half of their presumptive share). They are also taken into account when calculating a beneficiary's final entitlement from a trust. The adding back of funds advanced is called hotchpot. As a result it is common for trust deeds to allow a greater proportion of the trust fund to be advanced and that any sums paid will not be taken into account when making future capital distributions.

Power to appoint capital

6.26 Trustees would usually have the power to appoint capital either to the beneficiaries or perhaps to other trusts which have been established for the benefit of those beneficiaries. In addition, there may also be the power to appoint capital to separate funds within the same trust which can create tax advantages as the assets subject to the appointment do not leave the trust and therefore there is no transfer (if there were this would usually trigger a taxable situation.)

6.27 Usually the power to appoint would be very wide and can extend to the entirety of the trust fund. If this is the case, the trustees would often have the power to appoint funds to one or more of the beneficiaries in any proportion as they think fit.

6.28 Hotchpot does not usually apply to this method of payment.

Power to delegate

6.29 Trustees will usually be empowered by the deed (and always by statute) to appoint agents to assist them with the administration of the trust property. This enables trustees to appoint, for example, bankers, accountants, solicitors and investment managers.

6.30 Appointing an agent does not mean that the trustee can delegate his decision making powers. If he does he will be in breach of trust. However, the trustee can delegate his discretionary powers for a limited period of time by executing a power of attorney. Such an action is usually reserved for the situation where the trustee is likely to be absent from the country for a prolonged period and his absence could affect the administration of the trust. The trustee would still be liable for the actions of the attorney during the period of the attorney's appointment.

Power to invest

6.31   Usually the trustee will have wide powers of investment. If the deed is silent he can invest trust funds but only in accordance with local statutory provisions which will generally be restrictive.

Power to appoint trustees

6.32   Trustees would usually have the power to appoint new or additional trustees. We shall return to this in the next Section.

Power to add and remove beneficiaries

6.33   Usually the trustees will have the power to appoint additional beneficiaries in discretionary trusts as well as the power to exclude beneficiaries.

Power to change the proper law

6.34   The trustees of offshore trusts will usually be empowered to change the proper law of a trust, an area which we shall return to in detail in Unit 10.

Power to receive additional trust property

6.35   A great number of offshore trusts are created with a nominal initial trust property, e.g. £100. The trustee will therefore be given the power to receive additional property from the settlor, or from any other party, which he will hold under the same trusts as the initial property which he received.

Power to appoint protectors

6.36   The trustee would often be empowered to appoint the trust protector in a discretionary trust, a position which we cover in detail in Unit 11.

Power to incorporate companies

6.37   Many offshore trust deeds contain a clause which enables the trustees to incorporate underlying companies and for those companies to be assets of the trust.

Power to insure

6.38   Although most countries have statutory powers covering the insurance arrangements for trust property, the extent of the cover which the trustees can arrange would usually be restricted to loss or damage by fire. It is therefore advisable for the trust deed to contain a power which enables the trustees to arrange wide and comprehensive cover.

Power to give receipts

6.39   A clause would often be included in a trust deed enabling the trustees to give valid receipts for the transfer in or sale proceeds of all types of property, especially realty. Some statutory provisions restrict trustees receiving certain assets (e.g. a sole trustee can often be restricted from providing a valid receipt for the proceeds of the sale of land). A clause which gives the trustees power to receive any property is often useful.

Power to terminate the trust

6.40   It is usual for trustees to be given the power to terminate a trust ahead of the expiry of the perpetuity period or duration period as set out in the trust deed.

Student Activity 3

Find a copy of an offshore trust deed (perhaps one which you are currently administering) and list the powers which have been given to the trustees. Make a note against each suggesting why the trustee may want to have that particular power.

The Appointment, Retirement and Removal of Trustees

6.41   Most offshore trust deeds will contain provisions which cover the procedures required for a trustee to be appointed or removed and also how they can retire. However, if the deed is silent on these issues there will always be the statutory provisions to fall back on.

6.42   Each centre will have its own statutory requirements but in general terms the statutory provisions would usually be drafted along the following lines.

Statutory provisions
Statutory Power of Appointment

6.43   Usually, the statute would first mention that the power to appoint a new trustee would pass to the person nominated in the trust deed. However, if there is no such person the power would usually pass to the present, surviving or continuing trustee or the personal representative of the last surviving trustee.

Situations When the Statutory Power of Appointment Would be Exercised

6.44   Again, the provisions will vary but usually a new trustee would be required to be appointed if the present trustee died, remained out of the particular jurisdiction for more than a specific period of time (e.g. 1 year), wished to be discharged from his role, refused to act, was incapable of acting or if he was a minor.

Retirement

6.45   A trustee may retire although there must be a successor or continuing trustee in place to enable the retirement to be valid.

Removal

6.46   The statutory grounds under which a trustee can be removed have already been mentioned when we looked at the circumstances under which a new trustee must be appointed. To summarise, a trustee can be removed on his death, if he refuses to act, is unfit or incapable of acting or if he is a minor.

Vesting of Trust Property

6.47   Usually, the trust law of a centre will state that if the retirement and appointment of a trustee is performed by a deed or instrument, trust property will be deemed to have vested in the new trustee, unless of course further documentation is required by law to effect a transfer (such as a stock transfer form for an investment).

Usual express provisions

6.48 In most cases the trustee will have an express power in the trust deed to appoint a replacement or additional trustee. However, there is a growing trend that this power is given to a trust protector or in some trusts, to the settlor. We shall consider the possible effects of the power to appoint and remove trustees vesting in the settlor or the trust protector in Unit 11.

The number of trustees

6.49 This is important. Most trust deeds will specify the minimum number of trustees required but if not, the local trust statute should cover this point. Usually, the trust law of a centre will state that two trustees will be required for local trusts which are created for the benefit of minors or for those trusts which are to own realty.

6.50 However, the trust laws of most centres will allow local trust corporations to act as sole trustees of most types of trust (perhaps the only exception being non-charitable purpose trusts), although there may be a requirement that the trust corporation would have to be approved (which might involve having to meet certain capital requirements).

6.51 There is a potential problem if the local trustee wishes to retire and a trust corporation from another centre wishes to be appointed. The proposed trustee might not meet the criteria of a trust corporation in the centre where the trust is based and the result would be that the current trustee could not retire as the appointment of his replacement would be invalid.

The Use of Co-Trustees

6.52 Some clients prefer more than one trustee to be appointed to manage their trust and will insist that co-trustees are appointed.

6.53 As we saw when considering the duties of trustees, if more than one is appointed they must act unanimously and unless the trust deed specifies, a majority decision will not bind the minority.

6.54 Usually, a co-trustee is appointed in those cases where a trust corporation is not involved. They are therefore most commonly found in those trusts where the client has appointed trusted advisers to act (such as partners in a particular legal or accountancy practice). Often a member of the settlor's family is appointed alongside a 'professional' trustee (which in this context has been taken to mean someone who provides trustee services as part of their livelihood and who is paid for their services).

6.55 More than one trustee can help in the decision making process, usually by assisting discussions concerning the merits of a particular distribution or the exercise of an administrative power. This is usually the case where a family member, who is aware of the settlor's intentions and wishes, is appointed alongside a professional trustee.

6.56 However, they can also create potential problems. For example, if one of the trustees is resident offshore and the other is located onshore, the tax authorities in the onshore centre might decide the trust is taxable in that jurisdiction on the basis that part of the management and control is exercised from that location.

6.57   In addition to possible taxation problems, the settlor should also be aware of potential administration problems which can stem from the duty of the trustees to act together. Depending on the number and location of the co-trustees, it could be a difficult task to obtain the consent of them all before a particular action is taken. As a result, distributions could be delayed, as could the simple appointment of an agent, such as an investment adviser or banker.

The Appeal of Trust Corporations

6.58   Before moving on to the role and rights of the settlor, we should consider the use and appeal of trust corporations in offshore centres, as although it is possible for individuals to be appointed, it is much more common for a corporate entity to be used for offshore trusts. In this Section we shall look at a few of the factors and reasons why this is the case.

Licencing requirements

6.59   In some centres a trustee has to be licensed and there would usually be a capital adequacy requirement which often only a corporate trustee could meet.

Continuity

6.60   Unlike individuals, a corporation can continue in perpetuity and so the death or transfer of an employee will not affect the continuence of the trusteeship, nor one would hope the quality of the service.

6.61   In addition, a trust corporation will seldom change location. It may move offices within the offshore centre but it would rarely decide to relocate to another jurisdiction. There will therefore be continuity in terms of residence in the offshore centre chosen for ther trust.

Multi-jurisdictional

6.62   Many trust corporations have operations in more than one centre. This can provide a greater base of experience and knowledge of the offshore industry and also provides an opportunity for the trust to migrate to another office of the organisation in the event of a trigger event under a flee clause provision. A flee clause is one under which the law of the trust or residence of the trustees will change on the happening of a predetermined event, such as civil unrest, in the offshore centre originally chosen.

Expertise

6.63   Trust companies pride themselves on posessing a high degree of expertise as well as the necessary resources to service trust business effectively and efficiently.

6.64   Many trust corporations also possess investment departments which can be used to provide investment management services. In some cases they will also be affiliated to a bank or a company management function which can mean that the entire management and administration of an offshore structure can be conducted under the same roof. This is a factor which can create certain efficiencies and cost savings.

Internal audit

6.65   Trust companies will usually be subject to external audit requirements and in addition, they will also have in place internal controls and checks to ensure that the service is being delivered' efficiently as well as effectively. Many of the larger institutions will have internal audit departments which help police the various offices and can play a very useful trouble shooting role.

Documentation

6.66 Corporate trustees tend to offer clients standard trust deeds which can be amended as required. The deeds should have been the subject of a thorough review by local advocates or lawyers and as a result, a client can buy a deed 'off the shelf' safe in the knowledge that the terms and conditions have been pre-approved by an external legal adviser.

6.67 The client should still, of course, obtain his own legal (and tax) advice prior to the creation of a trust, although this review need not be concerned with the provisions contained in the standard deed.

Security

6.68 Many settlors favour trust corporations because of the security aspect. If there was a dispute and the trustees were found to be at fault, it would probably be easier for the beneficiaries to obtain financial recourse from a negligent trust corporation than from an individual who was acting as trustee.

7 The Rights and Role of the Settlor

7.1 Many trustees believe that the settlor of a trust will retain certain rights over the trust property. However, unless the trust deed specifically provides them with certain powers, the settlor of a trust will have no rights whatsoever over the administration of the trust or the trust property.

7.2 We look at some of the possible options which are available to settlors who want to exert some control or have some say in the conduct of the trust in Unit 11.

8 The Rights of the Beneficiaries

8.1 It is sometimes possible for trustees to forget that the beneficiaries of a trust have certain rights. Although most of these rights should be a matter of applying common sense on the part of the trustees, it is often the most obvious issues which are most commonly missed.

Student Activity 4

Make a list of the rights which you believe a beneficiary of a trust will have and compare it with the points contained in the following section.

8.2   The 'common sense' rights are as follows:

i)   A beneficiary has the right to be treated fairly by the trustees;

ii)   A beneficiary has the right to receive distributions from the correct part of the fund (e.g. an income beneficiary should receive only income payments).

A further right, which is not often employed, is:

iii)   Where all the beneficiaries are sui juris (in other words, they are all over the age of majority and all have full capacity) and are between them absolutely entitled to the trust property, they have the right to request that the trustees terminate the trust and pay the trust funds to them.

8.3   However, the area which can cause the greatest administrative problems and give rise to the most debate is the right of the beneficiaries to receive information relating to the trust and their interests.

Disclosure of Information to Trust Beneficiaries

8.4   It is generally accepted that trust beneficiaries have a right to request and receive information relating to their interest under the trust. For example, the life tenant of a fixed trust is entitled to be told the extent of his interest, how much income is being generated on the trust fund and also the capital value of that fund. Similarly, the remainderman has a right to know what the capital value is as one day he will receive a capital benefit. Consequently, in fixed trusts, beneficiaries usually receive copies of the trust accounts.

8.5   However, the position concerning discretionary beneficiaries is not as clear cut because they only receive a benefit at the discretion of the trustees. Once a payment has been made to them they cease to have an interest, unless the trustees decide to exercise their discretion in their favour again in the future.

8.6   The Irish case of *Chaine-Nickson* v. *Bank of Ireland* (1976) clarified the general position as it was decided that the rights of a discretionary beneficiary are no different from those of a beneficiary of a fixed trust. As a result, it would be reasonable for the trustees to release accounting information and possibly a copy of the trust deed following a request from a discretionary beneficiary. However, that does not mean that the trustees should proceed and release such details without further consideration, as several cases have since made it clear that the right to such information is not absolute and can be refused in certain situations.

8.7   For example, the beneficiary might require the accounts as part of an investigation by an onshore revenue authority or the details might be requested to enable the beneficiary to initiate proceedings against the trustee or settlor. In such situations, the trustees should refuse (which was one of the many points raised in the Cayman Islands case of *Lemos* v. *Coutts & Co* [1992-93]).

8.8   Another consideration is whether there are any statutory restrictions in place which restrict the release of information, such as there is in respect of exempted trusts in the Cayman Islands where it can be an offence to release information to the beneficiaries.

8.9   Apart from accounting details, the discretionary beneficiaries might also request copies of the paperwork which records how the trustees have exercised their discretion. For example, they might want to know why the trustee has acted in a particular manner. The UK case of *Re Londonderry's Settlement* (1964) held that the beneficiaries right to information did not extend to documents concerning the exercise by the trustee of their discretions and as a result the trustees would, in most cases, refuse such a request.

8.10   Similarly, the contents of a letter of wishes might be requested but again the trustee would try to rely on the *Re Londonderry Case* to refuse such a request.

8.11   However, documents such as the letter of wishes and minutes of trustee's meetings may have to be released under the rights to discovery in hostile litigation (the case of *Talbot v. Marshfield* [1885] refers).

8.12   The possibility that the contents of a letter of wishes might become public knowledge has led to some advisers suggesting that their clients request the trustees to record their wishes in a file note which the trustees then sign. This is often referred to as a memorandum of wishes and such a document can, in some cases, fall outside a discovery order.

       We return to letters of wishes, their use and effect in Unit 11.

Restriction on release of information

8.13   Some practitioners include specific provisions in their trust deeds removing the right of beneficiaries to receive and even request information relating to a trust. The wording would have to be carefully drafted as such a provision could be argued to be contrary to the usual rights of the beneficiaries.

8.14   It is also worth mentioning the Cayman Islands exempted trusts. This type of trust is registered with the Registrar of Trusts and once registered, it would be an offence to release information to beneficiaries without the consent of the Registrar of Trusts as the right to enforce the trust will be vested in the Registrar.

Objects of a power

8.15   Whilst on the subject of beneficiaries, it is worth mentioning that the persons who can benefit only as a result of the trustees exercising a power in their favour, such as the power to appoint capital if the trustees so decide, will have less rights to information than those discretionary beneficiaries who can benefit subject to the trustees exercising a discretion in their favour.

8.16   Often you will find that an offshore discretionary trust will only convey benefits to persons under a power which makes those persons the objects of a power rather than the objects of the trust. This is done primarily to reduce the rights to information which those persons would otherwise enjoy if they were discretionary beneficiaries.

The Right to Control the Trustees

8.17   Finally, unless the trust deed states otherwise, the beneficiaries have no right to influence the trustees in the performance of their duties or powers. Similarly, unless the deed states otherwise, the beneficiaries will not have the right to remove or appoint trustees.

8.18   In most instances they do however, have the right to enforce the terms of the trust against the trustees.

Summary

Now that you have read this Unit you should be able to

- Explain what a trust is

- Explain the difference between an express and a resulting trust

- Outline the requirements of the 'three certainties'

- List five factors which might affect the validity of a trust

- List five possible uses of an offshore trust

- Describe the features of a non-charitable purpose trust

- List five duties usually expected of a trustee

- Suggest ten powers a trustee might wish to have in a trust

- Outline who usually has the power to appoint a new trustee

- Summarise the usual rights of a beneficiary to information relating to the trust

Self-assessment Questions

1. Define a trust and include a summary of the usual parties involved in the creation of a trust.

2. Write brief notes on the difference between an express trust and a resulting trust.

3. In order for an offshore trust to be valid it must meet certain requirements. Apart from the three certainties, list three other criteria which must be met.

4. Explain what is meant by the term 'perpetuity period' and state how this is usually addressed in offshore trust deeds.

5. An offshore trust can be used for a variety of reasons. Write brief notes on five such uses.

6. Briefly explain why a client from a civil law country might wish to create a trust in the Cayman Islands.

7. Write brief notes describing the features and usual operation of a non-charitable purpose trust.

8. You have been asked to present a training session to your trust colleagues on the duties expected of an offshore trustee. List the main areas which you would cover in your presentation.

9. List five powers which you as a trustee would wish to see included in the terms of an offshore trust deed and write brief notes to explain why you would want those powers.

10. A beneficiary of a discretionary trust has contacted you for a copy of the trust deed, a copy of the previous year's financial statements and a copy of the letter of wishes. How would you respond?

Unit 10

Offshore Trust Administration
Part Two – The Law and Recognition of Offshore Trusts, the Administration of Discretionary Trusts and Offshore Trust Accounting and Reviews

Objectives

At the end of this Unit you should be able to:

- State the matters usually covered by the proper law of a trust

- Describe how the proper law would usually be determined

- Outline the factors which should be considered prior to changing the proper law

- Explain how a flee clause would usually operate

- Comment on the purpose and effect of the Hague Convention on the recognition of trusts

- Describe the effect and usual contents of a letter of wishes

- List five powers usually given to a trust protector

- Explain how a trust protector might have fiduciary responsibilities

- Comment on why trustees should hold meetings and record their decisions

- List five things an administrator should consider and check when reviewing trust accounts

In this Unit we shall be covering a number of the practical issues which the trustees of an offshore trust will regularly encounter. The areas we will be looking at could be the subject of a series of study texts in themselves, such is the complexity of the issues involved. However, all this syllabus requires is a general understanding of the main issues and so we shall be concentrating on these.

We start by looking at the proper law of a trust then move on to the recognition of foreign trusts, the administration of discretionary trusts, trust accounting requirements and finally trust review procedures.

1 The Proper Law of a Trust

1.1 There are essentially two issues to consider in relation to the law of a trust. The first relates to which Court should be chosen to adjudicate any possible future disputes or problems relating to the trust. The second relates to which law should be chosen to govern the trust. The first covers what is commonly referred to as the forum (or jurisdiction) of the trust, whilst the second addresses what is commonly known as the proper law of the trust. In practice, both laws will usually be the same for ease of administrative convenience.

1.2 The syllabus requires us to concentrate on the proper law of a trust which the remainder of this section will address.

Matters Covered by the Proper Law

1.3 Generally speaking, the proper law of a trust will govern such matters as its validity (which will be the method of creation including, in some cases, the capacity of the settlor), its effect (which will usually cover such matters as whether it will be recognised outside that jurisdiction) and its administration (which would include the powers of the trustees and the rights of the beneficiaries).

The Choice of Proper Law

1.4 Deciding on the proper law of a particular trust should be a relatively straightforward process. It will usually be accepted as being the law which is specified under the terms of the trust deed. Alternatively, if the trust deed is silent on this issue, the proper law applied will usually be that with which the trust is most closely connected. This is not always easy to determine although such factors as where the administration of the trust is carried out, where the trust assets are held, the place of residence of the trustees and also where the beneficiaries are based would be considered.

1.5 It is possible for the trustees to be resident in a centre which is different from that chosen for the proper law. For example, a settlor might choose the Bahamas as providing the proper law of his trust and decide to appoint trustees who are resident in Jersey.

1.6 Whether a trust will be able to receive the protection of the laws of the centre chosen, where it has no direct connection with that centre (which would usually mean having trustees who are resident in that centre), is debatable. However, there may be good reasons why a different law is chosen from the centre where the trustees reside.

1.7 To avoid doubt, clients should be advised to choose the proper law of their trust based on where the trustees are to be resident. At least the courts of the centre would be more willing to afford protection to local trustees in the event of a dispute.

1.8 In most cases there would be no practical advantages in appointing onshore trustees where the proper law is offshore. In fact, there could be serious adverse consequences in doing so. Apart from the fact that the courts in the offshore centre would probably not wish to defend an action brought against a trust with no local connections, other than the use of its name for the purposes of naming the law, there are also general management and control and taxation issues to consider.

1.9   Firstly, as we have already established in earlier sections of this study text, the management and control of a trust will usually be determined where the trustees are resident. If the trustees (or even one of them) are resident onshore it is possible (if not likely) that the trust will be considered resident for tax purposes in that location, which could result in the trust incurring substantial tax liabilities.

1.10   Secondly, if there was a dispute concerning, say, the validity of the trust, the person bringing the action could choose to bring his petition in a court in the onshore centre on the basis that this is where the management and control is being exercised. If offshore trustees were chosen, and the proper law was also that of the centre where the trustees were resident, any action would, realistically, have to be commenced in the offshore centre concerned which would, in most cases, make it harder for the action to proceed.

Changing the Proper Law

1.11   Most offshore trust deeds contain a clause which covers the proper law of the trust. In addition, there will also usually be provisions which cover who has the power to change the proper law to that of another offshore centre.

The power to change the proper law

1.12   In most cases the power to change the proper law will be given to the trustees and would require them to execute a deed or declaration stating that the law has been changed from one centre to another. This is how the law is changed in the majority of cases and most practitioners view this as the most effective method. However, the only UK case which can be quoted on this subject is *Duke of Marlborough v. Attorney General (no 1)* (1945) which suggested that a change in the proper law cannot be made unless all the beneficiaries agree.

Situations where a change may be required

1.13   Perhaps the main reason a change might be required would be if the advantages or benefits of the original centre were diminished. This could be as a result of the centre introducing a system of taxation on local trusts, there being political unrest or perhaps as a result of another centre altering its laws, with the result that it now offers greater potential benefits than the original centre chosen.

Factors to consider prior to making a change

1.14   There are a number of factors which a trustee should consider before a change is made to the proper law and these are detailed below.

Trust Law of New Centre

1.15   Before any change is made, the trustees must ensure that the law to be chosen recognises trusts and that the trust provisions of the new centre will not be contravened. For example, the perpetuity period of a Jersey trust might be 100 years but in the Isle of Man the maximum fixed period of years is 80. A change of proper law from Jersey to the Isle of Man would create a problem as the perpetuity period would be offended, which in turn might render the trust invalid.

Beneficial Interests

1.16   The trustees should also check that the interests of the beneficiaries will not be altered under the provisions of the new law chosen.

Interpretation of Words

1.17 Some centres place a different interpretation on certain words compared with other centres and the trustees should therefore ensure that the terms of any provisions or powers are not altered as a result of a change in the proper law.

Establishing a Real Presence in the New Centre

1.18 If a change of proper law is to take place it might be advisable to appoint a trustee who is resident in the new centre to establish a real link with the jurisdiction concerned. As we mentioned earlier, the courts in an offshore centre would generally be more willing to provide support to a local trust if the trust has a real connection with that centre and often a resident trustee would be a major factor in this process.

Effecting the change

1.19 This should be by deed. When trustees are deciding on the wording of the documentation to change the proper law of a trust they may forget to include reference to the desire to move the law of the forum of the trust as well. It is therefore often advisable for the deed or declaration which is prepared to cover altering both the proper law as well as the law of the forum in an attempt to avoid any possible future doubts or problems.

Flee Clauses

1.20 Whilst on the subject of the proper law of a trust and how (and why) it might be changed, we should take a look at a widely used devise in offshore trusts which is commonly referred to as a 'flee clause'.

1.21 A flee clause is one which attempts to switch the management and administration of a trust to another centre on the occurence of a particular event, such as civil unrest or the introduction of taxation, in the original centre chosen.

1.22 Usually, such a clause will state that on the happening of a predetermined event the trustees will automatically retire and new, specified trustees in another centre will be appointed. Often the clause will also specify that the proper law and law of the forum will be changed at the same time as the change in trustees.

1.23 Once again, the centre chosen which the trust will flee to should have comparable trust laws so as to avoid any possible future conflicts. The trustees in the emergency centre will also require careful vetting, although in practice a flee clause is only used where the original trustees have representation (or as is usually the case, other offices) in more than one location. The flee centre will, therefore, be one where the trustees have another office.

1.24 Another possible problem which should be considered is the transfer of the trust property to the new trustee on the happening of the specified event. Unless this can take place almost immediately the validity of the transfer might be in question. A possible solution which is sometimes used is the assets being held through an underlying company. On the change of trustees all that would be required to transfer the trust property would be an alteration to the nominee declaration recording the beneficial ownership of the company.

Dual Laws

1.25 Before leaving this topic we should mention that it is also possible to include provisions in a trust deed which attempt to apply the proper law over one part of the trust property and another law over the remainder. Similarly, different laws may be selected for different administration functions or powers.

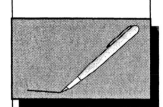

Student Activity 1

Obtain a copy of an offshore trust deed (preferably one with which you have had some involvement) and summarise the provisions which cover the choice and alteration of the proper law of that trust. If the deed is silent, how has the proper law been determined?

2   The Recognition of Offshore Trusts

2.1   Although trusts are not recognised in most civil law countries they are a familiar and popular concept with common law jurisdictions. However, not all common law countries have the same basic trust concepts which led to some debate as to whether a trust established in one country would be recognised and accepted in another.

The Hague Convention on the Law Applicable to Trusts (1984)

2.2   This Convention attempted to simplify matters with the main intention being to facilitate the recognition by one country of trusts created by the law of another. The Convention also attempted to provide a common set of criteria for determining which law should govern a trust.

2.3   The Convention was adopted in draft in 1984 by delegates from 32 member states and came into force on 1 January 1992. So far it has been ratified by Australia, Canada, Italy and the UK. It is only binding on those states who have signed and ratified it and in all likelihood these will be few in number for some years.

2.4   The implications of the Convention will in the short-term be undramatic. However, its main effect has been to provide a reason for a number of onshore and especially offshore jurisdictions to re-examine their trust laws and introduce reforms to facilitate the recognition of foreign trusts. Using the UK as an example, it introduced the Recognition of Trusts Act 1987 and the Recognition of Trusts Act 1987 (Overseas Territories) Order 1989 extending the Convention and Act to any colony, the Channel Islands and the Isle of Man.

2.5   The majority of offshore centres which provide trust services have enacted their own legislation that is similar in nature to the UK statute, which in turn was similar to the terms of the Hague Convention.

2.6   The following is a summary of the main provisions of the Hague Convention which students should be familiar with.

Articles 6 – 10

2.7   These deal with the choice of 'applicable law' of a trust and contain provisions which help determine the proper law of a trust in the event of the deed being silent on this matter. We looked at these when covering the proper law in the earlier Section.

Article 11

2.8 This dealt with specific aspects of the recognition of a trust and in particular noted that the trust property of a valid trust will constitute a separate fund. It also mentioned that the trustee of a valid trust may sue and be sued in his capacity as trustee.

2.9 Article 11 also stated that the recognition of a trust would imply that the personal creditors of the trustee have no rights or claims over trust property and that trust assets would not form part of the trustee's estate on death.

Article 15

2.10 This section mentioned that the recognition of a trust may be limited or even excluded if, for example, the trust attempted to defeat succession rights or the rights of creditors which exists under the laws of another state.

2.11 This therefore raises a question over the ability to use a trust for creditor or forced heirship protection purposes, an area which we shall return to in Unit 11.

Article 18

2.12 This confirms that the terms of the Convention may be disregarded where they are incompatible with public policy.

3 The Administration of Discretionary Trusts

3.1 Although a wide variety of trusts can be created in offshore centres there is no doubt that the most widely used type is the discretionary trust. In view of their popularity discretionary trusts are a very important part of the syllabus and students should be particularly aware of the many administration issues which this type of vehicle creates. This is the purpose of this Section.

The Appeal of Discretionary Trusts

3.2 The popularity of this type of trust is centred around its flexibility, not only for the settlor but also for the trustees. Settlors generally prefer this type of vehicle as it enables them to make provision for a wide variety of beneficiaries, including those who may not even be born. In addition, the trustees will usually be given the ability to add beneficiaries (and also to exclude them if the need arises) which further makes it possible for the changing circumstances of beneficiaries to be taken into account when distributions are contemplated.

3.3 Trustees tend to prefer discretionary trusts because of the wide powers which they are generally given. However, it is the nature of this freedom which can create very real administrative problems.

Likely Beneficiaries

3.4 Clearly, each case will be different although it would be usual to find that the beneficiaries of an offshore discretionary trust will be the settlor, his family and dependants. That is not to say, of course, that others would not also be included in the list of possible recipients of the trust funds.

3.5 As already mentioned above, in most trust deeds the trustees will be given the power to add to, or delete from, the list of discretionary beneficiaries. This can create additional confidentiality benefits as the trust deed need only contain a single named beneficiary (perhaps a charity) and the names of the 'intended' beneficiaries can be added by a supplementary deed at a later date. This is a widely used device offshore although it does create further considerations which we shall return to when we look at 'blind trusts' (which this type of arrangement is often referred to) in Unit 11.

3.6 Many settlors are happy to be included as a discretionary beneficiary on the basis that, if approached by the tax authorities in their home country, they might be able to argue that they can only receive benefit at the discretion of the trustees. This argument might be sufficient to avoid tax on the income or capital gains of the trust property on the basis that they have no absolute right to receive a benefit. However, this argument should not be relied upon in all cases as in some onshore locations, the settlor, who is also a beneficiary of his discretionary trust, will be assessed to tax on the trust property.

Types of Power Given to the Trustees

3.7 Most discretionary trust deeds will give the trustees very wide powers over the trust property. This will not only include who to make distributions to, when to make them and the amount to pay, but also who to appoint as an agent or adviser and when to terminate the trust. The trustee will therefore have, in most cases, almost absolute discretion over the trust property.

Concerns of the Settlor

3.8 It should come as no surprise that some settlors are reluctant to allow their trustees such wide powers. After all, what (or who) could stop them from exercising their discretions in a manner which the settlor never intended or generally disapproves of?

3.9 To provide, or offer, some comfort, there are two main ways in which a settlor may be able to have some say in the way in which his discretionary trust is being administered, which we shall consider next.

Letters of Wishes
Purpose of a letter of wishes

3.10 Trustees of discretionary trusts will usually have very little information concerning the circumstances and requirements of the discretionary beneficiaries. Without this type of information it can be difficult for the trustees to reach a decision when considering the exercise of many of their discretions, particularly when it comes to distributions. The settlor can, however, offer the trustees some assistance by preparing a letter setting out his wishes in respect of how he would like the trust administered and in particular, who he would like to benefit.

3.11 Most settlors of discretionary trusts prepare a letter of wishes, as this private letter to the trustees is usually called, but unfortunately, many settlors and indeed some trustees and financial planners, mistake the purpose and effect of such a letter.

Effect of a letter of wishes

3.12 Settlors should be advised that a letter of wishes is not a legally binding document and that the terms need not be followed by the trustees. In turn, the trustees and the settlor's advisers should remember that the main purpose of the letter is to provide the trustees with additional information (which may or may not help them in their decision making process) and that they can choose to take an action or reach a decision which is not covered by, or is perhaps contrary to, a wish which is expressed in the letter.

3.13   It is important that offshore trusts are not administered purely in accordance with the terms of a letter of wishes. The trustees should not be pressured by the settlor. If a letter of wishes is followed blindly by the trustees and the trust or a disposition of property is attacked, there is a strong possibility that the trust might be declared invalid and the entire arrangement treated as a sham on the basis that the trustees never intended to exercise any of their powers by an independent and active mental process, and the settlor never intended the trustees to exercise the powers given to them under the terms of the trust deed.

Sham trusts are covered in more detail in Unit 11.

Usual contents of a letter of wishes

3.14   The actual contents will vary from case to case but generally such a letter would start by stating that it is not intended to bind the trustees in any way and that it is not intended to create a separate trust. A reference to the letter not creating a separate trust might be included, as some practitioners have argued that certain trusts have been administered in accordance with the provisions of a letter of wishes and not in accordance with the terms of the trust deed. If this is the case the letter would take on the nature of a trust itself. Such a phrase is intended to prevent this claim being made.

3.15   After confirming the lack of effect which the letter will have, the settlor would then usually go on to mention who he would like the trustees to benefit and in what proportions. He might also mention that he may decide to change the terms of his letter in the future and also include reference to who he would like the trustees to communicate with after his death. Usually, this would be the settlor's spouse or one of his children.

3.16   Letters are generally signed by the settlor, although not usually in the presence of a witness as to do so might create the impression that the letter was intended to have legal effect (and perhaps be likened to a will).

Disclosure of the terms of a letter of wishes

3.17   At the time of writing the only case which specifically dealt with the rights of a beneficiary to receive a copy of the letter of wishes was heard in Australia (*Hartigan Nominees Pty Ltd* v. *Ridge* (1992)). In this case it was decided that the letter of wishes need not be disclosed to the beneficiaries on the basis that it was a confidential letter between the settlor and the trustees and confidentiality should normally be respected.

3.18   However, if there was hostile litigation against the trustees and the beneficiaries were trying to prove that the trustees had exercised their discretions improperly (perhaps by following, or refusing to follow, the terms of a letter of wishes), a letter might have to be produced to the beneficiaries (the case of *Talbot* v. *Marshfield* (1885) refers).

3.19   In view of the issues raised by the *Hartigan Case* many practitioners now request settlors to include in their letters of wishes a note to the effect that the letter is confidential.

Memorandum of wishes

3.20   Some offshore service providers suggest that instead of a settlor signing a letter setting out his wishes in relation to the administration of the trust, the trustees should record the settlor's wishes in a file note which is then placed with the trust records. A copy of the note is then sent to the settlor for his review but he is not asked to sign it.

3.21 Such a note, which is usually referred to as a memorandum of wishes, is becoming an increasingly popular alternative to the letter of wishes. This is mainly because it would probably be harder for a note to be subject to a disclosure order in the event of a dispute, on the basis that it is internal correspondence of the trustees (hence the use of the word 'memorandum') and not correspondence from the settlor, which can often be more easily produced.

Student Activity 2

Assuming you had just created an offshore discretionary trust, prepare a letter of wishes to the trustees outlining how you would like them to administer the trust. How would you feel if the trustees then said that they could not guarantee that they would follow your wishes?

The Trust Protector

3.22 Many offshore discretionary trust deeds, particularly those created within the last ten years, will contain provisions which cover the appointment and powers of the trust protector.

Role of the trust protector

3.23 This is difficult to define as such a position is not widely referred to in trust statutes, except in a few rare exceptions such as the BVI. However, it is generally accepted that the role of the protector is to oversee the actions of the trustees and also to provide them with an insight and understanding into the wishes of the settlor, and in some cases, the wishes of the beneficiaries.

3.24 The protector may also be appointed to act as a central point of liaison between the beneficiaries and the trustees and to resolve any disputes which may arise from time to time.

3.25 The position of protector is not the same as the position of trustee. For example, the legal ownership of the trust property is held by the trustee who is also responsible for the management and control of the trust and its property. The protector, on the other hand, is not the registered or legal owner of the trust property and would not, in most circumstances, be involved with the day-to-day management of the trust. He will, however, be expected to fulfil certain duties and responsibilities and will also be given certain powers under the terms of the trust deed.

Reasons why a protector may be required

3.26 A settlor might decide to include a protector for a number of reasons. Perhaps the most common are:

i)   He is concerned that the trustee will fail to exercise his powers and duties in a satisfactory manner and would like a third party to keep watch over the trustee's actions;

ii)   He is concerned that the trustee may not pay attention to his wishes (although as we have already mentioned the trustee is not under any obligation to do so);

iii) He would like certain powers to be withheld from the trustees;

iv)   He would like a third party to act as moderator, and the main point of contact, between the beneficiaries and the trustees.

Person usually appointed

3.27   Often the protector will be a close friend, a relative or adviser of the settlor and will usually be resident in an onshore centre. Indeed, this person might have been a good candidate for the role of trustee had it not been for the need to appoint trustees from an offshore centre.

3.28   Basically, any individual who has the necessary capacity to manage his own affairs could be appointed as a trust protector, although in view of the powers which they would often be given, careful thought should be given to the appointment. In addition, the nature of the duties and responsibilities of the protector should be explained to them prior to their appointment as, depending on the terms of the deed, they may be reluctant to have fiduciary responsibilities.

3.29   In some trusts, you will also find that the protector will be a corporate body, perhaps a limited liability company which has been registered or incorporated in an offshore centre.

Method of appointment

3.30   The trust deed should be checked to see what the requirements are for the appointment of the first and subsequent trust protectors. It will usually also cover the retirement and removal of such a person.

3.31   Usually, the trustees will have the power to appoint and remove the trust protector and this would often be achieved by a deed or declaration. It is common to find that the first protector is appointed on the creation of the trust. In some cases, the settlor may wish to retain the power of appointment and removal but as we shall see later in this Section, this may not be advisable, depending on the extent of the powers which the protector has been given.

Usual powers of the trust protector

3.32   The trust deed must specify what powers the protector will have as there are generally no statutory powers which will be available in default. Once again, they will vary from case to case although the following is a list of the common powers which are often dispensed:

i)   To remove and appoint the trustees;

ii)   To approve a change of proper law;

iii) To approve to the addition or removal of beneficiaries;

iv)   To approve proposed trust distributions;

v) To approve the appointment of an agent or adviser;

vi) To approve investment recommendations;

vii) To appoint replacement protectors;

viii) To approve a proposal to terminate the trust.

3.33 Ideally, if a protector is appointed he should only be given the power to approve the proposed actions of the trustees and not be given powers which could be construed as enabling him to manage or control the trust property. His powers should certainly not be greater than those of the trustees. If they were, there would be an argument to suggest that the protector would have the management and control of the trust property, possibly making him a 'quasi trustee', which in turn might make the trust resident for tax purposes in the centre where the protector is located.

3.34 The first power which was quoted above (to remove and appoint the trustees) might also create problems if the settlor retained the power to appoint and remove the protector. This is because the settlor would effectively be able to control the trustees which could in turn make the trust resident for tax purposes in the country or jurisdiction where the settlor is resident, regardless of the residence of the trustees or the protector.

Fiduciary powers

3.35 There has been much debate in recent years as to whether the protector's powers are held in a fiduciary or personal capacity. A detailed discussion of the legal aspects are beyond the scope of this syllabus but in general terms the debate will centre around the nature and extent of the powers which the protector has been given under the terms of the trust deed, and also whether the protector can benefit.

3.36 Firstly, a 'fiduciary power' is generally accepted to be one which has been conferred on a person for the benefit of others. Clearly, if the protector has powers which enable him to affect the interests of the beneficiaries (i.e. the power to approve trust distributions) then he will have fiduciary powers and will, as a result, be expected to fulfil the duties which are expected of those with such powers (an area which we shall return to later in this Section). However, whether the protector can benefit should now be considered.

3.37 If the protector is a beneficiary of the trust, it can be argued that his powers will enable him to protect his own interests and as a result, it is doubtful whether he would owe any fiduciary duties. Alternatively, if the protector is not a beneficiary and only others can benefit, he will be expected (and required) to exercise those powers which are given to him in the best interests of the beneficiaries. The Bahamian case of *Rawson Trust* v. *Pearlman* (1990) covered these areas.

We shall now look at some recent cases which covered the powers and general duties of trust protectors.

The 'Star Trusts' case (1994)

3.38 *Jurgen von Knieriem* v. *Bermuda Trust Company Limited* (1994), or the *Star Trusts* as it is commonly referred to, was a case which was heard in Bermuda and centred on the powers of the protector (Mr. von Knieriem) and his attempts to replace the trustees (Bermuda Trust Company Limited). In addition to having the power to remove trustees, the protector also had the power to appoint trustees.

3.39   The trustees believed that their removal was not in the best interests of the beneficiaries and after much discussion applied to the court for directions. The trustees hoped to show that the protector, who could not be a beneficiary, had fiduciary powers and as such had to exercise them properly.

3.40   The court, in fact, approved the actions of the protector and agreed to the removal of the trustees and appointment of another trust company. However, what was interesting was the fact that the court referred to a number of decisions made in the UK and in particular the case of *Re Skeats Settlement* (1889) in which it was decided that a power to appoint new trustees was a fiduciary power.

3.41   Although the *Star Trusts Case* did not specifically state that the powers of a protector are fiduciary, the discussions which it created led practitioners to agree that the protectors' powers can be fiduciary, depending of course, on the terms of the trust deed.

3.42   The case also highlighted the need for trustees to assess whether the protector is acting in the interests of the beneficiaries when exercising the powers given to him. If in doubt, the trustees should seek direction from the court on how to proceed.

Steele v. Paz Limited (1995)
3.43   This is a case from the Isle of Man which at the time of writing is still addressing a number of very wide issues. The area which is of particular interest to us in this Unit is the views of the court which confirmed that, in the case in question, the protector had fiduciary responsibilities and that these should be fulfilled with the best interests of the beneficiaries (rather than the settlor) in mind.

3.44   This is interesting as many advisers see the protector as being the 'settlor's man', when in fact, according to the findings of one part of this case, the protector should be acting for the beneficiaries much in the same way as the trustees would be expected to.

3.45   It was also interesting to note that in this case the protector had the power to appoint beneficiaries but as a protector had not been appointed the court decided that it had to appoint one to enable the trust to function.

Re the settlement between X and Blampied and Abacus (CI) Limited (1994)
3.46   Although this Jersey case had not been reported in detail at the time of writing it offers further insight into the role of the protector. One of the issues covered in this case concerns the protector and although it was agreed he did act in the best interests of the beneficiaries, some of his actions came close to being those usually expected of a trustee. It was noted that the role of the protector is not in fact the same as that expected and required of the trustee.

Further practical considerations
3.47   Whether a protector is required is a matter of personal choice by the settlor and we have already covered a number of areas which should be considered before

proceeding with such an appointment. However, before we leave this topic there are a few additional matters which should be considered and remembered.

i)   If the protector is to approve certain actions of the trustees, bear in mind that there may be time delays in receiving his consent.

ii) If the protector refuses his consent for a particular action, the trustees should not leave the matter at that. The trustees still have a duty to consider challenging his decision, a fact which the settlor should be made aware of at the time the possible position or appointment of a protector is discussed, otherwise the settlor might mistakingly think that the protector has the final word on such matters.

iii) If the protector is given powers which are too wide, he may be considered a trustee. This could affect the overall management and control of the trust, which in turn may alter the residence of the trust for tax purposes. For this reason it is usually advisable for the protector of an offshore trust to be resident in an offshore centre. This is also a good argument why the settlor should not be appointed as the protector of his trust, especially if the protector's powers are wide and he resides onshore.

iv) The trust deed should include provisions to enable the protector to charge and to receive a fee for his services.

v)   Finally, if the settlor is reluctant for the protector to be given fiduciary responsibilities, or the protector is reluctant to have these responsibilities placed upon him, the trust deed should specify that the protector will not be acting in a fiduciary capacity.

Student Activity 3

Select an offshore trust deed which contains trust protector provisions. Summarise the method of appointment, retirement and removal and also summarise the powers which have been given to the protector. Are there any provisions which might affect the management and control of the trustees or perhaps involve the settlor in this process?

Committee of Wishes

3.48   Some settlors decide that instead of appointing a single trust protector, they would prefer instead to appoint a number of people to perform this role. Usually, the term which is associated with this type of arrangement is a committee of wishes.

3.49   The matters which we addressed in relation to the trust protector should also be applied to a committee of wishes, although in view of the fact that the committee will usually comprise a number of individuals, the decision making process can be hindered and delayed far more than by appointing a sole trust protector to provide the trustees with assistance and possibly guidance.

Trustee Meetings – The Decision Making Process

3.50   As we have already mentioned, the trustees of a discretionary trust will have very wide powers and responsibilities and any decisions which they reach must be in the interests of the beneficiaries.

3.51 It is important that trustees, particularly those of discretionary trusts, record the decisions which they have taken. Perhaps the most effective method is to hold a meeting of the trustees and for the matters discussed to be recorded in the minutes of that meeting.

3.52 If there is only one trustee appointed, any decisions which are taken should still be minuted although there may not necessarily be a meeting at which the decision was made. A record similar to a written resolution for a company would seem appropriate in the circumstances.

3.53 The majority of offshore trusts have corporate trustees and although there may only be one trustee appointed in a particular case (that of the corporate body), it would be advisable for decisions to be taken by meetings at which at least two authorised representatives of the trust company are present.

3.54 Without a written record of the decisions which have been taken, there would be no evidence to suggest that the trustees exercised a particular discretion as a result of an active mental process. The trustees must show that they were responsible for actions taken, especially in relation to trust distributions, and the minute of a meeting can help to achieve this.

3.55 A trustee is not usually required to release or provide copies of minutes of meetings which are held. The case of *Re Londonderry's Settlement* (1964) supports this as it was held that the beneficiaries' rights to trust documents did not extend to documents which contained information on how the trustees have reached any decisions.

3.56 Despite being useful, students should remember that the processes of holding a meeting and then preparing the minutes of that meeting are not in themselves sufficient proof that the trustees acted in the best interests of the beneficiaries, nor that they reached a decision by using an active mental process. The case of *Rahman* v. *Chase Bank (C.I.) Trust Company Limited* (1991), which we cover in detail in Unit 11, was a case in point as the court was critical of the trustees attempts to produce minutes of meetings, which were supposedly held in 1978, which were considered to be 'housekeeping' documents and not, in the court's opinion, evidence of a genuine decision on the part of the trustees.

4 The Usual Structure (Contents) of an Offshore Discretionary Trust Deed

4.1 In Unit 9 we looked at some of the provisions which are usually included in offshore trust deeds relating to the powers of the trustees. We shall now look at how an offshore discretionary trust deed would often be structured.

The Parties to the Deed
4.2 The first part of the deed would usually cover who the settlor and the trustees are. In some cases another party may be mentioned although this is not particularly common in trust deeds (but is very common in deeds of retirement and appointment).

The Recitals

4.3 This section will include wording to the effect that the settlor intends to create a trust and will often specify the overall purpose of the trust (which might be to benefit the settlor's family).

Definitions

4.4 Most deeds will contain a section which defines the meaning of terms which are included in the deed. For example, the term 'Beneficiaries' will be defined and an explanation given as to who (or what) will or can benefit. Other terms which are usually defined, and which the trustees should pay particular attention to include the 'Perpetuity (Trust Duration) Period', and the 'Trust Fund'.

Provisions and Powers

4.5 The next section would usually contain details of how the trust property is to be held and distributed. In addition, the powers of the trustees would be included in this section. In this section it should clearly state that the trustees have discretionary powers and that the interests of the beneficiaries will also be of a discretionary nature.

Schedules

4.6 In an attempt to simplify trust deeds it is usual for a deed to contain schedules which are referred to in the deed. They are commonly used to list the beneficiaries or perhaps the trustee's powers.

Execution Page

4.7 Usually, although not always, the deed will be executed by the parties at the end of the document. All parties to the deed should sign or seal and their execution of the deed should be witnessed.

5 Trust Accounting Principles for Offshore Trusts

5.1 Finally in this Unit we shall look at some of the main accounting issues which trustees of offshore trusts should be familiar with (although much of what follows will equally apply to trustees of onshore trusts).

5.2 Students are not expected to complete trust accounts nor post-accounting entries in the examination. They are, however, expected to understand some of the fundamental trust accounting principles and also know what type of information should be recorded in the accounts which trustees prepare.

Purpose of Trust Accounts

5.3 In general terms, trust accounts serve the following purposes:

a) They provide trustees with the ability to check that the terms of the trust have been complied with;

b) They help to explain to beneficiaries how their entitlements have been calculated and also how the trust property has been accounted for;

c) They assist the trustees with the general management and control of the trust assets by recording the present state of affairs (which is particularly useful with regard to trust investments);

d)   They enable the trustees to fulfil their statutory duty to keep adequate accounting records which most offshore centres impose;

e)   They provide information which is required for taxation purposes. Although most offshore trusts are not taxed locally, beneficiaries who receive distributions from a trust may need to submit accounting information to their tax authorities.

Information Usually Contained in Trust Accounts

5.4   The precise details will vary from case to case but in general terms the following information would usually be contained in a set of trust accounts.

Brief history of the trust

5.5   A number of trustees will include a brief summary of the terms of the trust together with a note of any events (such as a substantial capital distribution) which have led to the position reflected in the current accounts.

The date of the accounts

5.6   The period which the accounts cover should be noted. Although most onshore trusts have their accounts prepared to coincide with fiscal years, many offshore trusts tend to have accounts prepared on the anniversary date.

A balance sheet

5.7   The purpose of this should be self-evident.

A capital account and an income account

5.8   It is an established trust accounting principle that capital items and income items must be recorded separately. This is often essential because different classes of beneficiaries may have different interests in the trust property (as is the case with fixed trusts).

5.9   Capital assets should be recorded in the capital account, so too should transactions of a capital nature, such as the appointment of capital. The assets are usually included at their book value (which is the acquisition value) and often a separate note is made of the current market value of those assets.

5.10   Similarly, income items (such as dividend receipts and maintenance payments) should be recorded in the income account.

5.11   In most cases, the trustees fees and expenses will be debited from income, although most deeds will allow this type of expenditure to be taken from either income or capital.

Separate schedules

5.12   Usually, trust investments are recorded in a separate schedule which is referred to in the capital account. Any income which the investments earned would then be matched with the figure quoted in the income account. Realised gains or losses from the disposal of an investment would also be recorded in this separate schedule and the net position would be noted in the capital account.

5.13   Separate schedules may also be used for other asset types, such as realty or assurance policies.

5.14 If surplus income is to be accumulated in accordance with the terms of the trust deed, a separate schedule will be included detailing the amount of income which has been accumulated during the period under review, plus income which has been accumulated in previous years.

Accounts and Trust Reviews

5.15 Trustees have a choice when it comes to the preparation of the accounts. They can either complete the details themselves or appoint an agent (usually an accountant) to carry out this function. Whichever method is chosen will not detract from the need for the accounts to be reviewed on completion.

5.16 Trustees will have their own system and procedures for the review of trust accounts. Indeed, those of you who administer offshore trusts will no doubt have had some exposure to your organisation's policies regarding this area of the business. However, for those of you who may not be familiar with this area of trust administration, a list is provided below of the matters which are often covered in the review of offshore trust accounts.

5.17 As you will see, this list extends beyond simply checking the figures recorded in the accounts. It is intended to provide the framework of a checklist to enable administrators and trustees to assess how the trust has been administered during the period under consideration and also to make sure that the required records and paperwork are in place.

5.18 The review of the trust accounts is also an ideal time to conduct a thorough review of all aspects of the administration of the trust. This regular review, which should take place at least annually, is a task which some practitioners ignore but such a procedure can be of tremendous benefit as it can help to reduce risk by alerting the trustees to potential problems before they materialise into matters of serious concern.

5.19 The following is a list of points to review when checking annual trust accounts:

   a) The trust deed should be read to check that the summary contained in the accounts is correct. Even if there is no trust summary, reading the deed is essential to check that any distributions which have been made were in accordance with the terms of the trust.

      Similarly, all distributions or other actions of the trustees should be covered in the minutes of meetings which would have been held by the trustees at the time the action was sanctioned. The files should be reviewed to make sure that there are minutes (or similar written records of the trustees' decisions) which correspond to the actions taken. If required, a subsequent meeting of the trustees could be held to discuss and ratify those decisions which were taken but not recorded at the time. Ratification can be a useful solution in some cases but it is not good practice as it is far better to hold meetings and record the findings of those meetings prior to, or at the same time as the trustees take action.

   b) Bank statements might be looked at, usually to check that the brought forward and carried forward figures are correctly shown in the accounts.

c) If distributions have been made, the files should be reviewed to make sure they contain suitable receipts from the recipients. If any receipts are missing they should be followed up.

d) If investments are held, the administrator should check that share certificates or similar documentary evidence of ownership is held for each stock recorded in the accounts. In addition, a check might also be made on the market value figure shown in the accounts by comparing this with the valuation figure prepared by the investment managers or advisers.

e) Dividend counterfoils (or the equivalent evidence of a receipt of income) should also be on the file and possibly checked off against entries which appear in the income account. The counterfoils can be used in certain cases to reclaim tax which might have been deducted from the income payment at source.

f) Any assets which have not been valued recently (perhaps in the last 12 months) should be looked at and a decision taken whether a market value should now be conducted. Similarly, all liabilities should also be given a realistic current value where possible.

g) If realty is held, the accounts review time might be an opportunity to check that the insurance cover is adequate and that premiums are up to date. In addition, the whereabouts of the deeds or other proof of ownership should be verified and if necessary, a market valuation undertaken.

h) Similarly, if any household effects or other chattels are held by the trustees (included in this general description could be a multitude of items such as yachts, motor vehicles, oil paintings and jewellery), they too should be reviewed and assurances received on their value, the suitability of the insurance arrangements, as well as their safe keeping.

i) If the trust owns shares in an underlying company it would be prudent to make enquiries as to the value of the those shares and also enquire as to the recent activities of the company.

j) If loans are either due to, or payable by, the trustees a check should be made that supporting loan documentation (either a loan agreement or at least a written confirmation of the loan position as at a recent date) is on file. The terms of the loan(s) should also be reviewed and possibly a plan for repayment implemented.

   If the loan is interest bearing, a check should be made that interest has been received or paid on the due dates.

k) Any future events which will have a bearing on the administration of the trust (such as a beneficiary attaining a particular age and receiving an absolute right to a share of the income) should be diarised as otherwise the trustees might miss the event and possibly be in breach of trust.

l) The trustee should check that the fees which have been charged have been based on the correct fee scale and that an invoice for the right amount has been issued. The trustees may also want to make sure that the fee has been collected.

m) The mathematics in the accounts should be checked. It can be very easy to concentrate on reviewing the status of the underlying assets and forget to check whether the figures add up and balance.

n) The accounts review is also a good time to check the trust records and make sure that the details held on the various beneficiaries are current. A 'family tree' might be a useful addition to the records where the beneficiaries are mainly from a particular family, which would often be the settlor's family.

   Supporting birth, marriage and death certificates should also be requested and copies held in the file.

   The trust records should also contain a copy of the trust deed as well as copies of any supplementary deeds, plus copies of any other documents which the trustees might need or have used to assist them in their duties (this will include a copy of the letter (or memorandum) of wishes).

o) The items held by the trustees in their own safe custody system should be reconciled. Some items should be held in a secure place (preferably in a fire proof area and under at least single lock and key). These would include the original trust deed, the originals of any supplementary deeds and the original letter (or memorandum) of wishes. Other items may also be held under secure conditions but copies should always be retained in the trust records as 'working' copies.

p) Usually, after all the matters have been reviewed, the trustees will meet and sign the accounts (an action which would often be recorded by a minute of a meeting).

Student Activity 4

If your organisation has an annual review procedure for the trusts which it administers, obtain a copy of the checklist/worksheet and compare it to the points covered in this section. If your organisation does not have an annual review procedure, perhaps you might like to draft one for the approval of your trust department manager.

Audit

5.20 The accounts for offshore trusts are rarely audited as there are no statutory requirements to this effect. However, some service providers will insist that all accounts for which they provide trustees are audited at least every 3 years.

5.21 Usually, the trust deed will empower the trustees to request an audit if they feel it appropriate.

Right to Receive a Copy of the Accounts

5.22 We briefly touched upon this in Unit 9 and to recap, the beneficiaries generally have the right to request a copy of the trust accounts (although in certain situations such a request may be refused by the trustees).

5.23 Co-trustees should receive a copy of the figures and so too should the protector, depending on the extent of the powers which they have been given.

5.24 The settlor has no right to receive such information, unless the deed specifies otherwise, or unless he is a beneficiary, the trust protector or a co-trustee.

Valuation and Revaluation of Specific Assets

5.25 Some assets are easier to value than others. For example, quoted stocks and shares are relatively easy to value whilst the shares in unquoted companies (in particular private limited companies) are very difficult to put a price on. In addition, an asset might be quoted or valued in a particular currency which is different from the currency in which the accounts are prepared.

5.26 These issues can create accounting problems for trustees. A detailed discussion of the principles which should be applied for these matters is outside the scope of the syllabus but in general terms the trustees would be wise to proceed along the following lines.

Valuation of unquoted shares

5.27 It is common to find that an offshore trust will own the issued shares of an underlying private limited company. In such cases the market valuation of the shares of the company would be determined by the value of the underlying assets which the company owns.

5.28 The annual accounts of the company should provide this figure and would certainly be a useful basis on which to value the trust's ownership.

Currency valuations

5.29 If an asset is valued in a currency which is not the base currency of the trust (e.g. the accounts are prepared in US$ and an asset is held in the UK which is valued in GBP), the asset should be revalued, based on the rate of exchange which exists between the two currencies at the date of the accounts. Any gain or loss would usually be posted to capital account.

Common Accounting Terms

5.30 Finally, there are three commonly used accounting terms which administrators should be familiar with. They often cause confusion as the words are so similar.

Appointment

5.31 This is the term which is applied to the payment of capital under a particular power in the trust deed.

Apportionment

5.32 This is applied to the situation where funds are received which comprise both income and capital (e.g. on the sale of a fixed interest stock where the proceeds comprise capital plus accrued income). A calculation has to be made to determine which amount is transferred to capital and which portion passes to income.

Appropriation

5.33 Most trust deeds empower the trustees to transfer property to a beneficiary in lieu of cash. If an asset is taken in specie the term often applied is appropriation.

Summary

Now that you have read this Unit you should be able to:

● Describe the matters covered by the proper law of a trust

● Explain how the proper law would usually be determined

● List those factors to consider prior to changing the proper law

● Explain how a flee clause would usually operate

● Comment on the purpose and effect of the Hague Convention on the recognition of trusts

● Explain the purpose of a letter of wishes and list the usual contents

● List five powers commonly given to a trust protector

● Explain the fiduciary responsibilities of a trust protector

● Comment on the need for trustee meetings and minutes

● List five checks an administrator should carry out when reviewing trust accounts

179

Self-assessment Questions

1. A trust deed does not state which proper law is to be applied. Explain how the choice of law might be determined in such a situation.

2. Provide two examples of situations why the proper law of a trust might be altered and explain how such a change might be achieved.

3. You are discussing the terms of your organisation's standard trust deed with a potential new client. Briefly explain the purpose of the flee clause which is included in the deed.

4. Summarise the possible attractions of discretionary trusts for settlors as well as for the trustees.

5. A settlor of an offshore discretionary trust has forwarded to the trustees a letter of wishes and has asked them to confirm that they will follow the terms which he has set out in the letter. Advise the trustees accordingly.

6. Outline the usual contents of a letter of wishes and suggest why a memorandum from the trustees might be more appropriate.

7. Outline the usual powers which are given to the trust protector and provide one example of the type of power which should not generally be given to this person.

8. Write brief notes on the findings of the following cases as they relate to trust protectors:

    a) *The Star Trusts*

    b) *Steele* v. *Paz*

9. Comment on the purpose of trustees holding meetings and then recording the decisions of those meetings.

10. Prepare a list of the administration issues which could be reviewed at the same time as checking the annual trust accounts.

Unit 11

Offshore Trust Administration
Part Three – Common Administration Issues and Risk Reduction

Objectives

At the end of this Unit you should be able to:

- Comment on the advisability of the settlor being appointed as trust protector

- List five possible benefits of a private trust company acting as trustee

- Highlight the duties and responsibilities of trustees which have a majority interest in an underlying company

- Briefly describe the duties of a trustee in relation to the investment of trust property

- Explain the duties of a trustee in appointing an agent

- Summarise the decisions of at least two recent court cases involving the extent of trustees' indemnities

- Describe the problems which could be associated with blind trusts and dummy settlors

- List the areas of concern with creditor protection trusts

- Briefly describe the effect of the *Lemos Case*

- List at least six ways to avoid sham trusts

In this final Unit on offshore trusts we shall cover a number of administration issues which are commonly faced by trustees. As you will see, many of these issues can create potential problems for the trustees as well as the beneficiaries and the settlor. Students should, therefore, be aware of how these potential risks can be avoided.

We start by looking at the role which the settlor of a trust might want to take on.

1   The Role of the Settlor

1.1   A number of settlors, particularly of offshore discretionary trusts, will want to retain some level of involvement in the administration and management of their trust and may suggest (some in fact demand) that they be given some say in the decision-making process.

1.2   As we have mentioned on a number of occasions in this study text, the residence of a trust for tax purposes will usually be determined by where the management and control lies. To avoid possible problems, the management and control of an offshore trust should be exercised by trustees who are resident in an offshore centre, preferably in the centre chosen as providing the proper law. However, if someone other than the trustees are making the decisions and managing the assets, the residence of the trust will, in all probability, be deemed to be where the management and control is actually being exercised. If the settlor, through his wish to have a say in the decision making process, effectively has these powers then serious and damaging consequences could result.

With that warning in mind, let us look at how the settlor might want to retain an involvement.

Appointed as Co-Trustee

1.3   Generally, it would not be advisable for the settlor of an offshore trust to be appointed a co-trustee alongside an offshore trustee. This is because all the trustees will have equal powers and responsibilities in relation to the management and control of the trust and its property, and as a result the trust might be deemed to be resident where the settlor is located. If he is resident onshore, serious tax consequences could result.

1.4   Another possible problem could relate to the jurisdiction of the courts in the event of a dispute or claim. If all the trustees are resident in an offshore centre and the trust has the proper law of that jurisdiction, any claim or action would have to be heard or defended by a court in that centre and there is a strong likelihood that the local court would do what it could to protect that trust and the trustees (depending on the circumstances of the action).

1.5   However, if one of the trustees (in this case the settlor) is located outside that centre, it would be possible for an attack on the trust to be made in the court where that trustee is resident. The protection offered under the laws of the offshore centre chosen could therefore be undermined if the settlor was appointed co-trustee and he was resident in a country which did not offer the same protections under its trust legislation.

Appointed as Trust Protector

1.6   The role of the trust protector and resulting administration issues has been covered in Unit 10, and you will recall that the powers which the protector is given will determine whether he can be seen to exercise management and control over the trustees and the trust property.

1.7   Generally speaking, wide powers should not be given to the trust protector, and the potential problems which could result if he did have an active input into the trust would be made worse if the settlor is appointed to this role.

1.8   The power to remove and appoint trustees (which is often passed to the trust protector) should be avoided as the settlor (in his capacity as protector) would directly be able to control the trust by being able to control who acts as trustee.

Completing a Letter of Wishes

1.9   We also covered this topic in Unit 10 and you will recall that such a letter has no binding effect and as a result, it should not affect the trustee's decision-making powers and their overall powers of management and control.

1.10   The settlor of a discretionary trust should be encouraged to complete a letter of wishes if he feels it will provide him with comfort in the knowledge that he has been able to provide the trustees with guidance and advice in relation to how they may wish to exercise their discretion.

1.11   The trustees should not, as we have already mentioned, follow the terms blindly, nor should they indicate to the settlor that they will follow the terms without consideration.

Appointed Investment Adviser or Other Agent

1.12   There is generally no restriction on who can be appointed as investment adviser or as any other designated agent, provided that the person who the trustee appoints is suitably qualified or experienced in the area concerned. As a result the settlor could be appointed to such a position. However, once again the trustees should look at the extent of the powers such an agent has been given and in particular whether they can be perceived as being able to exercise management and control over the trust property. If they do, perhaps the settlor is not the most suitable choice.

1.13   If the settlor demands to have some say in the investment of the trust funds, many practitioners would suggest that the settlor be named as investment adviser under the terms of the trust deed. However, as an alternative to this, the settlor could be asked to set out his ideas on the investment parameters in a side letter to the trustees, the existence of which would then be referred to in the trust deed under the investment clause.

We return to investment advisers and the duty of the trustee in relation to the appointment of agents later in this Unit.

Appointed as a Beneficiary

1.14   The settlor could, of course, benefit under the terms of the trust which he has created but he should consider whether there would be any possible taxation consequences of having an interest (either absolutely or at discretion) in property which he has placed into trust.

Private Trustee Company

1.15   It would seem appropriate to mention here the possibility of the client creating a private limited company to act as trustee of his trust. Under this arrangement a company would be incorporated with the sole purpose of acting as trustee of the client's trust. Although the idea is nothing new, in recent years there seems to have been a resurgence in the use of companies in this manner, particularly in Bermuda and the Cayman Islands.

1.16   There are a number of possible advantages to a settlor appointing a private trustee company as trustee of his trust, although as we shall also see, there are some potential problems:

Control

1.17   The settlor could be appointed to the board of the company (as too could members of his family and his advisers) which would enable him to have control over the trustee functions. However, if challenged it is doubtful whether this type of arrangement would create any tax savings, in view of the fact that the settlor would have retained the management and control of the trust property through his role as director of the trustee company.

Cost savings

1.18 A fee for acting as trustee would not be charged and the only expenses which would have to be met would be the cost of incorporating the company and keeping it in good standing. There may be a requirement that the company has to be licenced to act as trustee (and possibly have a locally licenced trust company to act as its agent) and if this is the case additional cost would be involved.

Limited liability

1.19 In theory, a limited liability company with no assets of its own would be better able to take on the trusteeship of assets which might be viewed as being of a speculative nature. In addition, if the trust is designed to provide creditor protection, a private trustee company might be a better option to act as trustee in view of its limited liability features.

Confidentiality

1.20 Private limited companies, especially those in offshore centres, can be structured to maintain confidentiality (as we have already seen when discussing companies earlier in this study text). They also prevent the possible worry over secrecy which some settlors have when appointing outside trustees.

1.21 It has been common practice in Bermuda for a purpose trust to own the shares in a private trustee company which would further increase the confidentiality possibilities.

Flexibility

1.22 The fact that the settlor can control the trustee company provides greater scope for flexibility and will enable the trustee to act in a manner which perhaps an outside trustee might be unable (or reluctant) to do.

2 Offshore Trusts Owning Underlying Companies – The Benefits and Risks

2.1 A great many offshore trusts own shares in underlying (usually offshore) private limited companies. Earlier in this study text we looked at the possible financial planning benefits which offshore companies can provide and we also covered why multi-company structures are often used.

2.2 Before we look at some of the administration issues which company ownership can create for trustees, we should perhaps mention why the trust/company structure is so popular.

Possible Benefits

2.3 The following summarises the main benefits commonly associated with a trust/company structure:

Limited liability

2.4 The limited liability feature of a company reduces risk and also enables property to be held in the structure which might not be considered a suitable 'directly held' trust asset (e.g. high risk investments or assets of a wasting nature).

Separate legal entity

2.5 A company is a separate legal entity and any legal actions which may be brought against it or the assets which it holds could, in theory, be restricted to the company and not extend to the trust or other companies in the structure. The risk of attack on the rest of the assets in an offshore structure can therefore be 'ring fenced' by using a company, or a number of different companies, depending on the nature and number of assets to be placed under the ultimate control of the trustees.

Asset holding

2.6 Certain types of assets cannot be registered in the names of the trustees and a company provides a useful and practical asset holding alternative.

Confidentiality

2.7 The ownership by the trustees would be confidential and would only usually be recorded by a nominee declaration.

Tax reasons

2.8 There may be tax savings available in holding property in an offshore company, with the shares of that company in turn being owned by the trustees of an offshore trust. For example, the shares of an offshore company are excluded property for UK inheritance tax (IHT) purposes; UK real estate which is owned by an offshore company can take that property out of the IHT tax net. Ultimate ownership by an offshore trust adds further weight to the possible tax savings available in some onshore centres.

2.9 In addition, under US estate tax legislation, on the death of a grantor, tax is payable on US situs assets which are held in trust. If an underlying company is used to hold the US situs assets there would be no tax to pay on the death of the settlor.

Possible Risks

2.10 The risks centre on the duties expected of trustees particularly where the trustee owns a controlling interest in an underlying company. A controlling interest would arise, for example, where the trust owns at least 51% of the issued shares in the underlying company. Most offshore trusts which own shares in an underlying company tend to own 100% of the issued shares of that company.

2.11 The duties expected of the trustees can perhaps be best explained by looking at two well reported UK cases.

Lucking's Will Trusts 1967

2.12 This case considered the level of information and involvement which the trustee should have in relation to the management and affairs of a company which it owned.

2.13 A sole trustee appointed a manager (who later became a director) to run the company's business. Unfortunately, losses were incurred as a result of the misconduct of the manager (who was drawing from the assets of the company), and the trustee was held liable because of his failure to adequately supervise the activities of the manager.

2.14 The duties of a trustee which holds the majority interest of an underlying company were examined and a 'reasonable man' test was applied to decide how trustees should act in such circumstances. Here is a summary of the findings and suggestions:

i) A reasonably prudent man acting as trustee would not content himself with obtaining the information which is generally available to the shareholders, but would instead seek to obtain information usually available to the directors.

ii) The trustee should seek to become represented on the board of directors of the company, perhaps as Managing Director or as a non-executive director (with the management delegated to someone else).

iii) If the trustee cannot be appointed to the board he should seek to find someone to represent him and his interests.

Bartlett v. Barclays Bank Trust Co. Limited (1980)
2.15 The case of *Bartlett* v. *Barclays Bank Trust Co. Limited* (1980) extended the principles raised in *Re Lucking*.

2.16 In this case the trustees had absolute power of investment and decided to invest money (through a company) in a building development project in London. They had bought in to the project at prices in excess of the value of the real estate in the hope that planning permission would be granted which, if it was, would have greatly increased the value of the project and therefore the investment. However, the company lost approximately £500,000 and the trustees were held liable for their actions which the court decided amounted to gambling with trust property.

2.17 The 'reasonable man' test was again applied and the findings extended the position which was summarised in *Re Lucking*. It was mentioned that trustees who own the controlling interest in an underlying company should also obtain copies of the agenda and minutes of board meetings, copies of monthly management accounts and in the case of a trading company, quarterly accounts.

2.18 The *Bartlett Case* also confirmed that a higher duty of care is owed by a professional corporate trustee and that such a trustee would be liable for breach of trust if loss was caused because it neglected to use the special skill and care which it professed to have.

A Possible Solution
2.19 Many offshore trust deeds will contain a clause which is designed to reduce the duties and responsibilities of the trustees in relation to their control over underlying companies. There has been considerable debate on this issue following the findings of the cases which we covered earlier in this Section. However, many practitioners believe that a provision which allows the trustees not to interfere in the running of an underlying company, unless they have actual knowledge of the mismanagement of that company, might provide some protection.

Student Activity 1

From your portfolio of cases, select an offshore trust which owns the majority of shares in an underlying offshore private limited company. What information do you have on file concerning the activities of that company and to what extent are the trustees involved in the decision making process? Alternatively, if you do not have such an example in your current case load, what information do you think the file should contain for such a situation?

3   The Investment of Trust Funds

3.1   The majority of offshore trust deeds will contain provisions which cover the investment of trust funds. Indeed, it would be usual to find that the trustees have been given 'absolute discretion' over the investments, thus enabling them to manage the trust assets as they see fit.

3.2   Failure to include investment powers in the deed would result in the trustees having to follow the investment guidelines that are handed down by statute, which are generally restrictive, difficult to follow and in some cases outdated (the Trustee Investment Act 1961 is perhaps a case in point).

The Duty of the Trustees

3.3   In general terms, a trustee has a duty to preserve the value of the trust property by following a prudent policy which a reasonable man would be expected to choose. Some centres have extended this general duty under their trust laws. Jersey provides a useful example of this where trustees are also expected to enhance the value of the fund.

3.4   The trustees' general duty to act in the best interests of the beneficiaries applies to the investment of trust funds, just as it does to those other areas of management which we have covered in other Sections of this study text.

How, then, should the trustee proceed to satisfy his duties?

Set objectives

3.5   The trustees should set investment objectives which they or the appointed managers will follow as quickly as possible. Usually, a trust portfolio would be managed on a conservative basis with a long-term view. However, the trust deed may allow the trustees to follow different objectives, perhaps in respect of different parts of the trust fund.

Appoint adviser

3.6   Although a trustee might be awarded wide powers of investment it is likely that instead of managing the funds himself he will appoint someone to perform this task for him. However, this appointment carries with it certain duties and responsibilities which the trustees should be aware of. We consider these in more detail later in this Section.

Speculation

3.7   Despite powers which may be contained in the trust deed to the contrary, a trustee is under a duty to avoid speculative investments. If he does invest in a speculative manner he may be able to rely on the terms of the trust deed which permit him to do so, although this may not provide the comfort or support which he may hope for. We return to indemnity clauses later in this Unit.

Interests of the beneficiaries

3.8   When deciding on the investment strategy to follow, the trustees should consider the interests of all of the beneficiaries and not concentrate on the needs or requests of, say, a life tenant at the expense of the interests of the remaindermen (or vice versa).

3.9   The case of *Learoyd* v. *Whitely* (1887) covered this very point.

Diversification

3.10   The trustees should, where possible, diversify the trust portfolio to reduce the exposure to risk.

3.11   This may involve dividing the portfolio into different sectors (such as industrial stocks, chemicals, fixed interest, stores etc.), investing in different markets in different countries and investing in different currencies.

3.12   In addition, when considering what investments to make, the trustees should put aside their own personal interests and views and must not refrain from making an investment purely by reason of the views they hold.

3.13   Diversification may not always be possible, perhaps because the value of the funds is too small. Nor indeed is diversification always practical. The trustees should also refrain from diversifying for the sake of it and take a sensible approach when looking at risk reduction. Those trustees who invest US$50,000 by purchasing 50 holdings of a value of US$1,000 each just to spread the risk will face considerable administration problems, not least when valuing the funds and making sure income has been received.

Preservation rather than gain

3.14   *Nestle* v. *National Westminster Bank plc* (1994) is often quoted and concerned the accountability of a trustee for the performance of a trust fund. The plaintiff complained that the trust fund had not performed as well as she thought it should have done (over a period of almost 70 years) and brought an action against the trustees for breach of trust.

3.15   Eventually, the case was dismissed but one of the issues which were raised was that trustees cannot be expected to guarantee returns or results and that the preservation of a trust fund is more important than seeking to increase its value.

Review

3.16   The trustees have a general duty to review the investments which have been made or acquired and they should establish a procedure which enables them to perform this task at least twice a year, and of course more regularly if the size or nature of the assets dictates.

3.17 The review process should not only cover the market value of the investments, but also the diversification of the portfolio, the yields received and anticipated and the needs and future requirements of the beneficiaries.

Appointment of an Investment Manager/Adviser

3.18 Who to appoint to advise on, or manage, trust investments is an important decision and can also be a difficult one as there are a large number of organisations and institutions to choose from.

Features required

3.19 The adviser or manager chosen should be professionally qualified in this field, suitably experienced and competent to act.

Services required

3.20 The trustees should decide which services they will require. Most will require a person to manage the investments on a discretionary basis (usually because the trustees will lack the necessary knowledge or experience to act in this manner), although some would only need assistance with placing or arranging deals because they make the decisions for themselves.

3.21 If an investment manager is appointed on a discretionary basis, the trustees might be at risk unless the trust deed allows the trustees to make such an appointment. Usually, the power to invest does not extend to passing the discretion to another party. If the deed is silent, the trustees might still decide to proceed with a discretionary investment management agreement on the basis that it is in the interests of the beneficiaries, but the appointment should be reviewed at least annually and the manager asked to produce contract notes and valuations in a timely manner.

Information provided to the manager/adviser

3.22 Assuming the trustees will require help with the management of the portfolio, they will need to furnish the service provider with sufficient information to enable them to make suggestions on the most suitable course of action to follow. The trustees should therefore provide the agent with details of the assets to be managed, together with other information such as the nature of the trust (i.e. discretionary or fixed), details of any anticipated capital distributions and the income requirements of the beneficiaries (or trustees to cover the fees and expenses).

Management agreement

3.23 The trustees will have to agree (unanimously) to the appointment. A meeting of the trustees should be held to reach this decision and minutes of that meeting should be taken to record what was discussed.

3.24 In addition, an agreement or contract between the trustees and the service provider should also be executed to formalise the arrangement and to set out the terms under which the agent is to act.

Settlor as investment manager

3.25 Some settlors want to be involved in the management of the trust assets. This is of course possible and may even be advisable, especially if the settlor has experience of investment-related matters. However, the extent of the powers which the settlor would have over those assets would be an important issue because if he is able to manage or control those funds he might jeopardise the residence of the trust for tax purposes.

Investment Letter

3.26 We briefly touched on this subject in Section 1.13 of this Unit, but it is worth returning to it again here. A letter from the settlor to the trustees, setting out how he would like the investments to be managed or the funds themselves invested, is a useful option for the trustees to consider where a settlor wants involvement in the investment matters. To have effect, and to provide the trustees with a level of protection (and perhaps indemnification) the existence of the letter should be mentioned under the terms of the trust deed.

4   The Appointment of Agents

4.1 The majority of trust deeds will contain provisions which will enable the trustees to appoint agents to assist them with the administration of the trust. If the deed is silent on this issue there will generally be powers available to the trustees under the local statutory provisions in the centre concerned.

4.2 Provided the trustee has appointed an agent in good faith, he will not usually be responsible for the default of that agent. This is a principle which was covered under Sections 23 (1) and 30 of the UK Trustee Act 1925 which also went on to mention that a trustee shall only be answerable and accountable for his own acts, neglects or defaults and not for those of his agents unless the same happens through his own wilful default. A number of offshore centres have adopted similar provisions in their local trust laws.

4.3 An appointment is considered to be made in good faith if the trustees carefully vet the service provider prior to appointment and are happy that he has the necessary experience and qualifications to act in the role envisaged. This will therefore mean that the usual protection offered under various trust statutes, and which is often built into the terms of trust deeds, will not be available to the trustees unless they are able to justify their choice of agent.

4.4 Usually, appointing the settlor to a particular position will not satisfy the 'good faith' test although the trust deed may authorise the trustees to do this. However, if any appointment is not considered to be in the interests of the beneficiaries it should be rescinded and another agent appointed.

5   Trustees Indemnities

5.1 In this Section we shall consider the indemnity provisions which are usually incorporated in offshore trust deeds. These provisions are aimed at providing the trustees with additional powers (over and above those which one would normally expect a trustee to have) and more importantly, to give them a degree of protection in the event of a future dispute concerning their exercise of a particular power.

Matters Which Would Usually Require an Indemnity Clause

5.2 The list will, of course, vary depending on the circumstances of a particular trust and the trustees attitude to certain areas of potential risk. However, it would be fair to say that trustees of offshore trusts would usually seek an indemnity in respect of the following:

a)   Investing the trust funds;

b)   The actions of agents and investment managers appointed by the trustees;

c)   The activities of underlying companies.

Some trustees also seek to be indemnified for all and any of their actions, particularly the exercise of a discretionary power.

Usual Effect of an Indemnity Clause

5.3   This is a difficult area to comment on. There are those who believe that if a trust deed allows the trustees to act in a particular manner, the trustees cannot be held responsible for any actions or losses which result as they have been given express powers to act in this way. On the other hand, there are those who believe that a trustee cannot be totally indemnified in relation to their actions as to do so would be in direct conflict with the fiduciary nature of the position. After all, the beneficiaries have a right to enforce the terms of the trust against the trustees and therefore the trustees must be accountable for their actions.

5.4   There have been a number of recent court cases which have attempted to address and also test the effectiveness of indemnity provisions in trust deeds. The main cases, and points, which students should be aware of are covered below.

Midland Bank Trustee (Jersey) Limited and Others v. Federated Pension Services (1994)

5.5   This case concerned the investment of trust funds which was delayed because the trustees (Federated Pension Services) believed that planned purchase orders could not be placed until certain regulatory formalities had been complied with. In fact, it transpired that there were no regulatory concerns and the funds could have been invested. Unfortunately for the trustees, the stock market prices went against them during this delay and they were sued for the alleged loss, calculated on the gains the fund would have made if the investments had been placed.

5.6   The trustees agreed that they had been in breach of trust but thought they would be protected under the indemnity provisions built into the trust deed. However, the court held that such clauses should be construed against the trustee and in particular, any ambiguities (which there were in this case) should be resolved against the trustee.

5.7   In addition, the local law in Jersey was also applied which provided that nothing in a trust deed shall release a trustee from his own fraud, wilful misconduct or gross negligence. The court found that the trustees had been guilty of gross negligence and as a result would not be covered by the indemnity provisions.

5.8   The fact that they were professional trustees also made matters worse for the trustees as the court noted that a higher degree of skill and care was due from them and they failed to deliver in these areas.

Midland Bank v. Wyatt (1994)

5.9   This case also confirmed that trust corporations (in particular) should be wary of relying on indemnities in a trust deed. Professional trustees generally owe a higher duty of care than individuals who act as trustees, and if they advertise the benefits of their expertise and experience, more will be expected of them.

Chaine-Nickson v. Bank of Ireland (1976)

5.10   One of the findings of this case was that if there are wide indemnities in place which attempt to remove the usual obligations and duties expected of trustees, it is likely that such provisions would be set aside.

Bartlett v. Barclays Bank Trust Co. Limited (1980)

5.11   We looked at this case in an earlier Section but it is worth mentioning again as there was an indemnity included in the trust deed which the trustees attempted to rely on. The clause basically stated that the trustees should be viewed as the absolute owners of investments which were held in the trust (including the shares in the underlying private company) and as a result, had the power to engage in speculative and hazardous investments. However, the court failed to accept this defence and noted that such general provisions should not be relied upon by trustees and that a reasonable man would not expect them to be included in a trust situation.

West v. Lazard Brothers (Jersey) Limited (1993)

5.12   There were a number of issues raised in this case but the one with which we are specifically concerned in this Section relates to the wide indemnities which the trustees were given. The findings in this case emphasised that courts (particularly those in offshore centres) will probably be reluctant to allow general indemnity provisions to stand, perhaps for the following reasons:

i)   To indemnify the trustees completely might make the trust invalid;

ii)   Wide indemnities may be objected to on the basis that they are contrary to public policy.

Armitage v. Nurse (1995)

5.13   This case was different from the others previously mentioned as it was suggested that trustees may, in fact, be able to rely on wide indemnity provisions provided they were not guilty of 'actual fraud'. Such a statement is, of course, open to wide interpretation but it does show that the courts may, in certain circumstances, adopt a stance which differs from that generally adopted in the other cases referred to in this Section.

Indemnities from the Settlor in his Personal Capacity

5.14   In addition to obtaining indemnities in the trust deed, some trustees also seek to obtain an undertaking from the settlor in respect of actions which they undertake in the course of administration. For example, the settlor may want the trustees to purchase a particular investment which the trustees believe to be speculative. Instead of refusing, they may decide instead to proceed but obtain an indemnity from the settlor designed to cover them should the investment make a loss and an action for breach of trust later be brought by the beneficiaries.

5.15   Alternatively, the trustees may decide to obtain an indemnity from the beneficiaries which they could use to prevent them from being sued for breach of trust in respect of a particular action at a later date. This may, perhaps, be a better option as it is the beneficiaries who would have the right to bring an action against the trustees. However, it may be difficult for the trustees to obtain an undertaking from all of the beneficiaries, which would be the only safe option, especially in a discretionary trust where some of the beneficiaries may not be ascertained (nor indeed born).

5.16 At the time of writing, the effectiveness of indemnities from settlors and beneficiaries has yet to be sufficiently tested by the courts. It is therefore difficult to establish whether this type of protection is desirable or indeed effective.

How the Trustees Should View Indemnities

5.17 Generally speaking, if a trustee fails to perform his over-riding duty to the beneficiaries, it is doubtful whether he will be able to rely on the indemnities which he may have built into a trust deed or which are provided by the settlor.

5.18 In addition, if the trustee fails to supervise the actions of his agent to a level which would be expected of a reasonable man, he may also be liable for the agent's actions, irrespective of any clauses or terms which may be contained in the deed to the contrary.

5.19 Having said that, it is reasonable that the trustees should request, and indeed be granted, some form of protection which they could rely upon in the event of an unwarranted claim arising from a disgruntled beneficiary. However, it would be extremely unwise, if not dangerous, for the trustees to believe that they can be indemnified for all their actions, and clauses which are designed to provide such a scenario should be viewed, at the very least, with caution.

Student Activity 2

Select an offshore trust deed which contains provisions which are intended to indemnify the trustees. Summarise those provisions and comment on whether any are too wide (or perhaps not wide enough).

6 Confidential Offshore Trust Arrangements

6.1 As we have already mentioned, a trust is usually created by a settlor executing a trust deed along with the trustees.

6.2 However, some settlors are concerned that their names are included in the trust deed and may suggest to the trustees that an alternative method of creating the trust is followed. Some of you may already be familiar with the use of declarations of trust and dummy settlors. Indeed, some of you may be administering trusts created in this manner. In this Section we shall cover both issues and also look at another common offshore device which is the blind trust.

Declarations of Trust

6.3 Under a declaration of trust, the client is not named as the settlor but instead the trustee prepares a trust deed under which he declares that he has received or holds property which he will retain in accordance with the terms of the trust deed. The trustee is essentially the settlor but the client should agree the terms of the deed and must have the necessary intention to want the trustees to create the trust on his instructions.

6.4　This is a useful device if the identity of the client is to be kept secret and is a much better alternative than the use of the dummy settlor (which we cover below).

6.5　Another advantage of a declaration of trust is that as the trustees are creating the trust, it would usually prevent the need to send the deed to outside parties for execution. This can save time, enable a trust to be executed in a much more efficient manner and also increases the confidentiality aspect.

6.6　It should be noted that not all service providers are prepared to provide trustee services for this type of arrangement, usually because they are concerned about the motive behind the client's desire not to be named as settlor.

6.7　In addition, clients who wish to create such a trust should also consider the fact that their involvement in the drafting process and their introduction of funds into the structure would probably lead to them being treated as the settlor in the event of an enquiry or dispute arising.

Dummy Settlors

6.8　Some settlors are reluctant to have their names included in the trust deed and to get around this problem, another person or corporation will be named in the deed as the settlor and will execute the deed in this capacity. This person or corporation will merely be acting on behalf of the true client, who would have agreed the terms of the trust deed and will be providing the trust property. In this situation, the person or corporation who creates the trust is often referred to as a dummy settlor.

6.9　Although this is a popular technique with some advisers and trustees, it brings into question the validity of the trust, as the person who creates the trust could be seen as lacking the necessary certainty of intention as he was merely acting on the instructions of another. As a consequence, a trust created in this manner might not stand up to an attack.

6.10　As we mentioned above, when looking at declarations of trust, the involvement of the true client in the drafting process and the use of his property would, in all likelihood, lead to him being treated as the settlor in the event of an enquiry or dispute.

Blind Trusts

6.11　A blind trust is usually one where a charitable organisation has been named as the sole beneficiary of a discretionary trust. The trust deed would then include powers, usually given to the trustee, to enable other beneficiaries to be added at a later date.

6.12　The settlor (or client if it is a declaration of trust) would then request (usually by letter of wishes) that the 'real' beneficiaries be added after the trust has been created. This is seen by many settlors, and indeed advisers, as a very effective means of maintaining the confidentiality of the structure as the 'intended' beneficiaries are not named in the deed.

6.13 This type of arrangement has increased in popularity but there is a possibility that a trust created in this manner could be attacked as being invalid on the grounds that the certainty of intention was missing on the basis there was no intention to benefit the named charity. A possible solution which some practitioners use is for the trustees to make a distribution to the named charity thus proving the intention to benefit it.

6.14 However, there is another possible problem which the trustees should be aware of and this is the fact that in many centres a trust which names a charity as sole beneficiary may have to be reported to the Attorney General who would usually have jurisdiction over charitable trusts. If a report is not made to the Attorney General it might be difficult for the trustees to argue in a dispute over the validity of the trust that it was ever intended for the charity to benefit.

7 Special Types of Offshore Trust

7.1 In Unit 9 we mentioned that offshore trusts, from some centres, can be used to provide protection against creditors and also against the claims of family members in civil law countries. In this Section we shall look at these 'special' trusts in more detail.

Offshore Creditor Protection Trusts

7.2 All trusts provide asset protection but some are aimed specifically at protecting assets from future unknown creditors or from claims which may arise on the bankruptcy of the settlor. They are a popular device, particularly with professionals who have a high risk of litigation, such as doctors, dentists and surgeons in the USA.

Choice of centre

7.3 Creditor protection trusts should only be created in a centre which has introduced specific legislation aimed at offering protection from creditors. Examples include the Cayman Islands, the Bahamas, the Cook Islands and Gibraltar.

Features of a creditor protection trust

7.4 The actual provisions will, of course, vary between centres but this type of trust generally provides the following features and possible benefits:

● Most onshore centres have legislation in place which enables transfers into trusts to be made void or voidable if a claim is made against the settlor by a creditor or if the settlor is declared bankrupt within a certain period of time, which can be up to ten years from the date of the transfer.

● Those offshore centres which have implemented legislation will refuse to accept claims which are received within a much shorter time frame and the onus will be on the creditor to prove his case.

Let us now look at the Cook Islands and the Cayman Islands as examples:

The Cook Islands: This was the first centre to introduce creditor protection legislation in September, 1989 and its laws provide that a local trust will not be void or voidable in the event of the settlor's bankruptcy or as a result of claims received from creditors. There are exceptions in the case of fraud but the onus is on the creditor to show that the international trust was established with the intent to defraud the creditor and that as a result of the transfer into trust, the settlor became insolvent. These points must be proved beyond a reasonable doubt and are, as a result, a major hurdle to those with a claim, but if the claim is successful the creditor will receive funds from the trust to cover his debt but the trust itself will not be made void or voidable.

A transfer is deemed not to be fraudulent if it is made more than two years after the creditor's cause of action arose or where the creditor fails to bring an action within one year of the transfer. In addition, any action must be commenced in the Cook Islands within two years of the transfer.

The local law also refuses to recognise any foreign judgement which may be made against the settlor, trustee or protector.

However, the recent case of *515 South Orange Grove Owners Association and Others v. Orange Grove Partners and Others* (1995) has cast some doubt on the use of the Cook Islands as a creditor protection centre. In that case the presiding judge was very critical of the use of such trusts in the Cook Islands and found in favour of the creditors on the basis that the two year limitation period should begin, not from the date the trust was created, but from the date of the judgement in California which led to the action which was heard in the Cook Islands.

As a result of this case the laws in the Cook Islands were altered to clarify the cause of action date.

The Cayman Islands: This was the second centre to introduce specific legislation and the provisions are similar in many ways to the laws of the Cook Islands. However, in Cayman the limitation period is 6 years (as opposed to two in the Cook Islands) and if a claim is successful the creditor will have first charge over the trust property in its entirety, which could make the trust void or voidable (compare this with the situation in the previous centre).

● Transfers to defeat the claims of existing creditors will most certainly be considered to be fraudulent and will not be protected under offshore provisions. It is only claims arising after the transfer of property has taken place which creates the planning opportunities.

Matters service providers should consider

7.5 In view of the purpose of this type of trust, service providers who have been approached to act as trustees of a creditor protection trust should proceed with caution. Here are some areas which they may wish to consider prior to agreeing to act as trustees:

i) Full 'know your client' procedures should be followed because if it is later found that the client was attempting to defraud known and current creditors, the trust would not only be illegal (under the laws of all the offshore centres) but the adviser and the trustee might be criminally liable for their involvement in the fraudulent operation and perhaps charged with conspiracy.

ii) The client should be asked to execute a declaration or affidavit confirming that he has no pending (or current) creditors, claims or legal actions against him.

iii) A declaration or affidavit of solvency should also be obtained.

iv) The client should be advised to retain sufficient funds outside the trust to meet personal expenses or cash requirements. This could be used as a defence that the trust did not contain all his assets and that he had personal funds available.

v) The source of funds should be verified and perhaps the client asked to confirm (again by declaration or affidavit) that they were not received as the result of money laundering or other criminal activities.

vi) The service provider may wish to consider arranging separate indemnity insurance in respect of this type of business.

vii) Finally, and perhaps most importantly, exercise common sense and if you suspect that the trust is an attempt to defraud existing creditors, do not take on the business.

Offshore Forced Heirship Protection Trusts

7.6   Forced heirship is a means by which a State imposes control over an individual's power to make testamentary dispositions. In such cases an individual's spouse and children will usually be entitled, by law, to at least a fixed share of his estate on death. Some offshore centres have introduced legislation which is designed to protect local trusts and trust property from the claims of 'forced heirs' as the family members are usually referred to.

Choice of centre

7.7   A number of offshore centres, such as the Cayman Islands, the Bahamas, Bermuda, Cyprus, Guernsey, Jersey and the Isle of Man have introduced legislation.

Features and potential benefits

7.8   We should start by looking at what succession rights are applied in some onshore areas:

i) Strict Forced Heirship Succession Rights
The individual has testamentary power over only part of his estate (such as in France, Italy, Spain, Scotland, Sweden, Denmark, Eastern Europe, South America and the Islamic states).

ii) Forced Heirship in Indefeasible Shares
The individual has full testamentary power over his entire estate but certain family members must receive at least a minimum share as prescribed by local law. (Several of the states in the USA have this restriction.)

iii) Judicial Adjustment
The individual has full testamentary power but certain family members have the right to apply to the court for financial provision which the court can grant at its discretion. (This is the situation in, for example, England and China.)

7.9   Making lifetime transfers will not necessarily avoid heirship rights as the value of any gifts made will usually be added to the value of a deceased person's estate and the shares of the 'forced heirs' will be calculated on this combined value. Gifts which have been made might be clawed back from the donees under court orders and the funds recovered paid to the heirs who have the enforceable rights.

7.10 The legislation which some offshore centres have introduced will, of course, vary but the essential elements are the same. Basically, under the laws of those centres, no trust which is governed by the local trust laws and no transfer of property into such trusts will be void, voidable, liable to be set aside or defective in any fashion. The capacity of any settlor shall not be questioned even if the law of any foreign jurisdiction does not recognise the trust, or a transfer avoids or defeats any heirship rights.

Matters the service provider should consider

7.11 Those who are approached to act as trustees of such a trust must not only follow the usual 'know your client' policies and procedures but should also consider other factors which may affect the protection afforded by the trust.

i) The statutory protection does not extend to the lex situs of property and as a result, assets transferred into a trust designed to offer forced heirship protection should not be held or located in a country or region which has or recognises forced heirship laws.

ii) Any distributions which are made by the trustees to beneficiaries who reside in a country which has or recognises forced heirship laws might be seized by the court in that country in the event of a dispute. Those funds might then be transferred to the persons who are entitled under the forced heirship rules in the settlor's country.

iii) If the trustee has an office or branch in a country which recognises the claims of forced heirs, there is a possibility that the court in the country where the office or branch is located might initiate proceedings against that office or branch in an attempt to recover funds or receive compensation which could not be obtained against the trustee or trust property in the offshore centre.

Lemos and Others v. Coutts & Co. (Cayman) Limited and Others (1994)

7.12 A number of administration issues were brought to the fore in this case which centred on a Greek businessman who created a Cayman Islands discretionary trust and placed into it the majority of his liquid assets.

7.13 The intention was that the settlor's sons were not to benefit and a Cayman Islands trust was chosen because of the legislation in place which does not recognise the claims of forced heirs (in this case the sons). On the client's death the sons attempted to have the trust set aside on the basis that it was invalid under Greek law.

7.14 The sons commenced proceedings in the Cayman Islands (against the trustees) and also in Greece (again against the trustees but also against others who were considered to be involved in the creation of the trust). A number of issues were raised, one of which was the possibility that an action would be brought in Greece against the parent company of the trustees (National Westminster Bank plc) on the basis that the parent company owned property in Greece which could be seized to settle the sons' claims.

7.15   In the end, the trustees decided to settle out of court on terms which were considered to favour the sons (although at the time of writing exact details have not been made public). Despite the fact that some practitioners have suggested that the special provisions in Cayman failed to fully protect the trustees, there is an argument to suggest that the sons would have received much more had the trust not been created there and so the anti-forced heirship provisions achieved some success.

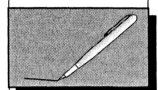

Student Activity 3

Select two offshore centres which have introduced anti-forced heirship measures and compare and contrast the provisions which apply. How do they differ from the general points which were made earlier in this Section?

8   Sham Trusts – What They Are and How to Avoid Them

8.1   No review of offshore trust administration issues would be complete without mentioning sham trusts and in particular the case of *Rahman v. Chase Bank Trust Company (CI) Ltd. and Others* (1991). Students should be aware of what might be considered a sham trust and more importantly, how to avoid them.

Definition of a 'Sham Trust'

8.2   There are three possible definitions of a sham trust.

●   Firstly, a sham trust could be one where the provisions in the trust deed do not create a valid trust, either because the powers which are retained by the settlor are too wide giving him what amounts to an absolute interest, or the 'trust' contravenes the local legal requirements for a valid trust.

●   Secondly, a sham trust could be one where the settlor and trustee agree that the trust will be administered in a manner which differs from the provisions contained in the trust deed.

●   Thirdly, a sham trust could arise were the settlor lacked the necessary intention to create a trust. This could be through incapacity or duress although a lack of intention could also be proved if the settlor failed to understand the terms and effects of the trust which he executed. When you consider the length and complexity of many trust deeds, perhaps the trust salesman should stop and ask himself whether the client sitting in front of him really understands what it is he has been asked to sign. If he does not, the trust could be attacked as a sham because of his failure to take time to explain the terms and effects of the trust deed.

Example of a Sham Trust Situation

8.3   The following is a simple example of a situation which could be attacked as being a sham trust.

8.4   A settlor and trustee execute a trust deed under which the trustee has a number of wide discretionary powers, including the power to distribute capital and income. However, the settlor has issued a letter of wishes which sets out how he would like the trustees to act. The settlor confirms that it was never his intention that the trustees would exercise any power without his authority and that they were only to make distributions in accordance with the provisions of the letter of wishes. The trustees in turn confirm that they will refer to the settlor on all maters and in particular that they will follow the contents of the letter of wishes.

8.5   The settlor never intended the trustees to have the powers which the deed gave them and the trustees never intended to exercise any of those powers.

8.6   If attacked, the trust would, in all likelihood, be set aside as a sham.

8.7   The following Section looks at an actual sham trust case.

Rahman v. Chase Bank Trust Company (CI) Ltd. and Others (1991)

8.8   The plaintiff was the widow of Mr. Rahman ('KAR'). KAR had created a Jersey trust with Chase Bank Trust Company (CI) Ltd. ('Chase') as the trustees in 1977 and the widow was claiming that the trust was invalid and that KAR's property belonged to his estate. The trust deed contained a number of provisions which included the following:

●   During KAR's lifetime he had a power of appointment over the trust fund and income which he could exercise with the trustee's consent. He also had a limited power of appointment over the property which did not require any consent from the trustees;

●   KAR had a life interest in the income;

●   KAR had power to appoint trusts, effective on his death;

●   The trustee had power to pay or apply capital or income to KAR and to regard only his interests;

●   The trustees could only exercise a number of powers with KAR's consent.

8.9   The Court decided that the settlement and the transfers to the trustee were wholly invalid and of no effect under the laws of Jersey on two grounds:

i)   The powers breached the Jersey maxim of 'donner et retenir ne vaut rien' which basically means that a donor's retention of a power to destroy a gift or to alter the gift renders it null and void. This is no longer part of Jersey law.

ii)   The settlement was a sham which KAR did not intend to have legal effect, on the basis he exercised control over the trustee and he treated the assets comprised in the trust fund as his own and the trustee was treated as no more than his nominee or agent.

8.10   The Court also referred to the fact that the trustee received letters from KAR which were clearly instructions rather than requests, and that these instructions were followed blindly by the trustee without exercising any thought or deliberation. The trustee did produce written evidence to show that they had recorded some decisions but the Court was critical of the minutes and resolutions as they did not evidence a genuine trustee decision.

8.11 The Court also noted that on a number of occasions KAR wrote to the trustee referring to 'my funds' and that the trustee had failed to correct KAR and remind him that they were in fact the trustee's funds and should not be thought of as his own property.

Avoiding Sham Trusts

8.12 The list which follows contains areas of advice which all service providers who offer trustee services should consider if they wish to avoid creating a sham trust situation.

Student Activity 4

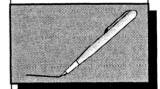

Before you read the following list, prepare your own list of points which trustees and service providers should consider or follow to avoid creating a sham trust, or turning an existing trust into a possible sham situation. Did you include any areas which were not covered by the list?

a) The trustees and the settlor should both accept the reality of the trust and have an intention to be bound by the terms of the trust deed. Perhaps this could be achieved by the settlor confirming in writing his intentions to create a binding trust, and that he accepts and understands the powers which will be given to the trustees. The trustees could then countersign this.

b) The trustees must control, and be seen to control, the trust property.

c) Settlors should not be given powers which give them elements of management and control.

d) Trustees should be seen to have exercised their discretionary powers by using an active mental process. Trustee meetings and the preparation of minutes of those meetings will help but are not the sole solution to this issue.

e) Avoid the use of phrases in letters of wishes or letters to the trustee which can be seen as instructing or directing the trustees.

f) Discourage the settlor from calling the trust 'my trust' or referring to the trust property as 'my property'. If he does refer to the trust or the trust property in this manner, correct him (preferably in writing).

g) Avoid the use of dummy settlors.

h) Avoid giving the protector wide powers which could affect or reduce the powers and discretions of the trustees (especially if the settlor is also the protector).

i) Avoid creating blind trusts or at the very least, obtain from the settlor full details of why such a trust is requested. If you proceed, consider making a token distribution to the named charity to show that there was an intention to benefit it.

j) Be aware of the additional risks and liabilities associated with creditor protection and forced heirship protection trusts and remember that they could also be attacked as a sham unless they are correctly administered. Remember that the local trust provisions in place in an offshore centre might not always offer the protection which the client requires.

k) Keep indemnity provisions in trust deeds reasonable. Too many wide exculpation clauses which fully indemnify the trustees for all actions could create a sham situation.

9 Trust Litigation in Offshore Centres

9.1 As you should by now appreciate, offshore trusts can provide a number of planning opportunities which cannot be offered by onshore trusts. They are also often used in complex financial and taxation planning arrangements which can involve substantial amounts of assets. In addition, offshore trusts may not be recognised as being valid under the laws of the settlor or the beneficiaries. It is no wonder that offshore trust litigation is on the increase.

9.2 In this text we have covered many of the more publicised cases which have been heard to date in various Courts and although they may have been few and far between, make no mistake that many more disputes involving offshore trusts are currently being discussed between lawyers or in Chambers.

9.3 Litigation may centre around a contention that a trust is a sham and we looked at possible ways of minimising this risk earlier in this Unit. However, litigation can also arise from the actions, or inactions, of the trustees. Such an attack would usually manifest itself as a claim against the trustees for breach of trust or perhaps for negligence.

9.4 The following are examples of actions or steps which offshore trust personnel should take to minimise the risk of a trust which they have dealings with being the subject of litigation.

i) Make sure that any 'standard' trust documentation has recently been reviewed by a law firm in the centre concerned and that the terms and powers are valid.

ii) Understand the pitfalls which can be associated with discretionary trusts and take appropriate action to ensure that these are avoided (refer to Unit 10 which covered this area in detail).

iii) If you suspect that a beneficiary or a third party is considering attacking the trust, obtain legal advice as quickly as possible. Remember that the advice which you receive may be information which the beneficiary has a right to have a copy of.

iv) If you suspect that a problem has arisen which might lead to litigation at a later date, take the initiative and obtain legal advice as corrective action may prevent the problem from materialising. Again, this advice may have to be disclosed so exercise care when wording the application for advice.

v) Treat with caution the prospective client who wants to create a trust but who refuses to obtain separate legal or taxation advice.

vi) Creditor protection trusts and forced heirship trusts should only be created after comprehensive due diligence has been performed. Both types of trust should be approached by trustees with caution (and both were covered in detail earlier in this Unit).

vii) Where possible, try to restrict the information which the trustees must (or should) release to beneficiaries. As mentioned in Unit 10, some practitioners include provisions in their standard trust deeds which are aimed at preventing the trustees from being able to release information to beneficiaries. Such provisions should be carefully worded.

viii) Finally, always exercise care and use common sense when making decisions which affect the beneficiaries or the trust property.

9.5 These points may not prevent a rogue beneficiary from attacking a trust but if you follow all, or some of them, you should at least have a sound foundation for your defence!

10 Account Opening – Risk Reduction Measures

10.1 We have already covered the information which a service provider would usually request from a new client when we looked at money laundering prevention. In addition to running the standard checks, those who provide trustee services would also be wise to have further procedures in place which specifically address new trust business.

10.2 In particular, service providers should have a questionnaire or similar form which they can send to a new trust client which, once completed, will provide them with sufficient information to enable them to prepare a draft trust deed for approval by the client, and possibly his advisers.

10.3 Without this information, the service provider might create a trust which failed to meet the requirements of the client and if this was the case, the trust could be attacked as a sham, caused by the service provider's to failure to ask the right and reasonable questions.

10.4 This 'trust request form' (as some agents refer to it) should contain at least the following basic information:

i) The type of trust which is required (i.e. Guernsey discretionary trust);

ii) The main reason for creating the trust. Preferably copies of legal or tax advice will be made available to the trustees to support this reason;

iii) The name and address of the intended trustees (to prevent any doubt). Professional trustees may also request that the client confirms in writing that he agrees the scale of fees which is to be applied;

iv) The names and addresses of the beneficiaries. One would usually expect these details to be included in the trust deed although the client might want to include some with the rest being added at a later date. Often a service provider will request copies of supporting birth and marriage certificates if it is considered to be appropriate.

The client might also be asked to confirm whether there should be powers included in the deed to allow for additional beneficiaries to be added and if so, by whom;

v) Whether the agent's standard trust deed can be used and if not, who is to draft the proposed trust deed. If the deed is not provided by the agent it would be usual for the agent to insist that separate legal advice be obtained in the offshore centre concerned to confirm that the provisions of the trust meet local requirements. The danger here is that a lawyer in an onshore centre might draft a deed which creates a valid trust in one centre but the provisions are such that the trust would not be valid in another centre;

vi) Whether a trust protector is required. If so, the client should complete the details of the person to be appointed, who he would like to be given the power to remove and appoint protectors in the future and also whether there are any specific duties or powers which the client would like the protector to have;

vii) A full description of the initial trust property as well as details of other property which may be added later (together with details showing from whom any additional property is likely to be received). Any speculative or high risk assets which the client would like to place into the trust should also be highlighted at this stage;

viii) Whether any trust distributions are anticipated in the near future (clearly these will then have to be approved by the trustees at a later date);

ix) Whether the client will also be completing a letter of wishes or asking the trustees to execute a memorandum of wishes (if it is a discretionary trust).

10.5 Some practitioners will argue that if a settlor has signed a trust deed, he must have read the contents of that deed and therefore accepted the terms. This is not to be relied on and the trustees should ask the settlor to confirm in writing that he has fully read and understood the deed prior to executing it. In addition, the trustees should in particular draw the settlor's attention to any exclusion or indemnity clauses that have been included which are aimed at providing the trustees with a level of protection. You will recall that both issues were covered earlier in this Unit when we looked at sham trusts and trustee indemnities.

10.6 Similarly, with declarations of trust, the client should be sent a copy of the draft deed prior to the trustees executing an engrossment and he should be asked to confirm in writing that the terms and provisions are in accordance with the instructions which he provided.

11 The Regulation of Offshore Trusts and Trustees

11.1 Many offshore centres have introduced legislation which prevents persons, and particularly corporations, from conducting trustee business unless they are licenced to act in this capacity. Examples of centres which have this restriction include the Bahamas, Bermuda, BVI, the Cayman Islands, Gibraltar, Madeira, Malta, Mauritius, the Turks and Caicos Islands and Vanuatu.

11.2 Perhaps the noticeable exceptions to the requirement for trustees to be licenced are the Isle of Man, Jersey and Guernsey, although they have considered the implementation of some form of regulation in this area.

11.3 Those centres which have licencing requirements will usually expect professional corporate trustees to meet certain minimum capital requirements as well as proof that they have sufficient expertise. Often there will also be different categories of licences, such as unrestricted (where they can act as trustees of any trust) or restricted (where they can only act as trustees for those cases which are recorded on the licence).

11.4 As trust litigation, or the risk of such litigation, increases so too no doubt will the number of offshore centres which implement regulatory controls over their trust (and also managed company) providers.

Summary

Now that you have read this Unit you should be able to:

- Comment on the advisability of the settlor being appointed as trust protector

- List five possible benefits of a private trust company acting as trustee

- Highlight the duties and responsibilities of trustees which have a majority interest in an underlying company

- Briefly describe the duties of a trustee in relation to the investment of trust property

- Explain the duties of a trustee in appointing an agent

- Summarise the decisions of at least two recent court cases involving the extent of trustees' indemnities

- Describe the problems which could be associated with blind trusts and dummy settlors

- List the areas of concern with creditor protection trusts

- Briefly describe the effect of the *Lemos Case*

- List at least six ways to avoid sham trusts

Self-assessment Questions

1. A prospective trust client has asked you whether he could be appointed as a trust protector of his trust. Comment on this proposal.

2. List the options which may be available to a settlor of an offshore trust to enable him to have some say in the administration (and possibly management) of that trust.

3. Your organisation is the trustee of an offshore trust which is the majority shareholder of an offshore private limited company. List the information which you would require to fulfil your duty as trustee.

4. Briefly describe how the issues surrounding the cases of *Learoyd* v. *Whitely* (1887) and *Nestle* v. *National Westminster Bank plc* (1994) may affect the manner in which trustees of offshore trusts invest trust property.

5. List the areas in which the trustees of an offshore trust might require an indemnity.

6. An offshore trust deed contains very wide indemnity provisions which are designed to exclude the trustees from any liability in respect of their actions in the management and administration of the trust. Comment on the advisability of such provisions.

7. A potential trust client would like to create an offshore trust but is concerned that his name may have to be included in the trust deed as settlor. Briefly explain what options might be available and highlight any possible objections which the service provider might raise.

8. Briefly describe the general features of a creditor protection trust which might be of interest to those individuals who work in professions which are prone to litigation.

9. Describe what is meant by the term 'sham trust' and explain what actions the trustees can take to avoid such a situation occurring.

10. List the informaiton which a service provider would usually request from a client who is interested in establishing an offshore trust.

Unit 12

Offshore Investment Services

Objectives

At the end of this Unit you should be able to:

- Summarise the features of the different investment services usually provided from offshore centres

- Outline the usual advantages for clients in having their investments managed offshore

- List the information a service provider would require to formulate a portfolio

- Understand the three main investment strategies available

- Describe how a portfolio would usually be structured to meet the objectives of certain client types

- Explain how a potential currency risk could be reduced

- Describe the usual features offered by custody services providers

- List the topics and terms usually contained in a client agreement

- Summarise how investment services are usually regulated in those centres which have implemented supervisory controls

- Outline the usual requirements necessary to create an investment department in an offshore centre

The syllabus requires students to have an understanding of the investment services which are commonly provided from offshore centres. In addition, a basic understanding of how investment portfolios are constructed for clients is also required. This Unit covers these specific topics, although a more detailed appreciation of investment techniques, monitoring and portfolio construction is outside the scope of this course.

It should be remembered that the investment of trust funds was covered in an earlier Unit.

1 Investment Principles

1.1 In this Unit we cover a number of practical issues relating to the investment of assets in offshore centres. However, before we start to look at these topics it is important that we cover a number of the basic principles and also define a few of the more commonly used investment terms.

Definition of the Term 'Investment'

1.2   An investment is generally a type of asset into which a person or an entity has placed cash or other funds, in return for which they hope to receive an increase in the value of their assets, a return on their assets or security. Some investors hope for all three but realistically, only one, or possibly two, can be achieved for a particular investor.

Types of Investment

1.3   A number of common types of investment which students will encounter are covered below. The list is not exhaustive and from time to time you may encounter different types of investment vehicles which you may need to research or investigate further.

Liquid investments

1.4   These are investments which can be quickly sold or closed to receive the underlying funds on demand. They include bank deposits (such as fixed term accounts which could be closed on demand but with a loss of interest).

Gilts/government bonds

1.5   These are investments which have been issued or guaranteed by a government. In the UK such investments are called gilts whereas in other countries, such as the USA and in most European countries, they are called bonds.

1.6   These gilts or bonds are sold to the public or institutions for a number of reasons but perhaps the most common is to raise the necessary funds required to meet the cost of a particular project or government scheme.

1.7   They will be secured (or guaranteed) by the government which has issued them and will usually be issued for a fixed term (such as 5 years) after which time the investment will be repaid and cash returned to the investors. The date on which the funds are repaid is referred to as the maturity date. The rate of interest which is paid is referred to as the coupon and payment will be guaranteed and made on fixed dates (often 6 months apart).

1.8   On maturity, the investor will receive the 'par value' which will be the face value of the gilt or bond and not the amount which was invested. For example, a UK gilt will have a par value of GBP1.00 but it might be quoted at 95p. If 10,000 units (sometimes referred to as 'stock') were purchased and the holding matured in 5 years' time, the cash which will return to the investor on maturity will be GBP10,000.00 but it only cost him GBP9,500.00. Similarly, if the cost of the stock on acquisition was 105p, the investor would still only receive GBP10,000.00 on maturity even though the holding cost him GBP10,500.00.

1.9   Gilts and bonds will pay a fixed rate of interest to the holders. In addition some of these types of investment are index-linked which means that the value will be adjusted in line with the prevailing rate of inflation in the country concerned.

1.10   UK gilts are presently exempt from UK capital gains tax and some are also exempt from UK income tax.

1.11   Although gilts and bonds can achieve capital appreciation, they are usually purchased because of their security and the fact that income is guaranteed.

Equities

1.12 These are basically investments in quoted companies and can either be ordinary shares or preference shares.

1.13 Ordinary shares enable the investor to share in the profits of the company and gives them the right to receive a dividend (income payment out of realised profits of the company) if one is declared. Preference shares give the holder the right to receive a fixed rate of dividend which is payable in preference to any dividend which may be payable to the ordinary shareholders. Although preference shares have certain advantages, the entitlement of their holders to participate in the profits of the company will generally be less than those of the ordinary shareholders.

1.14 As equities provide the opportunity to participate in the profits of a company, they are usually purchased for capital appreciation purposes, although they do also provide some income return by way of dividends.

1.15 Dividend income from equities usually has tax (withholding tax) deducted at source by the company and the tax position of the shareholder will decide whether this tax can be reclaimed. Usually, the withholding tax on dividend income paid to an offshore vehicle (such as a company or to the trustees of a trust) cannot be reclaimed, unless the offshore centre where the vehicle is based has a double taxation treaty in place with the remitting country.

Loan stocks

1.16 Companies often raise cash by way of loans and a loan stock is basically a loan which an investor has made to the company, in return for which they will receive interest and on maturity of the loan they will receive back the par value of the stock.

1.17 They are similar to gilts and bonds but there is greater risk as they are not backed by a government. There are different types of loan stock such as debentures (which are usually secured against assets of the company), guaranteed stock (which are often secured by an outside guarantee) and unsecured stock (which offer more risk and therefore sometimes potential for higher return).

Collective investment schemes

1.18 These schemes acquire a basket of underlying investments in different gilts, equities and loan stock. Investors can then buy a share in the basket of the underlying assets (which is usually referred to as a unit).

1.19 Such schemes provide investors with the opportunity to hold a wide variety of different investments whilst at the same time having no direct investment in any of those different types as all they own will be a share of the total basket. They are therefore a popular method to achieve diversification, an area which we return to later in this Unit. Unit trusts and mutual funds are examples of collective investment schemes.

Other, More Speculative Types of Investment

1.20 In addition to the mainstream types of investments, students should also be familiar with the more speculative vehicles which exist.

Convertibles

1.21 These are usually loan stocks which can be converted by the investor to ordinary shares.

Warrants

1.22 If an investor purchases a warrant he is in effect buying the right to purchase shares in a company in the future at a fixed or agreed price.

Options (otherwise known as 'derivatives')

1.23 An option creates an opportunity to buy or sell shares (depending on the type of option acquired) at a fixed price in the future. Students may remember these were at the centre of the Barings Bank collapse but although they are very risky forms of investment, they can also achieve excellent returns.

Commonly Used Investment terms

1.24 Before we leave this Section it might be useful to go over a few of the more commonly used terms which you will no doubt come across from time to time.

Book value

1.25 This is the value of the investment when it was first acquired (either by purchase or transfer).

Market value

1.26 This is the value of an investment based on its current market price. If you were to sell it, the market value would be what you would receive for it.

Yield

1.27 The yield is the return which you can expect from a fixed interest security (such as a gilt or a bond). It will be determined by the price of the stock and the coupon, and in some cases the period of time before the stock reaches maturity.

1.28 The basic yield is known as the flat yield which is calculated by dividing the coupon by the market price and multiplying the total by 100. The redemption yield takes into account the time to maturity.

2 Structuring a Portfolio

2.1 Before we look at how a portfolio might be structured for different types of investors we should first examine the three strategies, or options, which are available.

Strategies Available

2.2 The strategy is essentially the goals or objectives which the client who is investing his funds will have. There are three basic options:

Capital appreciation

2.3 An increase in the capital value of the portfolio will be the priority and this would be achieved at the expense of income return. There would also be a high element of risk involved with this strategy as often with risk comes the chance of reward.

Income return

2.4 Income would be the priority and as a result, growth in the value of the capital would be sacrificed. There would generally be less exposure to risk with such a strategy and instead a greater element of security would be built into the portfolio.

Balance between capital growth and income return

2.5   This is often referred to as a 'middle of the road' policy as both income and capital are required, with equal importance placed on both factors. There will be some risk but there will also be a similar weighting for security.

The Structure of an Investment Portfolio

2.6   The structure of a portfolio will usually contain a combination of the following elements:

Liquidity

2.7   This will comprise short-term funds which are available immediately or at short notice, such as cash or bank deposit accounts.

Investments which provide security and/or income

2.8   An element of the portfolio would usually be invested in low risk vehicles which, by their very nature, should also provide at least a minimum income return.

Capital growth

2.9   Finally, a portion of the fund would usually be invested in holdings designed to increase the capital value of the fund. This segment is at greater risk but is often offset by the holdings acquired for security covered in the Sub-section above.

2.10   The split between the investments held for liquidity, security and capital appreciation will vary depending upon the objectives of the client. We examine some possible strategies for different types of personal investors in the following Section.

Possible Strategies for Different Types of Clients

2.11   This is a difficult area on which to comment as every client is different and their requirements and situations will vary. However, the following generalisations, and it must be stressed that this is all they are, might shed some light on what certain client types might be looking for.

Single person, no dependants and in employment

2.12   A long-term strategy for capital growth would usually be appropriate. Often such a portfolio is designed to provide a 'pension' fund for the client's old age. Current income requirements are probably being met by their employment income.

Married person, no children

2.13   Probably a similar strategy to the above will be required although if the couple are planning a child they might prefer a short to medium-term view to secure sufficient capital gains to meet future commitments.

Married with young children

2.14   A long-term view might be appropriate for part of the fund with the emphasis on capital growth. The aim might be to provide a fund to cover college or university fees in the future. However, in the short-term, income might be a problem (as young children are expensive, as many of you may already appreciate) and if this is the case the strategy might be better suited to a short to medium-term view to maximise income. The level of the employment income could be a factor here.

Married with older children

2.15   This might also be an expensive time, especially if the children are in tertiary education.

If so, income might be a priority. However, if the children are no longer dependants, a long-term view to provide capital growth for old age might be more appropriate.

On retirement

2.16 Usually, employment income will have ceased and the client's house paid for, so income will be the major requirement. Security is also important as this will be the client's retirement fund and must last him to the end of his days.

3 The Information Usually Required by Service Providers to Formulate an Investment Portfolio

3.1 Although the information required will vary between service providers, the following will usually be the minimum information requested to achieve the construction of an investment portfolio.

Personal Details of the Client and his Dependants

3.2 The age of the client, his address, his marital status, and if he is married, usually details of his spouse, are all important details. If there are children, the number and their ages will be needed.

Financial Position

3.3 The client should be asked to confirm what assets he holds, both in his sole name and jointly with others. The list should include all assets, including realty, bank deposits, investments or interests in trusts. Approximate values would also be useful.

3.4 His sources of income should also be ascertained, to include any earnings from employment, together with confirmation of his financial commitments, such as mortgage or loan repayments and school fees.

3.5 It would also be useful to know whether he has any pension arrangements or life assurance cover as without such provisions it would be wise to include some form of retirement planning in the strategy which is to be followed.

Taxation Situation

3.6 The client's tax position should be ascertained, to include confirmation of his highest rate of income tax and capital gain tax, his residence situation and his domicile position.

3.7 Students should be aware that some onshore investments are tax-free for certain individuals (such as UK government exempt gilts).

Investment Parameters

3.8 The client should be asked to clarify his investment objectives and whether he has a long, medium or short-term view.

Attitude to Risk

3.9 The client's attitude to risk should also be ascertained. Some investors will be nervous about the risk of losses whilst others are keen to invest in speculative securities.

Personal Preferences

3.10 The client should be asked whether he has any preferences relating to choice of investments. For example, some clients do not want to invest in companies which are connected with tobacco or drugs. He may also want to retain or invest in a particular company or its shares for sentimental reasons.

'Home' Currency

3.11 The currency of the client's country of residence may also be a determining factor. For example, if the client lives in the USA and regularly requires dollar payments to top up his income, there would be little point in having assets invested predominantly in sterling as sale proceeds would have to be converted to dollars, an exercise which would create exposure to potential currency losses.

Student Activity 1

What information does your organisation usually request from potential investment clients and how does it compare with the general points which we have covered?

4 Investment Services Provided from Offshore Centres

4.1 The services provided offshore will essentially be the same in nature as those provided from onshore centres. You will, therefore, tend to find the following on offer:

Execution Only Services

4.2 Some clients do not require investment advice or management but only want the facility to place trades. They therefore contact a broker, bank or other such service provider and instruct them to place the trade required on their behalf.

Advisory Management Services

4.3 Some clients are happy for their investments to be managed by an agent but they still want to retain control over decision-making processes, such as what to sell or purchase and when those orders should be placed. This is the essential feature of an advisory service as the client would be consulted on all investment matters. This can create additional work and administration time for the agent and often you will find that the fees which are charged for the provision of this type of service can be high and are often negotiated at the commencement of the relationship.

Discretionary Management Services

4.4 This is the most commonly used investment service in offshore centres. The service provider would be given complete control over the client's portfolio and would have absolute discretion over buying and selling decisions. The service provider would usually attend to all related administration issues such as the collection of dividends, dealing with corporate actions (such as rights issues) and arranging the safe custody of the certificates. The provision of custody services are dealt with later in this Unit.

4.5 Agents are generally more willing to provide this type of investment service as they will be able to perform a full management function with minimum interference.

5 The Advantages of Offshore Investment Services for Clients

Student Activity 2

Before you read the next section, prepare a list of the reasons why you think a client might want to have his investments managed in an offshore centre and compare it against the points which follow.

5.1 There are a number of reasons why a client might decide to have their investments managed offshore but perhaps the following are the most common.

Confidentiality

5.2 Offshore centres can generally provide a greater degree of confidentiality than onshore centres. Indeed, as we have already seen when looking at banking services in Unit 3, some centres have implemented legislation designed to provide statutory protection of information.

Taxation

5.3 Depending upon a client's taxation position, it might be possible for the income and capital gains generated from a portfolio which is registered and managed offshore to be retained by the agent in the offshore centre tax-free until such time as the income or capital is remitted to the client.

5.4 This method of tax deferral is a widely used and important tax planning device.

Regulation

5.5 The lack of regulation and reporting requirements relating to investment business in many offshore centres provides appeal to some clients who prefer their agents to proceed with their affairs with the minimum of outside interference or restriction.

Professional Management

5.6 Most offshore centres can boast a number of sophisticated and professional investment management service providers who have experienced and qualified staff with knowledge of a number of world markets.

Convenience

5.7 In view of the number and geographic spread of offshore centres, it is possible that a client might be closer, in terms of distance, to an offshore service provider than to an onshore service provider of equal experience and competence.

6 Possible Disadvantages for Clients

6.1 Despite the potential benefits there are also possible downsides to locating investment services in an offshore centre and these could include the following:

Lack of Regulation of Agents

6.2 Not all centres regulate or have a system to supervise the provision of offshore investment services. By appointing a service provider in an unregulated or unsupervised jurisdiction, there is a greater risk of that agent acting outside the scope of their powers and obligations under the terms of any client agreement which may have been executed. In addition, there might not be any redress available to the client under local law in the event of a default on the part of the agent.

Control

6.3 It can be very difficult for a client to monitor, or in some cases, control the actions of his investment agent if he is located in an offshore centre.

6.4 Contact (by telephone, fax or meeting) may also be another hurdle in view of the geographic distance which may exist between the client and his offshore adviser.

Reputation

6.5 The reputation of an offshore centre can change overnight if there were to be a scandal involving any aspect of its financial services sector. If the name of the centre where the client has placed the management of his investments is tarnished, the client may also be concerned for his reputation, simply by association.

Lack of a Local Stock Market

6.6 Very few offshore centres have their own stock market which means that most trades for offshore-based portfolios have to be placed via an onshore market. This can add to the expense.

Location of the Services/Client Information

6.7 Clients should also check where the investment services are being performed. This is important because some offshore investment management services are in fact being performed in onshore centres (perhaps in London or New York). This would not affect the quality or standard of service but there could be a confidentiality issue as client information would have to be held by the agent in the onshore centre which might make that information subject to onshore disclosure requirements. There might also be a management and control issue depending on the powers of the investment agent.

7 Offshore Custody Services

7.1 In addition to those investment services already mentioned, some banks and financial institutions also provide custody services. These are either provided to their clients as an addition to their discretionary investment management package or offered as a separate service to individuals. Often, institutions only require assistance with their custody requirements.

7.2 Custody services will generally comprise the following:

Registered Ownership

7.3 The client's investments will be registered in the name of the offshore custodian who will act as nominee for the beneficial owner of those securities.

7.4 It is usual for the offshore custodian to appoint agents in a number of onshore locations to act as sub-custodians in respect of securities which are registered or traded in those locations. Having the securities held by these sub-custodians in the country of origin of the securities or within the market where they are traded creates efficiencies with regard to the purchases and sales of those investments.

Settlement

7.5 The settlement of purchases and sales would be handled by the offshore custodian, usually through its network of correspondent banks. Settlement would usually be arranged in any currency but with the facility to convert the funds to another currency if required.

Income Collection

7.6 The custodian would receive dividends and other income payments on the client's securities on the due date and then credit the amounts received in accordance with the client's instructions. Once again, income would usually be collected in any currency although there would be the choice of having the income converted to another currency upon receipt.

Corporate Actions

7.7 Companies sometimes notify their shareholders that they will be carrying out a rights issue, or they may decide to offer shares instead of paying a dividend. The offshore custodian will receive notification of these and other such corporate actions and will either notify the client or his agent for instructions.

Reporting

7.8 The custodian will provide the client or his adviser with full accounting details as well as notification of trades, income receipts and transactions which have affected the holdings, such as certain corporate actions. Some service providers will be able to provide this information electronically.

8 Currency Risk Reduction

8.1 Those clients who choose to invest through an offshore centre will often have substantial sums under investment which will be purchased and held in a variety of different currencies. Fluctuations in exchange rates can therefore be a major concern and it is important that the adviser takes appropriate steps to mitigate those currency risks. Some of the main courses of action available are outlined below.

Regular Reviews and Checks

8.2 The following is a list of the reviews and checks which an investment adviser could make to try and reduce the currency risks:

i) Review the likely performance of the economy of the country which issued the investment;

ii) Check the level of interest rates and their likely movement in the short to medium-term;

iii) Review the state of the local stock market and the performance of the various indices;

iv) Follow recent movements in the foreign exchange rates and try and predict likely future movements.

8.3 However, even if all these precautions were taken, there is no guarantee that losses will not occur.

Currency Hedging

8.4 Capital gains which might build up following the purchase of a foreign stock could be eroded by a currency loss if the exchange rate fell between the client's 'home' country's currency and the currency of the foreign country which issued the stock.

8.5 This possible problem could be solved if the purchase of the foreign investment is financed by a loan taken out in the foreign country or at least in the foreign currency. If the exchange rate falls, the loan liability will also fall, whilst at the same time the client's funds are not affected and would be available for investment elsewhere.

Currency Swaps

8.6 This is an arrangement under which parties exchange sums of currency in different denominations which is backed by an agreement to re-exchange the currencies at the same exchange rate at a future date.

Back-to-Back Loans

8.7 This is an arrangement under which a client might deposit funds with an offshore bank and these funds would then be used as security for a loan made by the bank to the client, perhaps to finance an investment purchase. This could create certain tax savings as well as avoid exposure to currency risk.

Currency Options

8.8 These enable a purchaser to acquire an option to buy currency at a specified rate against delivery of another type of currency at any time within a certain period or on a fixed date in the future.

9 Risk Reduction by Diversification

9.1 Diversification is often the key to the mitigation of risk and as the saying goes, it is better not have all of your eggs in one basket!

9.2 There are a number of ways to achieve diversification and perhaps the most common are:

a) Holding a range of fixed interest as well as equity investments in a portfolio to provide a spread of holdings which offer both capital growth and income return;

b) Investing in different countries, currencies and markets;

c) Investing in a collective investment scheme or similar investment funds.

10 Client Agreements

10.1 Most offshore investment service providers will require their clients to execute an agreement setting out the terms and conditions which will be imposed. This will be particularly important with regard to discretionary investment management business. Those centres which have imposed regulatory investment controls will also often insist that a client agreement be executed in respect of any investment management business.

10.2 The terms and contents of an investment management agreement will vary between service providers but the following would usually be included in such documents for private individuals:

i) Nature of the services to be provided;

ii) The basis of the fees which will be payable, together with a note of the frequency they will be due;

iii) The manner in which the client can give instructions to the service provider;

iv) The arrangements for the holding of the client's money, registration and custody of the assets;

v) The client's requirements for the receipt of reports, contract notes and valuations;

vi) Investment parameters;

viii) Indemnification for the investment manager and a statement confirming the extent of his liability for his actions (although the indemnity would not extend to cover loss caused by fraud or wilful neglect on the part of the agent). We return to indemnification in the next Section;

vi) Arrangements for the termination of the agreement.

10.3 Certain changes will have to be made to the above to cater for agreements which will be required for trustees and corporate entities.

Student Activity 3

Compare the list above against the information contained in an investment management agreement which your organisation either issues or has recently signed.

Indemnification

10.4 An increasing number of service providers arrange indemnity insurance cover. This not only affords protection to the provider in the event of a claim but can also offer protection for their clients, as it might be possible for the clients to make a claim under this type of policy if the service provider defaults on his obligations as set out in the agreement.

10.5 Such insurance can help to alleviate the concerns of some clients and may also be favourably looked upon by the regulators (if there are any) in the offshore centre concerned.

10.6 However, remember that indemnity insurance cannot usually protect the service provider from poor or negligent investment decisions or management practises.

11 Regulation and Supervision of Investment Services in Offshore Centres

11.1 The standard and depth of the regulation of financial services varies between different offshore centres and this is certainly the case when you consider the regulation of investment business which is carried out and provided from offshore centres.

11.2 Each centre is responsible for implementing its own regulatory requirements. Some centres, such as those in Europe, require agents involved in the provision of investment services to be licensed although the majority of centres do not have specific regulatory requirements in place in relation to the provision of investment business.

11.3 In those centres where there is a system of regulation, the basic requirements which service providers must meet will usually be as follows:

i) They must be 'fit and proper' which will generally require them to be able to demonstrate integrity, solvency and competence;

ii) They should be able to show a proven track record in this area of finance and be able to provide a detailed business plan outlining their objectives;

iii) They must meet certain minimum asset requirements (the extent of which will be related to the nature of services which they wish to provide with, for example, managers of collective investment schemes having to maintain a higher level of tangible assets than those who are tied to selling a particular type of investment product);

iv) Clients' money must be properly segregated and designated accounts opened for each client;

v) Adequate arrangements must be made for the safe custody of clients' assets;

vi) They will be expected to act for clients only in accordance with the terms of the client agreement;

vii) There will often be a requirement that any advertisements which the service provider issues must not contain misleading or untrue statements;

viii) They will be expected to maintain procedures to ensure that they comply with the requirements of the regulatory provisions of the centre concerned.

As mentioned earlier in this Section, those centres which have implemented regulations will require those involved in the provision of investment services to be licensed. The fee payable to the licensing body will not only vary between centres but also according to the type of activities to be undertaken.

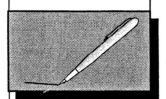

Student Activity 4

Select an offshore centre which has implemented investment regulations and make a note of the key provisions which are designed to provide investor protection. What are the areas which might encourage (or perhaps discourage) investment business in the centre chosen?

12 Investment Review Procedures

12.1 A review of the investments held in a particular portfolio whether it is in an offshore trust or company, or held for an individual, is a relatively simple procedure but one which can lead to potential problems if not conducted correctly.

12.2 To many practitioners, an investment review involves a comparison of the market value of the investments with the book value, to make sure that profits are being made, and a quick check of the income figure to make sure that it is in line with the return which was expected. This does, of course, provide valuable information but as we shall now see, other checks and reviews should also be performed at regular intervals.

Matters which should be the Subject of a Review

12.3 The following is a list of the areas which should be considered for every client, trust or company which holds investments.

Book values

12.4 The value of each investment at the time it was acquired or transferred into the portfolio should be recorded and if necessary, checked. This information is useful for tax purposes as it will enable the gains or losses made on the investment to be easily calculated. This figure is also useful for comparison purposes.

Current market price and market value

12.5 The administrator should also check that each investment has been priced and valued at current market rates. Those holdings which have not been valued (such as shares in private limited companies) should be the subject of a further review to ascertain the most recent valuation of the underlying assets of that company.

Income yield/return

12.6 The reviewer should check that the anticipated yield or income return is being achieved. This is particularly important in fixed trusts and in portfolios where a reasonable level of income is required.

Dividend/interest income

12.7 A check should be made that dividend and interest income has been received in accordance with the payment due dates and a note made of any tax which may have been deducted at source on the payment (as it might be possible to reclaim all or part). Receipts should be accompanied by a counterfoil which records full details of the amount distributed.

Strategy/objectives

12.8 The portfolio should be structured to meet the strategy and objectives which were set at the time the investments were acquired. The review process can highlight whether the aims are still being met and is also an ideal opportunity to reflect on whether those aims are still required or indeed still suitable.

Diversification

12.9 The administrator conducting the review should ensure that the portfolio is suitably diversified to reduce risk.

Liquidity and cash requirements

12.10 The amount of liquidity which will be required to meet short-term cash requirements should be determined and if necessary, shares or stocks should be sold to meet those needs. Similarly, the percentage of the portfolio which is liquid should be reviewed and an adjustment made if necessary. When interest rates are high, usually higher balances are retained on deposit although in times of lower interest rates, funds are generally committed to markets rather than to cash.

Indices

12.11 There should be a benchmark against which the performance of the portfolio is to be judged. The book value provides this to some extent but it would be preferable to compare the growth (or decline) in the portfolio against the trend in market indices (such as the Dow Jones Industrial or the FT-SE 100 Index).

Funds added or withdrawn

12.12 Such details should be recorded as otherwise it would not be possible to fairly judge the performance of the investments. For example, the current market value of the portfolio might be less than at the time of the previous review, but what the valuation may not state is that a substantial cash withdrawal was made 2 months ago. Similarly, the investments might show a gain compared to the previous valuation but only because of new funds which have been added.

Reconciliation of the certificates held

12.13 An important part of the review should be a reconciliation of the certificates which are held. Usually the ownership of an investment is evidenced by a certificate which corresponds to the number of shares, stock or units acquired. A check should therefore be made to ensure that the requisite number of certificates are held, either in the administrators' records or by a custodian appointed to hold the certificates on behalf of the client or beneficial owner of the portfolio.

Role of the investment managers and other agents

12.14 Last, but by no means least, the role and performance of the investment manager (if one has been appointed) should be considered. The administrator should weigh up the quality of the reports, information, valuations and advice received from the manager and also note the fees which have been charged. The review might also be a useful opportunity to check whether the terms of the management agreement require alteration.

12.15 If other agents have been appointed, e.g. custodians, their role should also be reviewed.

13 Establishing an Investment Department

13.1 Investment management activities in offshore (as well as onshore) centres are conducted by a variety of service providers such as stock brokers, banks, trust companies, insurance companies, law firms and accountants. Some, as we have already seen, have to be licensed and therefore subject to regulatory controls whereas others can perform these services without being supervised by the local authorities in the centre concerned.

13.2 The requirements to set up an investment department will therefore vary between centres as in some cases local licensing rules must be complied with. We have already looked at what the licensing requirements would generally cover and in this Section we shall look at a few of the issues which a service provider should consider before opening an investment department in an offshore centre.

Experienced Workforce
13.3 It is important that a service provider has experienced employees and a strong management team to enable it to perform the services which will be required. In offshore centres another consideration would be the ability of the agent to bring in workers from outside the centre. Many offshore centres impose controls over the employment of ex-pat workers and the agent should therefore ensure that there will be an available source of local labour as well as scope to import professional staff if necessary. The packages to be paid to the employees should also be considered and any 'hardship' features of the centre factored in.

Procedures
13.4 It should have in place detailed procedures and internal work practices in relation to all areas of the business to be conducted.

Research Facilities
13.5 The service provider should have at its disposal the facilities required to enable it to conduct thorough market and individual stock and share research. This may require the agent to purchase sophisticated computer equipment in order for it to obtain this information in-house or it might decide to develop relationships with other firms and use their research material, usually for a cost.

Segregation of Functions
13.6 Depending on the activities to be performed, the service provider may have to segregate the duties which he is to perform. For example, if the agent intends to deal or make a market in investments, there must be internal controls in place which will keep information which that section is privy to out of reach of other sections, in particular the section which selects holdings for clients' portfolios.

Technology

13.7 The service provider should also have in place the technology required to enable it to communicate efficiently with his clients, market-makers and other professionals in this field of finance. He must be able to produce and distribute reports and valuations in a clear, accurate and timely manner. The centre chosen should be able to support and maintain the technology required.

Premises

13.8 Suitable premises to accommodate the investment area would also be required. Some centres have available business premises but some have a shortage of office space.

Summary

Now that you have read this Unit you should be able to:

- Outline the features of the different investment services usually provided from offshore centres

- Describe the usual advantages for clients of offshore investment management services

- List the information a service provider would require from the client to enable him to formulate an investment portfolio

- Briefly describe the three main investment strategies

- Describe how to structure a portfolio to meet the needs of different client types

- Explain how to reduce currency risk

- Describe the features of custody services

- List the usual terms contained in a private client agreement

- Summarise how investment services are usually regulated

- Outline the usual requirements to create an investment department in an offshore centre

223

Self-assessment Questions

1. Write brief notes covering the main features of the investment services usually provided in offshore centres.

2. Explain to a potential client the benefits which might be associated with him having his investments managed in an offshore centre.

3. You are in a meeting with a new investment client. What information would you request in order to formulate an investment portfolio?

4. Describe the different investment objectives which a client could choose from.

5. Briefly describe, in general terms, how you might structure an investment portfolio for the following client types with a lump sum to invest:

    a) An unmarried client in employment;

    b) A client who has retired.

6. Outline the usual steps which an investment manager in an offshore centre would take to reduce exposure to currency risk.

7. Briefly describe the features and general advantages of the offshore custody services offered by some service providers.

8. List the usual information which you would expect a client agreement to contain.

9. Briefly describe the usual licensing requirements for the provision of investment business in those centres which have implemented a system of investment regulation.

10. Your bank is proposing to open an investment department in an offshore centre. Suggest areas which would require consideration prior to the creation of such an operation.

Unit 13

Offshore Pension Funds

Objectives

At the end of this Unit you should be able to:

- State the usual purpose of a pension fund
- Describe the usual structure of an offshore pension fund
- Summarise the role of the employer in a pension fund
- Contrast the roles of the actuary and accountant in a pension fund
- List six possible advantages in basing a pension fund in an offshore centre
- Briefly explain the taxation advantages of an offshore pension fund
- Outline the main investment considerations of a pension fund
- Summarise the usual duties expected of a trustee of an offshore pension fund
- Summarise the usual powers of a trustee of an offshore pension fund
- Comment on the selection of a trustee of an offshore pension fund

1   Purpose of a Pension Fund

1.1   A pension fund is an arrangement under which an organisation, such as a large multinational corporation, makes financial provisions for its past, present and future employees as well as its senior executives. Although pension funds act as vehicles for the payment of pension monies they are also used to pay general benefits to employees and executives.

2   Structure of an Offshore Pension Fund

2.1   A pension fund will be structured as a discretionary trust. The employer-company will be the settlor and its current, previous and future employees will be the discretionary beneficiaries. These 'beneficiaries' are generally referred to as members of a scheme.

2.2   There will be a trust deed which sets out the terms under which the pension contributions and/or the benefits are to be held. Often the terms of the trust are referred to as rules. There will, of course, be a trustee who will be given certain powers which will not be dissimilar to those given to trustees of private trusts.

2.3   If the trustees are located in an offshore centre, and the trust is governed by the laws of that centre, the pension fund will be considered to be resident in that centre and therefore 'offshore'.

3   Role of the Various Parties in an Offshore Pension Fund

The Employer
3.1   In addition to creating the pension fund, the employer would also be responsible for making sure that the correct amount of contributions are paid on time to the trustees, that he notifies the trustees of new members to be added to the pension fund and that he also advises the trustee of any amendments which are required to the rules of the fund (as set out in the trust deed).

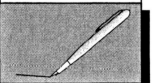

Student Activity 1

Based on the earlier Units on trusts, what do you believe would be the role of the trustee of an offshore pension fund?

The Trustee
3.2   The duties of a pension fund trustee will generally be similar to those which are expected of the trustees of a private trust. We covered the general duties of trustees in an earlier Unit and in Section 5 below we look at some of the specific duties and powers of the trustees of pension funds.

3.3   In an onshore pension fund it is usual for there to be a number of co-trustees, most of whom would be provided by the employer. Usually, many of the co-trustees would be senior executives of the employer and as a result, the employer will usually be able to exert a certain amount of control over the assets of the fund and distributions which are made. Such a situation can create a possible conflict of interest. For example, if the employer provides some or most of the board of trustees, those individuals may be expected to act in accordance with the interests of the company rather than in the interests of the beneficiaries of the pension fund.

3.4   Offshore pension funds, on the other hand, tend to have a sole corporate trustee appointed who would act closely with the employer but at the same time provide an independent viewpoint. A corporate trustee should, in theory, represent the interests of the employees to a greater extent than a trustee who is closely associated with the employer.

3.5   If the employer does wish to have representation on the board of trustees of an offshore fund, the representatives of the employer would usually act alongside the corporate trustee whose role would be to maintain impartiality.

The Administrator

3.6 The trustees would not always perform the day-to-day operations of the offshore pension fund and often you will find that an administrator will be appointed to assist with the day-to-day running of the fund. In such cases the administrator would provide the administration services which the trustee would otherwise have to undertake, such as the collection of income and dividends from the underlying investments, the production of valuations of the fund and the maintenance of pensioner records and the pensions and benefits paid.

The Investment Manager

3.7 The size of the contributions which are made into an offshore pension fund will usually be substantial as too will the pension or benefit payments required. The investment portfolios which underlie such funds will therefore be substantial and require expert management. Few trustees, perhaps with the exception of those banks who provide corporate trustee services, will be able to provide adequate investment management services and as a result it is usual to find that the investment management function is delegated to a suitably qualified and experienced agent.

3.8 Indeed, in view of the size of the assets under management, a committee may often be appointed which comprises a number of different investment managers who all participate in the decision making process.

The Actuary

3.9 The actuary is the person who will be appointed to calculate the amount of the contributions which are required to be placed into the fund to cover the expected distributions to employees and pensioners. After making his initial calculations, the actuary would continue to review the fund and its assets to determine whether any alterations are required to the level of funds going into or coming out of the fund.

The Accountant

3.10 An accountant would be appointed by the trustee to prepare the financial statements of the pension fund and to fulfil any other accounting requirements which may be required either under statute (i.e. under the trust law of the centre or under specific pension legislation such as that which is in place in Bermuda) or in accordance with the rules of the fund.

4 Possible Advantages of Offshore Pension Funds

4.1 There are a number of reasons why a company might decide to establish a pension fund in an offshore centre.

Student Activity 2

Before reading the following section make a list of the possible benefits which you believe might be available in establishing a pension fund in an offshore centre.

Taxation

4.2 The fund would be subject to the local taxation rules of the centre where the fund is resident. The residence of a fund would usually be determined by where the trustees are resident and if the trustees are located in an offshore centre the fund would, in general terms, be subject to the local tax regime of that centre. As offshore centres are either low or no tax centres there are, therefore, considerable tax planning opportunities for a company locating a pension fund in an offshore jurisdiction.

4.3 A further possible tax benefit provided by offshore centres is that distributions out of the pension fund to employees or pensioners would not be subject to withholding tax at source. As a result, employees or pensioners can receive gross distributions from the fund. The local taxation situation of the recipient might, of course, mean that they will be assessed to tax on such receipts in their country of residence but if they also live in a low tax location, there would be clear advantages to receiving a pension which has not suffered tax at source.

Regulation

4.4 There is very little regulation at the present time concerning the provision of offshore pension fund services. Indeed, there is also a lack of regulatory controls in onshore centres as well.

4.5 This lack of regulation means that an offshore pension fund will be able to take a more flexible approach to the investment of the assets and also to the payment of pensions and benefits.

4.6 Some centres have implemented measures which prevent corporate trustees from acting in any type of trust (including pension funds) unless they are licenced locally. This licencing requirement does at least provide some degree of control over those who can act as trustee of an offshore pension fund.

Contributions

4.7 Usually, there will be no restrictions on the extent of the contributions which can be made into an offshore pension fund. Similarly, there will not usually be any restrictions on the amount of benefits which an offshore pension fund can distribute to its members.

Uniformity

4.8 Offshore pension funds provide an opportunity for the employer to make uniform provisions for all its employees regardless of where those employees work or reside. Such provisions can also be made regardless of the pension laws or other local requirements which may be in place where the employer or the members are based.

Investment Strategies

4.9 Unlike onshore pension funds, there will not generally be restrictions imposed on an offshore pension fund in relation to the investment strategies which it may undertake.

Nor, in usual circumstances, will there be any restrictions on the types of investments such a fund may select for inclusion in its portfolio. Offshore pension funds can, therefore, expose a greater proportion of its assets in speculative investments which creates an increased opportunity for capital growth as well as higher income return.

Investment considerations are covered in a following Section.

Currency Protection

4.10 Offshore pension funds can usually pay pensions or benefits in any major currency. This can protect the recipients from currency variations which will occur.

Benefit Packages

4.11 An offshore fund could also be established to pay employees fringe benefits which arise in relation to their employment. It is usual for benefits, such as incentive schemes and share purchase options, to be restricted by onshore regulations but an offshore scheme would not be subject to such restrictions, thus enabling the employer to make greater benefit provisions for his employees than he could through an onshore fund.

Top-Up Provisions

4.12 It is usually possible for an employee of an offshore pension fund to make contributions into the fund to top up the contributions which his employer has made on his behalf, thus providing him with a larger pension entitlement on his retirement. Often the percentage amount which an employee can contribute will be greater than that which is permissible in an onshore fund.

5 The Investment of Offshore Pension Fund Assets

5.1 As already mentioned, pension funds will usually comprise a considerable amount of assets which in turn have to be invested to meet the employee requirements of the company concerned. Regular cash sums will also be contributed by the employer (and in some cases by the employees) and these sums must also be invested.

5.2 In general terms, the assets which comprise a pension fund should be invested with a long-term view and although the overall philosophy will be conservative there must be scope for capital appreciation in order to meet the future requirements of the members of the scheme, and indeed to cater for the addition of future members.

5.3 Many funds will also have current beneficiaries who will require regular distributions (such as a monthly salary) and as a result, there will be a need to ensure that the investments in those funds produce a sufficient level of income to meet the cash needs.

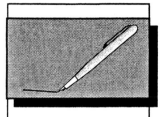

Student Activity 3

What information do you think the investment managers of an offshore pension fund will require to enable them to formulate an investment strategy?

6 Practical Issues Concerning the Role of the Trustees

6.1 We have already looked at the usual powers and duties of trustees in an earlier Unit. Although these general principles will also apply to the trustees of an offshore pension fund there are certain specific issues which the trustees of a fund should consider.

Duties of Pension Fund Trustees

6.2 In general terms, the trustee of a pension fund should make sure of the following:

a) That the contributions due from the employer and the employees are received and suitably invested;

b) That new members of the scheme are admitted in accordance with the terms of the trust (and often in accordance with the employer's rules);

c) That benefits are paid on time to the members and that they are paid at the correct rate;

d) They must safeguard the assets of the pension fund;

e) They must act in the interests of the members (and future members) of the fund;

f) They must act impartially (e.g. they must act fairly between the members of the fund);

g) That accounts are prepared (usually at least annually) and if necessary submitted to the employer and other interested parties;

h) To exercise their powers for a proper purpose. (We shall look at this next.)

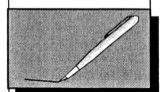

Student Activity 4

Compare the list of duties above with those expected of a trustee of a private trust. Where do you see similarities?

Powers of Pension Fund Trustees

6.3 The trust deed will set out the powers which the trustee can, if he decides, exercise although as we mentioned above the trustee is under a duty to exercise his powers only if they are for a 'proper' purpose. This would generally be for a purpose which is in the interests of the members and which is exercised in accordance with the terms of the trust deed.

6.4 It is worth mentioning again at this point that the trustee can exercise his powers 'if he so decides' because the trust will be a discretionary trust.

6.5 Some of the usual powers given to the trustees of an offshore pension fund are as follows:

a) To invest the assets as if they were the beneficial owners and if appropriate, to appoint an agent to assist them with this or any other management or administration function;

b) To decide, in certain circumstances, who is to receive benefits, how much and when (e.g. on the death of a member of the scheme or the lump sum payable on the retirement of a member of the scheme);

c) To decide on pension increases;

d) To decide whether the terms of the deed require amendment or in extreme circumstances for the trust to be terminated;

e) To decide when and how new members (beneficiaries) are to be added to the scheme;

f) To decide how to treat and account for additions which may be made to the scheme from time to time (perhaps by the employer or sometimes by the employee).

7 Selection of a Trustee

7.1 In view of the fact that offshore pension funds are not usually subject to regulation in offshore centres it is extremely important that the institution which wishes to establish a fund appoints a reputable and experienced trustee. They should also check that the agents who are then appointed by the trustees are also suitably qualified and experienced.

7.2 A locally incorporated or locally licensed bank or trust company would often be an ideal choice of trustee and the administrator and investment manager would often be a similarly licensed local institution.

7.3 The bank or trust company which is chosen would usually be of international standing and have operations in a number of offshore (and possibly onshore) locations. In view of the size of funds potentially under management it would also be reasonable to expect that the service provider chosen has a proven track record of high quality asset management.

231

Summary

Now that you have read this Unit you should be able to:

● Explain the usual purpose of a pension fund

● Outline the usual structure of a pension fund

● Describe the usual role of the employer in a pension fund

● Compare the role of the actuary with that of an accountant of a pension fund

● Provide six possible advantages in basing a pension fund in an offshore centre

● Outline the taxation advantages of an offshore pension fund

● Comment on the investment considerations of the trustee of a pension fund

● Summarise the usual duties expected of a trustee of an offshore pension fund

● Summarise the usual powers of the trustee of an offshore pension fund

● Provide an opinion as to the most suitable choice of trustee of an offshore pension fund

Self-assessment Questions

1. Briefly describe who might decide to create an offshore pension fund and state for whose benefit such a vehicle might be created.

2. List the parties who would usually be involved in an offshore pension fund.

3. Outline the usual role of the employer in the creation and future administration of an offshore pension fund.

4. Describe the potential taxation advantages of an offshore pension fund.

5. Outline the possible benefits of an offshore pension fund in relation to the payment of benefits and the receipt of contributions.

6. Describe to a potential client who is interested in establishing an offshore pension fund the investment considerations which you would have and the type of strategy you would follow.

7. List the duties expected of the trustee of an offshore pension fund.

8. List the powers usually given to the trustees of an offshore pension fund.

9. Comment on how offshore pension funds are usually regulated.

10. What type of service provider would you suggest as a suitable choice to act as the trustee of an offshore pension fund

Unit 14

Offshore Investment Funds

Objectives

At the end of this Unit you should be able to:

- Outline the role of the manager of a unit trust

- Briefly explain the difference between a roll-up fund and a distributor fund

- Describe the difference between an open-ended company and a unit trust

- List the parties usually involved in the running and administration of an offshore open-ended company

- Describe the usual structure of a closed-ended investment fund

- List three advantages of offshore investment funds for investors

- List three advantages of offshore investment funds for the promotor

- Outline how investment funds are usually regulated in those offshore centres which have implemented investment regulations

- Understand the terms 'UCITS' and 'Designated Territories' as applied to offshore investment funds

- State six possible areas which an investor might want to consider before selecting an offshore investment fund

1   Definition

1.1   An investment fund is a vehicle which holds a number of different investments. Investors are given the opportunity to invest in the fund by providing cash in exchange for a share in the underlying investments. Investors would not, however, receive a direct share of each stock held but would instead be given a share of the fund itself (often called a unit) which would comprise a proportion of all of the underlying investments held. Investors can therefore aquire an interest in a wide variety of investments by purchasing units in an investment fund.

1.2   For a fund to be classified as 'offshore' it would usually have to be operated from an offshore centre. This would normally require the management or administration to be conducted from an offshore centre. We return to this aspect in the Section on regulation later in this Unit.

1.3 There are different types of investment fund which are provided from offshore centres and the syllabus requires students to have a working knowledge of each type as well as a basic understanding of the possible advantages in establishing a fund in an offshore jurisdiction. Students should also be familiar with some of the practical issues which relate to the administration of offshore funds. This Unit will therefore concentrate on these main areas.

2 Open-ended Offshore Investment Funds

2.1 Investment funds are usually classified as being open-ended or closed-ended. Open-ended funds can be created as a unit trust, as an open-ended company or as a mutual fund. Together, they are sometimes referred to as collective investment schemes.

Unit Trusts

2.2 This is a type of trust. The promoter (who wants to create the fund) will be the settlor who executes a trust deed which will set out how the fund is to operate. A trustee and manager will be appointed. The trustee will be responsible for the safe keeping of the assets and for ensuring that the terms of the trust deed are followed. The manager, who will often be the promoter, will be responsible for the day-to-day administration of the fund and will report to the trustee. The trust property will represent the funds which have been received from the investors and the investors themselves will be the beneficiaries, although their interests will be in proportion to the funds which they have invested.

2.3 We shall now consider the roles of the trustee and the manager as well as looking at the roles of the other parties who will often be required.

The role of the trustee

2.4 The duties owed by the trustee of an investment fund are similar to those owed by the trustee of a private or pension trust. In most unit trusts the day-to-day administration of the fund will be conducted by the manager and as a result, the trustee will expect the manager to perform the duties which he would otherwise be responsible to fulfill.

2.5 The trustee should satisfy himself that the manager is fit and proper to act in this capacity and that the fund is administered in accordance with the trust deed and any other regulations which may apply in the offshore centre.

2.6 The trustee will be required to take control of the unit trust's assets and to be registered as their legal owner. He will have the power to appoint agents (such as bankers) to assist him with the proper and effective running of the fund and he will usually place the management of the investments with the manager who he has appointed. In some cases a trustee will also appoint a custodian to hold the underlying investments.

2.7 The trustee will also be responsible for checking the price and method of pricing of the fund and will oversee the distributions which are made to the investors. He will sometimes be responsible for maintaining the register of unit holders although this would usually be delegated to a registrar or custodian.

2.8   Usually, the trustee will be a corporate body who is approved to act in this capacity by the regulatory authorities in the offshore centre where the fund is based. The criteria for approval to act as the trustee will vary between centres but often a capital adequacy test is applied to make sure the corporate body has sufficient financial standing to act as trustee. Often an international bank will be appointed to fulfill this role. The position will usually require a licence which is issued by the local regulatory body.

We shall return to regulatory requirements later in this Unit.

The role of the manager

2.9   The manager will be under a duty to administer the fund in accordance with the terms of the trust deed as well as in accordance with local regulations which may apply to the unit trust. In view of the responsibilities which this will involve, the trustee should carefully check the suitability and expertise of the intended manager before proceeding with the appointment.

2.10   In addition to advising on the investments, the manager will also be responsible for making a market in the units of the trust and will be involved in selling units to the initial investors, eventually buying them back and then re-selling them to new investors. The manager will also advise on the possibility of issuing new units from time to time.

2.11   Usually, the manager will be a company which is incorporated in the offshore centre and will perhaps be owned by an overseas bank, insurance or investment company. The requirement that the manager be a local company enables the authorities in the offshore centre to have some jurisdiction over its activities. Once again, we shall return to regulatory issues as they relate to fund managers later in this Unit.

Other parties

2.12   In addition to the trustee and manager, a unit trust will usually have other parties who will perform specific functions as follows:

a)   An accountant to prepare financial statements and fulfill other accounting requirements as appropriate;

b)   An auditor to confirm the accuracy of the financial information produced;

c)   Registrars to record the investor details;

d)   A custodian who will be responsible for the physical safe keeping of the certificates which have been issued in respect of the underlying investments. In some cases the custodian may also be the registered owner of the investments and hold them on behalf of the trustee.

Trust expenses

2.13   The trust deed will usually contain fee charging provisions to enable the trustees to charge a fee for their services. Such provisions will also cover the payment of auditors expenses and fees of the registrars and will also enable the trustee to cover the cost of any legal advice which he may require on the structure.

237

2.14 The manager's fees will also be covered in the deed. Usually he will receive an initial fee (which is calculated on the value of the funds paid into the unit trust) plus an annual management fee which would normally be calculated on the market value of the fund.

2.15 The manager will also receive remuneration for his role in market making which will be the spread between the bid and offer prices. The bid price is the price at which the manager will buy units and the offer price is the price at which he will sell units.

Types of offshore unit trust
2.16 There are two main types of offshore unit trust:

i) Distributor Funds
These are unit trusts which pay a dividend to unit holders and subject to the terms of the trust deed, the fund cannot retain earnings.

ii) Roll-up Funds
These are unit trusts where income is not distributed but is instead added to capital, which is why they are sometimes referred to as accumulation units. No dividends are paid but instead revenues are added to capital. This in turn should increase the value of each unit.

Many investors prefer to invest in roll-up funds. If no dividends are paid, income tax will not be an issue for the investor and if there is any capital gains tax (or equivalent) to pay, it will be deferred until such time as the units are sold. However, some onshore centres, such as the UK, have introduced legislation which has reduced the taxation benefits previously offered by roll-up funds by making the disposal of units a chargeable event for income tax purposes.

Open-ended Companies
2.17 This type of fund is similar in some respects to a unit trust. It will own a basket of underlying investments and investors will be able to buy units in the vehicle, thus giving them exposure (through indirect ownership) to a wide base of different holdings.

2.18 However, an open-ended company, as the title suggests, is a corporate vehicle and will therefore have the general features of a company. As such it will have a separate legal identity and can continue in perpetuity. Instead of units, this vehicle will issue redeemable shares and there will not be a trustee controlling the fund as the management and control will be vested in the directors. Finally, there will not be a trust deed as the memorandum and articles of association of the company will govern the fund.

2.19 As this type of fund is a corporate entity it will only be available in those centres which have the required company legislation to permit such a vehicle to exist.

The structure
2.20 The directors will usually appoint a management company to assist with the administration of the company and possibly to manage the investments. They may also be involved with the preparation of accounts and valuations and the maintenance of the statutory records, although often an accountant will be appointed to assist with the preparation of financial information.

2.21 A custodian may be appointed to handle the custody of the investments and cash assets. The custodian may also be involved in the settling of trades which are placed within the fund.

2.22 In some instances the custodian might be referred to as a 'custodian trustee' and the function which is performed by the management company might be referred to as 'third party fund administration'.

2.23 The directors are often appointed by the promoters or if the promoter is, for example, an international bank, the directors might be senior officials of that bank.

2.24 The management company will usually be a company which has been incorporated in the offshore centre chosen for the fund and the custodian will usually have to be approved to act in such a position by the local regulatory authority. It is possible that the custodian might have to be a locally incorporated company. Regulatory issues will be covered again later in this Unit.

2.25 The company will usually issue redeemable shares which will also be participating shares, thus enabling investors to receive profits. Usually, these shares will not carry voting rights although some funds do permit investors to vote.

2.26 In addition, the company will often issue founder shares, usually to the promoters or management company, which will generally have voting rights but no rights to participate in the profits of the company. Such shares are not usually redeemable. In some funds the founder shares do not have voting rights.

2.27 The management company may also hold nominal shares which are used to replace the par value when redeemable shares are redeemed.

2.28 Some offshore funds have a stock market listing in certain onshore centres (e.g. London) but this can be an expensive process and such funds are generally only traded through markets which are made by the managers.

Types of open-ended companies
2.29 The two common types of funds are:

i)   Umbrella Funds
     A type of fund where there is a group of different underlying funds held within one main fund, enabling investors to make switches between funds at a cost-effective rate.

ii) Feeder Funds
     Funds under which the investors' monies might be invested in other funds.

Mutual Funds
2.30 These are similar to open-ended companies and were developed in the USA. They have a similar structure to open-ended companies mentioned above, indeed open-ended companies were in fact modelled on the mutual fund vehicle, and are aimed primarily at the US dollar market.

2.31 Offshore mutual funds are predominantly offered in Caribbean offshore centres, such as the Cayman Islands, but like all types of offshore investment funds covered earlier in this Unit, they cannot be sold to US citizens as they are not authorised investments in accordance with the requirments of the Securities and Exchange Commission.

3 Closed-ended Investment Funds

3.1 These are funds which do not offer redeemable shares and are commonly known as investment trusts.

Structure
3.2 The structure will be similar to that mentioned for open-ended investment companies. The directors will be responsible for the management of the company and they will usually appoint a management company to administer the fund. The administrator will usually be responsible for holding the assets and will perform a function similar to that of custodian as described earlier.

Types of Closed-ended Investment Companies
3.3 A number of international banks and finance houses offer their own in-house funds which are based on the investment trust vehicle.

3.4 The popularity of closed-ended funds has, in the main, been built on the ability of such vehicles to borrow and to gear up. This creates greater potential for higher returns although there is also the risk of the fund making a loss as borrowing and gearing are speculative actions.

Pricing
3.5 The pricing of closed-ended investment companies is similar to the pricing of the open-ended funds in that the key factor is the value of the underlying investments in the fund (often referred to as the Net Asset Vaue). However, other considerations must also be taken into account, notably the supply and demand of the shares.

3.6 Closed-ended funds will have a stock market quotation.

4 Advantages of Offshore Investment Funds for Investors

4.1 There are a number of reasons why an investor might find an offshore investment fund attractive and the following is a summary of those which are most commonly quoted.

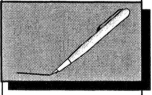

Student Activity 1

Prepare your own list of possible advantages before proceeding and then check it against the points which follow.

Possible Taxation Benefits

4.2   As we have already mentioned on a number of occasions in this workbook, offshore centres are either low or no tax centres and as a result, funds which are created in an offshore centre will not be subject to tax, either in respect of income earned or on capital gains which are realised within the scheme. Funds can therefore build up tax-free profits which can in turn be re-invested.

4.3   In addition, investors will not be liable to local capital gains tax on the disposal of units nor will they be subject to the deduction of withholding tax on the payment of income distributions.

4.4   Offshore funds provide planning potential as capital or income remittances could be delayed and made at times which would be favourable to the investor. The scope for tax deferral is one of the main reasons behind the growth in the offshore fund market.

4.5   Despite the possible tax benefits which offshore funds can provide, it should always be remembered that it is the tax position of the investor which will determine just how advantageous this type of vehicle could be.

Potential for Greater Returns

4.6   In view of the fact that the income and profits of the fund will generally be free from tax in the offshore centre where the fund is based, all the profits and income generated can be re-invested which creates greater potential for higher rates of return compared with onshore funds which are subject to local taxation.

Investment Strategies

4.7   High risk assets cannot generally be held in onshore funds in the light of fund regulations which exist. However, there are fewer restrictions concerning the types of asset which can be held in offshore funds and as a result 'riskier' assets, such as real estate, commodities, futures and options, can be included in offshore portfolios. This, in turn, increases the scope for higher returns although as you will appreciate, with risk comes the danger of making losses!

5   Advantages of Offshore Investment Funds for Promoters

5.1   Offshore funds not only provide potential benefits for investors but they also provide possible advantages for the promoters.

Student Activity 2

Prepare a list of possible advantages for the promoters before reading the following points.

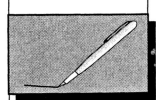

Regulation

5.2   Usually, the regulation of offshore funds is more flexible and less onerous than the regulations which govern onshore. This can create greater investment opportunities.

Taxation

5.3   We have already looked at the tax advantages which may be available to investors in the previous section and covered the likelihood that offshore funds will not be subject to taxation in the local centre. The potential for greater returns helps offshore funds attain more efficient economies of scale than they could achieve onshore.

Increased Revenue

5.4   In view of the possibility of higher returns the promoters of offshore funds may be able to charge higher fees than they could charge if they were offering onshore funds. In addition, the relaxed regulation which exists in some offshore centres reduces the costs which would otherwise be incurred to meet the level of supervisory requirments which are imposed in most onshore jurisdictions.

6   The Regulation of Offshore Investment Funds

6.1   Where the fund has been created, or more importantly where the management or administration of the fund is carried out, will determine how the fund will be regulated. Not all offshore centres have legislation in place which regulates this type of vehicle but in those centres which have imposed regulatory controls, it would be usual to find different classes of funds available and different rules applying to those classes.

Authorised Funds

6.2   These are funds which can be freely marketed to investors in a variety of different countries, including some which are onshore. We return to these in Section 8 below.

Restricted Funds

6.3   These are funds which have a restriction in respect of where they can be marketed.

6.4   Usually, a local trustee and manager will be required and both would have to be 'authorised' to act in accordance with local requirements. To be 'authorised' the trustee or manager would have to be the holder of a licence (such as an investment licence or a bank/trust company licence).

Exempt Restricted Funds

6.5   These are funds which have less than a certain number of participants (e.g. 50) and in view of this ownership restriction they are not subject to the same controls as restricted funds. Neither the trustee nor the manager of an exempt restricted fund will require a licence to act.

Closed-ended Companies

6.6   Usually, investment trusts are not regulated by offshore centres as they are publicly quoted investment funds. However, permission for the creation and administration of the fund might have to be obtained from the regulator in the centre chosen.

Student Activity 3

Select two offshore centres and compare how they regulate their investment fund industries.

7 General Marketing of Investment Funds

7.1 Although relaxed regulatory controls can be an advantage to promoters, administrators and investors alike, it can create problems if there is the desire for the fund to be marketed outside the offshore centre and in particular, if the fund is to be marketed in onshore centres.

7.2 Generally speaking, onshore centres will only allow funds to be marketed locally if those funds meet the regulatory requirements of that centre. This effectively excludes the majority of offshore funds as the level of regulation will be less than that which is expected and required onshore.

7.3 However, there are opportunities for offshore funds to market themselves in some onshore regions.

8 Marketing of Offshore Funds in Onshore Centres

8.1 Although at the time of writing, it is not possible to market an offshore investment fund in the USA (it is not even permissible for a US citizen to invest in such a fund), in certain circumstances it is possible for an offshore fund to be marketed in Europe, provided that is so authorised.

UCITS

8.2 The Undertaking for Collective Investment in Transferable Securities (UCITS) was a European Union initiative which intended to harmonise the regulatory controls of EU member states with the objective that collective investment funds could be freely marketed between those member states.

8.3 There are a number of requirements which must be met before a fund can qualify as a 'UCITS fund'. The main ones are as follows:

a) The assets must be held by a custodian who is authorised to act in this capacity in the centre where he is based;

b) The investments in the fund must be transferable securities listed on a recognised stock exchange;

c) It must meet certain reporting and liquidity requirements.

8.4 These funds must be set up in an EU member state, a fact which excludes the vast majority of offshore funds except those which are established in the Dublin International Finance Centre, Luxembourg or Gibraltar.

The UK Provisions and Designated Territories

8.5 A number of offshore funds can, however, be marketed in the UK as a result of Section 87 of the UK Financial Services Act 1986. Under this section the Secretary of State may allow certain Designated Territories to market their funds in the UK on the basis that the fund regulation in those territories meets the regulatory requirements of the UK.

8.6 Bermuda, Guernsey, the Isle of Man and Jersey are, at the time of writing, designated territories.

8.7 It is also possible that funds from countries which have Designated Territory status may be allowed to market in other onshore centres (apart from the UK) on the strength of the fact that their regulatory requirements meet UK standards. In such cases the fund wishing to market must seek authorisation in the country or countries concerned but there is no guarantee that permission will be granted.

9 Investment Strategies/Types of Funds

9.1 There are a wide variety of investment funds to choose from and the following will give you an indication of the type of underlying investments and strategies which different funds may choose and offer.

Single Class Funds

9.2 This type of fund will only have one class of investor (unit holder) and only one underlying investment portfolio.

Multi-Class Funds

9.3 Although there may only be one underlying investment portfolio, there will be different classes of investors (unit holders) with perhaps some receiving income distributions and others receiving units instead of income.

'Hub and Spoke' Funds

9.4 Also sometimes referred to as ' master and feeder' funds, this type of vehicle has two tiers. Firstly, there is the master fund which is aimed at high net worth institutional investors. Secondly, there is the feeder fund which invests in the master fund and is made up of investors who did not have sufficient capital to buy into the master fund as of right and they have had to combine their subscriptions to meet the necessary criteria.

Exotics

9.5 Basically, this type of fund is aimed at investors who are precluded from investing directly into specific types of investments. Instead, the fund buys those holdings which the investor would be unable to hold in for his own account.

Equity Funds (Common Stock Funds)

9.6 As the name suggests, such funds only invest in equities, usually from a particular country. Often these funds are geared to capital appreciation.

Fixed Interest Funds (Bond Funds)

9.7 In this case the underlying investments will be fixed interest holdings, either government issues or debentures issued by corporations. Often the strategy would be high income return. These are sometimes referred to as 'income funds'.

Commodities/Derivatives

9.8 These are high risk but there is a possibility of high capital rewards.

Tracker Funds

9.9 These are sometimes called index-linked funds and comprise investments which are chosen from a particular stock exchange index. The objective is that the underlying assets will perform as least as well as the market indices.

Realty Funds

9.10 As the name suggests, such funds hold real estate which can create considerable capital gains but on the other hand, because of the nature of the assets, they do carry high risk and are also very illiquid.

Balanced Funds

9.11 These have a mixture of equities and fixed interest holdings designed to provide a balance between income and capital growth.

Money Market Funds

9.12 These are funds which hold short-term instruments of the money market, such as certificates of deposit and treasury bills.

Student Activity 4

Obtain investment literature from an organisation which offers offshore investment funds and see whether there are any other types of funds which they provide.

10 Which Offshore Fund to Choose

10.1 This is, of course, down to individual choice although there are a few areas which a prospective investor might want to consider as part of the selection process.

Regulation

10.2 The investor should decide whether to place his assets in a fund which is administered in a regulated offshore centre or in a fund which is administered in an unregulated centre. The risk/reward ratio would be a key factor in deciding which centre to choose for the investment.

Reputation of the Service Provider

10.3 The investor should check who will be providing the various functions which are required under the structure. In particular, he should feel comfortable with the companies or institutions who will be acting in the roles of trustee, manager and custodian.

10.4 Some offshore centres have a relatively new fund industry wherereas other centres have a developed fund industry with a high level of local expertise.

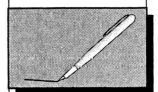

Marketability of the Fund

10.5   Some investors might prefer a fund to be widely marketed and as a result, might want to invest in a UCITS fund or in a centre which has designated territory status (if the UK is a key market area).

Taxation

10.6   There may be tax advantages if the client invested in a roll-up fund rather than in a distributor fund.

10.7   In addition, the client should consider whether his tax position would be improved if he invested directly into securities and equities so as to take advantage of double taxation treaties which may exist between his country of residence and other onshore (and possibly offshore) centres.

Investment Policies

10.8   Some offshore funds have aggressive investment policies geared to capital growth, whereas others have a more conservative approach.

Cost

10.9   The investor should check what the fund is likely to cost in terms of market price and also any subsequent fees to the managers.

10.10 The price movements of the fund over a reasonable period of time could be reviewed to ascertain whether there had been any major variances and if so, enquiries should be made as to why these variances occurred.

10.11 If it is a unit trust, the investor should also check the fee structure of the fund as often offshore funds will be more expensive than their onshore counterparts. Some also have an arrangement under which the initial fee is rebated or part-refunded to the investor.

Summary

Now that you have read this Unit you should be able to:

● Describe the usual role of the manager of a unit trust

● Explain the difference between a roll-up fund and a distributor fund

● Outline the difference between an open-ended company and a unit trust

● Describe the usual structure an offshore open-ended investment company

● Describe the usual structure of a closed-ended investment fund

● List the potential advantages to investors of offshore investment funds

● List the potential advantages to the promotors of offshore investment funds

● Outline the usual regulatory requirements of investment funds in those offshore centres which have implemented investment regulations

● Explain the terms 'UCITS' and 'Designated Territories' as applied to offshore investment funds

● State the criteria an investor might apply in the selection of an offshore investment fund.

247

Self-assessment Questions

1. Write brief notes on the usual structure of an offshore unit trust.

2. Compare the roles of the trustee and the manager of an offshore unit trust.

3. Comment on the difference between distributor and roll-up funds in relation to the treatment of income and suggest which one might be more suitable for a client who pays a high rate of income tax.

4. Describe how an open-ended company would usually be structured.

5. Outline the usual structure of a closed-ended fund and comment on the attractions which this type of fund may have for certain investors who are looking for capital growth.

6. Highlight three possible benefits which may exist for those who invest in offshore funds.

7. Write brief notes on the possible advantages which exist for the promoters of an offshore investment fund.

8. Some offshore centres have introduced legislation and rules which are designed to regulate their fund industries. Outline the usual regulatory requirements which such centres have implemented.

9. Explain what a UCITS fund is and describe the features of such a fund.

10. You are in a meeting with a prospective investor. Outline some of the areas which he may wish to consider before deciding on which offshore investment fund to include in his portfolio.

Appendix 1

Answers to Self-assessment Questions

Unit 1

1. Although there is no legal definition, the term 'offshore' has come to be applied to the situation where a financial transaction is carried out from a jurisdiction which is at least one step removed from the client who has initiated that transaction. The jurisdiction which will be chosen for the transaction will usually have low rates of taxation.

2. Generally, an offshore centre will have concessionary rates of taxation usually for, although not necessarily restricted to, individuals, corporate entities and trusts.

3. A fiduciary service is one which requires the agent or person who is providing the service to exercise certain duties and show certain responsibilities over the property or funds which are under his control. Examples include trustee services and managed company services.

4. The list could include taxation savings, exchange control problems, client confidentiality, minimal reporting requirements, first class legal system, local expertise, regulation, communications, geographic distance, attitude of local government, political and economic stability and general asset protection.

5. The list could have included the main or common language used in the offshore centre, the cost of the provision of services, the reputation of the centre, the centre's time zone and its climate.

6. Generally speaking, assets held offshore for the benefit of non-residents of that offshore centre will be free from income and capital taxes in that centre.

7. Regulation offshore is usually less onerous than that which is conducted onshore. Usually, there will be a requirement that service providers are licenced to conduct financial services in the centre concerned and often the centre will rely upon the local agents to carry out due diligence checks on their clients.

8. It is fair to say that for an offshore centre to develop it requires the support of the local government and politicians. Without this support it will not receive the capital to cover the initial start-up costs, nor will it be able to pass laws designed to attract international business. In addition, without backing from the government the centre will not attract foreign institutions wishing to provide services from that centre.

9. It is important for an offshore centre to have political and economic stability. Without these there could be political unrest and unemployment, both of which could lead to a loss of confidence in the centre concerned and a transfer of business elsewhere.

10. Some centres are more expensive than others and although cost is often a consideration for clients, so too are other factors such as the suitability of the laws in place, the quality of the service providers and the reputation of the centre. These are usually the areas which are quoted to those clients who are put off a particular centre because it is more expensive than others.

Unit 2

1. The client's residence situation might be determined as follows:

   a) By living in a particular country for a qualifying period (e.g. for at least 6 months);

   b) By making regular visits to a particular country and the length of his stays over a period of years (e.g. more than 3 months a year over 4 years could make him resident);

   c) Whether he has accommodation available for his use in a country and he visits that country during a tax year;

   d) Whether he is a citizen or national of a country and is only living outside of that country as a temporary measure (e.g. not to work but perhaps to travel short-term).

2. He would probably be considered to be domiciled in the country where he was born (referred to as his domicile of origin). He may have changed this domicile and acquired one of choice but to have done this he would usually have had to undertake a number of steps designed to severe all links with his domicile of origin and create new and substantial links with his intended new domicile (e.g. by selling his house and resigning from any clubs or associations of which he was a member in his country of origin and purchasing a house in the new intended location).

3. The list could have included tax on income, tax on capital, taxes on death, lifetime transfer tax, tax on investment income, stamp duty and indirect taxation.

4. The residence of a trust is usually determined by where the management and control of the trust lies. This is usually where the trustees are resident as they should have the management and control function.

5. Distributions out of a trust to a beneficiary will not usually have any tax implications for the trustees although the beneficiary might be liable to tax in respect of the funds which he receives. However, if regular capital payments are made to the beneficiary his tax district might consider that the payments are of an income rather than a capital nature and assess him to income tax. In addition, some countries levy tax on capital distributions by tracing back the gains which the trustees have made and assessing the beneficiary who receives capital which has arisen from realised gains in the trust.

6.   Generally speaking, where the management and control lies will usually be the place where the company will be considered to be resident for tax purposes. As the directors of the company should exercise the management and control of a company, the residence of a company will often be determined by where the board (sometimes where only one board member) resides.

7.   Offshore centres do not impose tax on individuals, trusts, companies or partnerships which are considered to be non-resident. In this context, non-resident is taken as meaning that the entity concerned is not based, resident, managed or trading in the offshore centre concerned.

8.   Usually, to take advantage of the tax benefits the trust would have to be created by a non-resident for the benefit of non-residents of that centre.

9.   As you suspect that the potential new client wants to use your services to evade tax, you should not accept the business as to do so might amount to conspiracy to evade tax. In addition, you may have to report the intention to evade to the local authorities, depending on the nature of the business which was proposed and whether tax crimes fall within your centre's list of reportable offences.

10.   This is a tax agreement between two countries which basically allows tax deducted at source from payments from one country to be offset against tax which would otherwise be payable by the taxpayer resident in the other country. The treaties determine in which country tax should be payable and ensure that a taxpayer is not assessed to tax twice on the same 'foreign' income. This is particularly useful in relation to the payment of investment income on overseas holdings where withholding tax is deducted at source as it would be difficult, if not impossible, for the investor to set off the tax deducted from his dividend against his local tax liability.

Unit 3

1.   The notes should have covered the following areas: low taxation, less regulation, cost, infrastructure and available work force.

2.   The usual attractions are the fact that tax will probably not be deducted from deposit interest, there may be statutory secrecy provisions in place, higher rates of interest might be possible, there are a large number of internationally known institutions represented offshore and in addition some banks are only represented offshore.

3.   A domestic licence is one which enables the bank to provide banking services to both local as well as foreign clients. A restricted licence, on the other hand, will often mean that the licence holder can only provide services for clients who are resident outside of the centre. An offshore licence is sometimes referred to as a licence which is required by a managed bank.

4.   The list could include a minimum capital requirement, a specified risk:asset ratio, a specified gearing ratio, the completion and filing of accounts, adequate internal controls and management information systems must be in place, there may be a 'four eyes' test, changes in the directors and officers must be notified to the regulators, charges over assets must be notified and licences will usually be issued and reviewed annually.

5. Cross border regulation has increased following the BCCI collapse and the findings of the Basle Committee. Such regulation makes it possible and easier for information to be passed between regulators in different centres which helps the authorities have a better understanding of the activities of institutions which are operating from more than one location.

6. The Offshore Group of Banking Supervisors was created in 1980 with its principal aim being to improve the supervisory systems and the general exchange of information which occurs offshore. It covers such matters as what information should be exchanged with onshore authorities, how to prevent money laundering and the use of offshore banks for criminal purposes generally, the importance of the role of external auditors in assisting with supervision and the criteria to be applied to assess a bank's financial position.

   This Group currently has 19 members and includes centres such as the Bahamas, Bermuda, the Cayman Islands, Cyprus, Gibraltar, Guernsey, Hong Kong, the Isle of Man, Jersey and Singapore.

7. Under common law, confidentiality may be regarded as arising in the following circumstances:

   i) By virtue of an express contract;

   ii) By virtue of a special relationship such as between a client and his lawyer or accountant; and

   iii) By virtue of the law of tort under which, for example, information with commercial value can, under certain circumstances, be protected.

8. The duty of secrecy was set out in the case of *Tournier* v. *National Provincial and Union Bank of England* (1924). This case established that the relationship between a banker and his client gave rise to a legal duty of confidence which involved non-disclosure of the client's affairs even after an account has been closed.

9. Any two from the following could have been chosen:

   i) By virtue of an express rule of law, such as a court order or a statute such as the UK's Criminal Justice Act;

   ii) Where there is a public duty to disclose, which would occur in cases of serious crime such as money laundering, drug trafficking etc;

   iii) Where the interests of the bank would require disclosure, such as a situation where a bank might sue a customer and state how much the customer owes in the writ; and

   iv) Where the client provides the bank with an expressed or implied authority to disclose, such as providing references or status enquiries.

10. Reference could have been made to the Bahamas, BVI, the Cayman Islands or Gibraltar and the fact that anyone in possession of confidential client information will be committing a criminal offence if it is divulged to any person who is not entitled to it.

Unit 4

1. A captive insurance company is a corporate entity, usually a private insurance company, which is created and controlled by either a parent company, a professional association or a group of businesses. The purpose of the captive insurance company will be to provide insurance for that parent company, professional association or group of businesses against certain risks.

2. Taxation benefits may be a consideration but should not be the main reason why a captive is contemplated. There should be other reasons why such a venture is planned otherwise any possible tax savings which might result could be lost under scrutiny by the tax authorities or regulators in the 'home' jurisdiction of the parent.

3. A managed captive should be considered which would be operated by a local agent who is authorised to provide 'managed' services. The agent would already have the structure, premises, equipment, expertise, experience and staff in place to service the business which saves the capital costs which would otherwise have to be incurred if a captive were to be started from scratch.

4. Certain information would usually be required by the department or authority in the offshore centre which governs and regulates captive insurance business. The required information would often include an application in the prescribed form, confirmation that the company meets the prescribed capital requirements, a business plan, confirmation that the directors and officers meet 'fit and proper' tests, the submission of regular reports, and on the conduct of the company, confirmation that the prescribed liquidity requirements are met and finally annual audited accounts.

5. Limited partners take a passive role in the firm and their liability is limited to such amounts as are set out in the partnership deed (which will usually be the amount they contributed to the partnership funds). General partners will be the partners who manage the firm and whose liability will be unlimited. General partners are often referred to as managing partners.

6. Generally speaking, a partnership is not assessed to tax but instead it is the individual partners who will be issued with assessments in respect of their shares of the income and profits of the partnership. A partnership is therefore transparent for tax purposes, it does not exist as a taxable entity as the liabilities and profits would be attached to the individual partners.

    In an offshore limited partnership it would be usual for the limited partners to be non-resident or international companies (or whatever the local equivalent may be) and the general partner will often be a locally incorporated resident company which has a resident director (and in some cases a suitably qualified company secretary). In those centres which impose taxation on corporate entities it would be usual for such a company to be permitted to apply for tax-exempt status (or the equivalent tax status) in the offshore centre concerned.

    As a limited partnership would usually be treated as a separate entity for tax purposes, in those centres which have corporation tax it would be advisable for it to apply for tax exemption. In centres which impose no direct taxation an annual 'registration' fee would be payable instead.

253

The partners of an offshore limited partnership would not, therefore, be assessed to local tax on their share of the profits and in addition, no withholding taxes would be payable on distributions made to non-resident partners. In addition, those partners would not be subject to any non-resident tax.

7. A limited partnership can be structured as a collective investment vehicle. The investors would in effect be the limited partners and the manager of the scheme would be the general partner. The limited partners would share in the profits (or losses) of the scheme whilst the general partner would receive a fee for managing the funds.

8. A 'flag of convenience' is often used to describe the situation where a vessel is registered in a country or state which is not the country or state where it was originally built or originally registered. Ship owners therefore have the option to choose the laws and regulations of another marine administration rather than be governed by those of their 'home' country.

Examples of centres which can be categorised as such are the Bahamas, Bermuda, BVI, the Cayman Islands, Cyprus, Gibraltar, Liberia, Madeira, Malta, Netherlands Antilles, Panama, Singapore and Vanuatu.

9. The list could have included confidentiality, to prevent political problems, to circumvent legal issues, potential tax savings and possible lower costs.

10. The list could have included the following: the name (or proposed name) of the ship, a certificate of survey detailing the parameters of the ship (type of ship, size, tonnage etc.), evidence of title of ownership, if the ship has not been registered previously, a copy of the Builder's Certificate will usually be required, details of the current registry (if applicable), the proposed use of the ship, details of the company which is to own the ship (or which owns the ship) and full names and addresses of the directors and officers, payment of the prescribed fees.

Unit 5

1. Placement is the physical disposal of the cash proceeds which have been received from the illegal activity (e.g. paying the cash into a bank account). Layering involves creating a complex layer of financial transactions so as to hide the true identity of the source of the funds (e.g. instructing the bank to wire the funds to an account with another bank and then instructing that second bank to transfer the funds on again). If the layering stage has been a success, the illegally obtained funds will now be integrated into the financial system and will appear to be legitimate funds.

2. A discussion centring on transactional services (wire transfers and draft payments) was required together with reference to lending facilities and letters of credit trades.

3. Two should have been chosen from trust services, corporate services, investment services, collective investment schemes and insurance services. Notes on the chosen service should then have been made and the points in Section 3 covered as appropriate.

4. A number of examples could have been provided. The lists contained in Section 4, points 4.3 and 4.4 contain many of the more common examples of suspicious transactions.

5. The list could have covered the purchasing of securities to be held by the financial institution in safe custody, where this does not appear appropriate given the customer's apparent standing, back-to-back deposit/loan transactions with subsidiaries of, or affiliates of, overseas financial institutions in known drug trafficking areas, requests by customers for investment management services where the source of the funds is unclear or not consistent with the customer's apparent standing, large or unusual settlements of securities in cash form and buying and selling of a security with no discernible purpose or in circumstances which appear unusual.

6. A number of countries and territories have teamed up to try and attack money laundering activities by allowing information to be freely exchanged in relation to known or suspected money launderers. Not all of the treaties which are in existence cover every laundering activity (e.g. in some cases the proceeds from tax evasion are not covered). An example of a treaty is the UK/USA Assistance Treaty of 1st April, 1989.

7. Under most local offshore requirements, offshore financial services providers will generally have to be in possession of fairly extensive information on a potential new client before they can provide any of the services which may be required. Once a service provider has collated this data they are said to have performed a 'know your client' check.

    The information which is obtained should provide the service provider with personal information on the client as well as details of his general financial situation and the motive behind him requiring services from an offshore centre.

    Regulatory bodies in offshore centres generally rely on service providers to perform satisfactory due diligence on clients who wish to conduct business through their offshore centre rather than perform their own checks.

8. The information would usually include proof of the identity of all beneficial owner(s) as well as of all the directors and authorised signatories of the company, copies of the certificate of incorporation, memorandum and articles of association (if the company is already in existence), details of the activities (or intended activities) of the company, proof of source of funds, possibly a copy of any taxation and/or legal advice obtained relating to the company's activities or intended activities.

9. This would usually include proof of the identity of the settlor or the client on whose instructions the trust was created, full details to confirm the identity of the trustees and the type of trust, the purpose of the trust (i.e. for the benefit of the client's family etc.), the source of funds and possibly a copy of any taxation or legal advice obtained prior to the creation of the trust.

10. The answer to this question will of course depend on the centre chosen.

Unit 6

1. A company exists as a separate legal entity and has its own legal personality which is distinct from its members and indeed from the ultimate beneficial owner. A company can sue and be sued in its own capacity, it can open a bank account, purchase property or execute a contract.

   A company also has what is known as perpetual succession, which means that a change of ownership, such as the death of a member or shareholder (or indeed the death of the beneficial owner), will not usually affect the continuance of the company. A company can only be terminated by legal process, such as voluntary liquidation or dissolution.

2. The residence of a company is usually determined by where it is managed and controlled. There could, therefore, be possible taxation benefits in a client incorporating a company in an offshore centre which has low or no corporate taxation (which is the situation in most offshore centres), for that company to be managed and controlled from that centre (which could be achieved by appointing local directors) and for the client to transfer the ownership of his assets to that company.

3. The answer will of course depend on the centre chosen although it is likely that the steps will be similar to those covered in Section 4.

4. Some companies may wish to conduct business activities in another country and often this will involve them having to establish a place of business in that other location.

   Registration would usually involve sending the following to the Registrar of Companies: a copy of the certificate of incorporation, copies of the memorandum and articles of association, details of the directors and officers plus the intended location of the business address in the centre concerned. It would also be advisable to check whether the company could be registered under its current name as there may already be a company registered under the same or very similar title. If there is a problem with the name, often a business name can be used instead for registration and business purposes in that centre.

5. The memorandum of association records the public face of the company and contains information which outside parties should be aware of if they wish to undertake business with the company. The articles of association contain the internal rules of the company and provides the basis for the administration of the company.

   Both documents combined are the company administrator's 'bible' and one or possibly both documents should be referred to before the company conducts any business, whether the business is of an external nature (such as signing a contract) or an internal matter (such as the holding of a directors' meeting).

6. Brief notes should have been prepared covering voluntary liquidation, dissolution and strike off (which are the usual options available).

7. The list could have included the general fiduciary duty, duty to avoid a conflict of interest, duty not to make a personal profit, the general duty of care, statutory duties which apply and any additional duties which may be imposed under the articles of association.

8. The list of powers should have covered many of the following, namely the power to borrow or charge assets, to open bank or custody accounts, to allot shares, to remove and appoint directors and other officers, to execute contracts, to declare dividends and to call meetings of the members.

9. A general discussion of the fact that in law there is no such thing as a 'nominee director' was required, with emphasis on the need for all directors (even of client companies) to understand that they will be bound by the usual duties expected of a director and that they can be liable and accountable for their actions (or inactions).

10. The members are the owners of the company and have certain rights and powers which can impact on the directors and are also rights and powers which the directors themselves will not usually have. Usually, the members will have the power to appoint and remove directors, the power to alter the memorandum and articles of association and the power to pass special resolutions at members' meetings which are used to authorise business such as the change of name of the company or placing the company into voluntary liquidation.

Unit 7

1. Answers should have referred to the special tax treatment of companies in offshore centres and covered such options as international companies, non-resident companies, tax-exempt companies, exempted companies and IBCs.

2. International Business Companies (or IBCs as they are commonly known) are offered by many of the centres in the Caribbean, such as the Bahamas, Barbados, Belize, and the Turks and Caicos Islands. They are therefore commonly found in no tax, as opposed to low tax, centres. Usually there are no requirements to have a local resident director and the filing requirements are less onerous. Corporate directors are usually permissible (which is not often the case with exempt companies) and usually sole directors are permissible.

   International companies are the European equivalent of the International Business Companies and are available in low tax centres such as Alderney, Gibraltar, Guernsey, Jersey and the Isle of Man. International companies can elect to pay tax locally at a fixed rate, usually up to 30% or 35%, instead of paying a nominal amount of tax (which would generally be at the same rate as the nominal tax paid by exempt companies). The filing requirements are similar to those of the exempt companies in those centres and usually corporate directors are not permitted.

3. Tax-exempt companies are not generally permitted to trade or perform business activities in the offshore centre concerned but the management and control would usually have to be conducted locally, or at the very least, there must be at least one member of the board of directors resident in the offshore centre. Tax-exempt

companies must not usually be beneficially owned by a local resident or by a local trust, unless the trust has a clause which specifically excludes local residents from benefiting.

4. The list will depend on the centre chosen but usually many of the areas covered in Section 2, points 2.4 to 2.29 would have to be provided to the Registrar.

5. The registered office will usually be the place where a company will keep its registers (of directors etc.). It would also be usual to find the common seal of the company kept there (if the company wanted to keep a seal) together with accounting records. The minute books recording the meetings of the directors and members would usually be retained there as well. The name of the company would also usually have to be recorded at its registered office in a situation where it can be viewed by the general public.

6. A client might prefer to choose a company in a centre which has minimal reporting requirements because he would like to take advantage of the increased levels of confidentiality which this could create. In addition, minimal reporting requirements should also mean less activity for the service provider and therefore lower costs.

    The most commonly quoted example would be the BVI.

7. Sometimes minimal reporting can create the impression that the company, and possibly the client behind that company, have something which they wish to hide. Another factor is that outside parties wishing to conduct business with such a company might be deterred from proceeding with the business anticipated on the basis that a routine check on the company's records filed at the local registry does not uncover much information on such matters as the directors or activities of the company (on the basis that such information is not required to be filed).

8. A number of services should have been mentioned such as incorporation services, provision of the registered office, provision of directors and officers, provision of nominee shareholders, maintenance of the corporate records and the preparation of annual accounts.

9. This would usually involve a new company questionnaire, a company management agreement and an indemnity.

10. The first step would be to determine how many companies the employee is on the board of, where those companies are located and how many other directors are appointed in those companies. The articles of association should be checked to see what provisions exist concerning the required number of directors.

    The next step would be to arrange for the employee to sign letters of resignation for those companies on which he is a director. Again, the articles should be checked to ascertain how a director can resign, which would usually be by letter addressed to the registered office requesting to resign from the board. Assuming a replacement director has to be appointed, the next stage would be to decide who to appoint and how this can be achieved. The articles should be the point of reference in respect of how to appoint and the organisation's internal rules and procedures would probably contain guidance on who to appoint.

The next step would usually be to hold a directors' meeting to accept the resignation of the employee on the various companies and to appoint his replacement. After this meeting has been held and the resolutions passed, the changes should be notified to interested parties, such as banks or other institutions who receive instructions from the company and who must know at all times who is authorised to sign on behalf of the company. In addition, the register of directors should be updated and in some centres the Registrar of Companies must also be notified of the changes. The companies databases should also be updated with the alterations.

The new director should receive some form of indemnification from his employer for acting in this new capacity and the outgoing director may also receive confirmation that he will be indemnified for future actions which may be brought against the company. The company's letterhead may also have to be amended and finally, the beneficial owner might also want to be notified of the changes.

Unit 8

1. The articles could be worded so that the management and control of the company lies with the directors and also with those members who have the shares. Neither the directors nor the shareholders would be able to receive any distributions from the company. The guarantee members would be eligible to receive dividends and loan payments at the discretion of the directors or voting members.

    Under this arrangement, the directors and the shareholders would have a role which would be similar in nature to that of the trustees of a discretionary trust, whilst the guarantee members would receive an interest which would be similar to that of a discretionary beneficiary.

    The articles could also include provisions for the appointment of a person who would oversee the actions of the shareholders and directors and by doing so would be similar to a protector.

2. The members, rather than the directors, would usually be involved in the management of a limited duration company. Any income which the company receives or any realised gains which it makes will be considered to be the income or gains of the members and not of the company.

3. The list might have included the ability to appoint sole directors and have single members, redomiciliation provisions, audit exemption, waiver of the need to submit accounts to the members, waiver of an objects clause in the memorandum of association, dispensing with a common seal, the ability to have written resolutions and the fact that bearer shares can be issued.

4. Usually, service providers would be reluctant to send bearer shares out of their office. Although the security aspect is a consideration (what if they were lost?) there is also the risk that ownership of the company could be transferred without the knowledge or approval of the service provider which could create serious problems.

5. A company cannot make a decision and instead decisions are made for it by the directors and the members. A simple answer but one which is often forgotten by the busy offshore administrator.

6. The nature of the business conducted at the AGM will usually be determined by the articles of association although it would usually include such business as the declaration of a dividend, considering and approving the annual accounts (which should have already been signed by the board), considering the directors' and, if applicable, the auditors' reports in the accounts and approving any alterations required to the board of directors.

   The business to be conducted at an EGM will be those matters, usually of an urgent nature, which would not or could not wait until the next AGM (such as the removal of a director).

7. This would usually include confirmation that the meeting was a directors' meeting, where and when it was held, the persons present and those absent, the appointment of the chairman, the reading and possibly approval of the minutes of the previous meeting before moving onto the business which was conducted at the current meeting, resolutions which were passed, a note that the meeting was terminated and finally the chairman's signature.

8. This question relates to the provision of split boards and the issues which this can create for service providers. These issues are covered Section 4 points 4.3 to 4.8 and the discussion should have centred on management and control for tax purposes, as well as how the agent would wish to retain control over the affairs of the company so that decisions could not be taken without his knowledge.

9. Again, management and control is an issue which would be determined by the extent of the powers to be given to the client. Answers should have covered the difference between a general and a special power of attorney and the fact that general powers should be avoided.

10. The main reasons which should have been covered were to reduce risk (by diversification), additional confidentiality possibilities which this could bring and the fact that in some cases the lex situs of an asset might require that a separate corporate vehicle be used to hold that asset.

Unit 9

1. A precise definition of a trust is difficult but generally speaking it is the relationship which exists when a person, called the trustee, is compelled in equity to hold property, called the trust property, for the benefit of persons, called the beneficiaries.

   The person who creates a trust is usually referred to as the settlor or in some countries he is called the grantor (e.g. USA). The settlor could be a beneficiary and even the trustee of his own trust.

   There can be more than one trustee and in some cases a trust protector may be appointed whose role would usually be to oversee the actions of the trustees and make sure that the settlor's intentions in establishing the trust are met.

2. An express trust is created as a result of a positive, intentional action on the part of the settlor, such as him executing a trust deed or other such instrument to create an intervivos trust. Another example of an express trust is a testamentary trust.

A resulting trust is a type of implied trust which is created as a result of what the law infers as being a person's intention. An example of a resulting trust would be where A transfers property to B without any indication that a gift was intended or has taken place. The property would therefore be held on a resulting trust for A, as on B's death the property would revert (be transferred back) to A. Another example would be where A transfers property to B to hold for C's lifetime. If there is no instruction as to what is to happen to that property on C's death, the property would be held on a resulting trust for A as on C's death, the property would return to A (or A's estate if he too has died).

3. The criteria includes such factors as the capacity of the settlor, the purpose of the trust, the need for the trust to be properly constituted and the duration of the trust.

4. Trust property must vest (or be transferred to or held for a beneficiary) within what is termed the perpetuity period (which is often referred to as the trust duration period). If the property is not vested within that time the trust would generally fail.

The maximum period for which vesting may be postponed starts from the creation of the trust and will vary depending upon the offshore centre concerned. However, many centres have chosen the options available under English trust law which is either the a period of a life in being plus 21 years or, as is more usually the case, a specific number of years not exceeding 80. Some have a longer period (ranging from 100 to 150 years) whilst a couple have abandoned the time period completely.

The fixed period is the most commonly used option.

5. The most common uses are covered in Section 4. Five should have been chosen and notes written on those points.

6. In Civil Law countries, such as South America, Central and Southern Europe and the Middle East, local laws are in place which require persons from those countries to leave a certain percentage of their assets on their death to certain heirs, usually their spouse and children.

This restriction on testamentary freedom can create problems for clients from those areas but it has also created opportunities for some offshore centres who have introduced legislation which encourages clients from those countries to create local trusts which would be protected from claims by forced heirs. Basically, under the laws of such centres as the Cayman Islands, the capacity of the settlor and the legality of the trust will be governed by the laws of the offshore centre and the rights of heirs and forced heirship laws will be ignored by the local courts.

7. These are discretionary trusts but are not created for the benefit of persons or charities (in other words, there are no beneficiaries) but they are instead created for a particular purpose. This purpose must be specific (clearly stated in the terms of the trust deed), reasonable and possible. In addition, the purpose must not be unlawful, immoral or contrary to public policy.

A trustee (who would usually be a trust corporation, a lawyer or an accountant), would be appointed and there would also be an enforcer appointed under the terms of the trust deed whose role would be to oversee the actions of the trustee. The powers of the enforcer would be similar to those of a protector but his fiduciary responsibilities would be governed by the statute which allows purpose trusts.

The duration of a purpose trust would usually have to comply with the local centres' perpetuity rules. There will usually be a provision in the trust deed to cover how the trust will terminate and also what is to happen to the balance of the trust property on termination.

Purpose trusts can be used for a variety of reasons such as to hold a particular asset, to assist in corporate financing schemes and to protect assets in high risk industries.

8.   The duties should have included those listed in Section 6, points 6.3 to 6.19. Please refer to these points when checking your answer.

9.   Similarly, please refer to Section 6, points 6.20 to 6.40 which cover the usual powers given to the trustees.

10. Answers should have covered the case of *Chaine-Nickson* v. *Bank of Ireland* (1976) and gone on to mention that it would usually be reasonable to release a copy of the trust deed to the beneficiaries and also a copy of the financial statements. However, a copy of the letter of wishes would not usually be produced and mention made of *Re Londonderry's Settlement* (1964).

Answers should then have gone on to mention that the beneficiaries' rights to certain information is not absolute and the trustees can refuse to provide details, for example where they know or suspect that trust information is to be used in hostile litigation against the trust or the trustees.

Unit 10

1.   The proper law of a trust will usually be the law which is specified under the terms of the trust deed. Alternatively, if the trust deed is silent on this issue the proper law which will be applied will usually be that with which the trust is most closely connected. This is not as easy to determine, although factors which would be considered in evidence would be where the administration of the trust is carried out, where the trust assets are held, the place of residence of the trustees and also where the beneficiaries are based.

2.   Perhaps the main reason why a change might be required would be if the advantages or benefits of the original centre were diminished. This could be as a result of the centre introducing a system of taxation on local trusts, there being political unrest or perhaps as a result of another centre altering its laws with the result that it now offers greater potential benefits than the original choice of centre.

In most cases the power to change the proper law will be given to the trustees under an express power in the deed and would require them to execute a deed or a declaration stating that the law has been changed from one centre to another. This is how the law is changed in the majority of cases. However, mention should have been made of the case of *Duke of Marlborough v. Attorney General (no 1) (1945)* which suggested that a change in the proper law cannot be made unless all the beneficiaries agree.

3. A flee clause is one which attempts to switch the management and administration of a trust to another centre on the happening of a particular event, such as civil unrest or the introduction of taxation, in the original centre chosen. Usually, such a clause will state that on the happening of a pre-determined event the trustees will automatically retire and new, specified trustees in another centre will be appointed. Often the clause will also specify that the proper law and law of the forum will be changed at the same time as the change in trustees.

4. The popularity of this type of trust is centred around its flexibility. Settlors generally prefer this type of vehicle as it enables them to make provision for a wide variety of beneficiaries, including those who may not even be born. In addition, the trustees will usually be given wide powers to administer and manage the trust which provides them with greater flexibility and control.

5. The settlor should be advised that his letter of wishes will not be a legally binding document and that the terms need not be followed by the trustees. In turn, the settlor should be advised that the main purpose of the letter is to provide the trustees with additional information (which may or may not help them in their decision making process) and that they can choose to take an action or reach a decision which is not covered by, or is perhaps contrary to, a wish which is expressed in the letter.

6. Generally, a letter of wishes would start by stating that it is not intended to bind the trustees in any way and that it is not intended to create a separate trust. After confirming the lack of effect which the letter will have, the settlor would then usually go on to mention who he would like the trustees to benefit and in what proportions. Often guidelines as to the investment of the trust property would also be included. He would also probably go on to mention that he may decide to change the terms of his letter in the future and also include reference to who he would like the trustees to listen to and take advice from after his death (e.g. the settlor's spouse of one of his children).

    Letters of wishes are generally signed by the settlor although not usually in the presence of a witness, as to do so might create the impression that the letter was intended to have legal effect (and perhaps be likened to a will).

7. The powers would often include to approve a change of proper law, to approve to the additional or removal of beneficiaries, to approve proposed trust distributions, to approve the appointment of an agent or adviser, to approve investment recommendations, to appoint replacement protectors and to approve a proposal to terminate the trust.

    One of the powers which the protector should not perhaps be given is the power to appoint and remove the trustees, especially if the settlor was the protector.

8. The findings of these cases can be found in Section 3, points 3.38 to 3.45. Please refer to these points when checking your answer.

9.   Answers should have referred to the need for the trustees to make (and be seen to have made) decisions which are the result of an active mental process. The holding of a meeting of the trustees indicates that the decision was the result of a discussion and the purpose of the minutes would be to record this decision-making process. However, it should also have been mentioned that the processes of holding a meeting and recording the decisions taken are not in themselves proof that the trustees exercised a due thought process.

10.   The list should have included many of those points covered in Section 5, point 5.19, which should be referred to for guidance.

Unit 11

1.   There are no statutory provisions which would prevent a settlor (which we can assume the client will become) being asspointed as the protector of his trust. However, the possible 'management and control' problems which this could create should have been mentioned and the fact that careful drafting of the protector's powers is a key issue.

2.   In addition to possibly being appointed trust protector the settlor might also decide on one or more of the following: to act as co-trustee, complete a letter of wishes, be appointed as investment adviser, be included as a beneficiary or use a private trustee company as trustee.

3.   Section 2, points 2.10 and 2.11 contain the information which the trustees should obtain, which are in essence the findings in *Lucking's Will Trusts* (1967) and *Bartlett v. Barclays Bank Trust Co. Limited* (1980).

4.   Both cases should have been outlined and the conclusions stated that the trustees should consider the interests of all the beneficiaries (*Learoyd* v. *Whitely*) and that trustees cannot be expected to guarantee return, only the preservation of the trust fund *Nestle* v. *National Westminster Bank plc*).

5.   Indemnities are often requested to cover such matters as investing the trust funds, the actions of agents and investment managers appointed by the trustees and the activities of underlying companies. Some trustees also seek to be indemnified for all and any of their actions, especially the exercise of a discretion.

6.   This question called for a discussion of the cases referred to in Section 5, points 5.3 to 5.13 and the matters which arose relating to the suitability and effect of indemnity provisions. Please refer back to that Section when checking your answer.

7.   The options available are the creation of a trust by declaration and the use of a dummy settlor to settle the trust.

        Not all service providers are prepared to provide trustee services for a declaration of trust, usually because they are concerned at the motive behind the client not wanting to be named as settlor. Dummy settlors are also frowned upon, not only because of the possible motive of the client but also because the validity of the trust might be brought into question on the basis that the settlor might lack the necessary intention to create a valid trust.

8. In most onshore centres, transfers into trust will be made void or voidable if a claim is made against the settlor by a creditor or if the settlor is declared bankrupt within a certain period of time, which can be up to ten years from the date of the transfer. Generally speaking, those offshore centres which have implemented legislation to protect against creditors will refuse to accept claims against a settlor. The time frame during which a claim must be made will also be much less and generally the onus will also be on the creditor to prove that the transfer into trust was intended to defraud him.

9. Section 8 contains a definition of 'sham trust' and also covers the points which trustees and administrators should be aware of to enable them to avoid sham trust situations. This is a particularly important area for practitioners and you should therefore refer back to that Section to check your answer.

10. The paperwork which is required for the take on of new business is an important area for practitioners to appreciate and the following is the information which would usually be requested, often in the format of a 'trust request' form: type of trust required, the reason for the trust, details of the settlor (to include the source of funds), details of the beneficiaries, whether a 'standard' trust deed is required, details of the trust protector (if required), whether any property is likely to be added in the future and also whether any distributions are proposed and, whether a letter of wishes would be required.

Unit 12

1. The services provided offshore will essentially be execution only services (where the clients contact a broker, bank or other such service provider and instruct them to place the trade required on their behalf), advisory management services (where the client would be consulted on all investment matters) and discretionary management services (under which the service provider would usually attend to all administration and management issues). The custody of the investments themselves would also usually be offered.

2. The usual advantages associated with having investments managed offshore are confidentiality, taxation, regulation, professional management and security.

3. The information would usually include the personal details of the client and his dependants, the client's financial position, his taxation situation, his investment parameters, his attitude to risk and any personal preferences he may have in relation to types of investments to be held.

4. The three strategies are to maximise capital, to achieve as high an income return as possible and finally to achieve capital appreciation whilst at the same time obtaining a reasonable income return (which is often described as a 'middle of the road' strategy).

5. a) A long-term strategy for capital growth would usually be appropriate. Often such a portfolio is designed to provide a 'pension' fund for the client's old age. Current income requirements are probably being met by their employment income.

b) As employment income would have ceased and usually the person's house already paid for, income will be the major requirement. Security is also important as this will be the client's retirement fund and must last him to the end of his days.

6. The strategies to reduce the exposure to currency risk would usually be currency hedging, currency swaps and arranging back-to-back loans (all three steps being covered in Section 6, point 6.2. In addition, regular reviews and checks of the currency positions and rates should be undertaken to assess possible exposure to risk.

7. A summary of the offshore custody services which are generally offered by service providers are covered in Section 7 which should be referred to.

8. An agreement would usually cover the nature of the services to be provided, the basis of the fees which will be payable together with a note of the frequency they will be due, the manner in which the client can give instructions to the service provider, the arrangements for the holding of the client's money, registration and custody of the assets, the client's requirements for the receipt of reports, contract notes and valuations, investment parameters, indemnification for the investment manager and a statement confirming the extent of his liability for his actions (although the indemnity would not extend to cover loss caused by fraud or wilful neglect on the part of the agent) and finally arrangements for the termination of the agreement.

9. Although not in place in all centres, the regulation of the providers of investment service would usually cover such matters as fit and proper tests, a proven track record in this area of finance, minimum asset and capital requirements, the segregation of clients' money and adequate safe custody arrangements. There will also usually be the requirements to implement proper and adequate training and compliance programmes.

10. The areas which should have been covered and expanded upon were the need for an experienced work force, implementation of procedures and compliance matters, the existence of research facilities, the segregation of functions, adequate technology and finding suitable premises.

Unit 13

1. A pension fund is an arrangement under which an organisation, such as a large multinational corporation, makes financial provisions for its past, present and future employees as well as its senior executives. Although pension funds act as vehicles for the payment of pension monies, they are also used to pay general benefits to employees and executives.

2. The parties would usually include the employer (settlor), the trustees, administrators, an investment manager, an actuary and an accountant. Their respective roles are covered in Section 3.

3. In addition to creating the pension fund, the employer would also be responsible for making sure that the correct amount of contributions are paid on time to the trustees,

that he notifies the trustees of new members to be added to the pension fund and that he also advises the trustee of any amendments which are required to the rules of the fund (as set out in the trust deed).

4. The fund would be subject to the local taxation rules of the centre where the fund is resident. The residence of a fund would usually be determined by where the trustees are resident and if the trustees are located in an offshore centre the fund would, in general terms, be subject to the local tax regime of that centre. As offshore centres are either low or no tax centres, there are considerable tax planning opportunities for a company locating a pension fund in an offshore jurisdiction.

    A further possible tax benefit provided by offshore pension funds is that distributions to employees or pensioners would not be subject to withholding tax at source. As a result, employees or pensioners can receive gross distributions from the fund. The local taxation situation of the recipient might, of course, mean that they will be assessed to tax on such receipts in their country of residence but if they also live in a low tax location there would be clear advantages to receiving a pension which has not suffered tax at source.

5. Usually, there will be no restrictions on the extent of contributions which can be made into an offshore pension fund. Similarly, there will not usually be any restrictions on the amount (or nature) of benefits which an offshore pension fund can pay out.

6. Pension funds will usually comprise a considerable amount of assets for investment to meet the requirements of the employees/pensioners. Regular cash sums will also be contributed by the employer (and also in some cases the employees) and these sums must also be invested. In general terms the assets should be invested with a long-term view and although a conservative view should be taken, there must be scope for capital appreciation to meet the future requirements of the members.

    Many funds will also have current pensioners who will require regular distributions (such as a monthly salary) and as a result, there will be a need to ensure that the investments in those funds produce a sufficient level of income so as to meet the cash needs.

7. A list of the duties of a pension fund trustee is contained in Section 6, point 6.2 and many of those areas should have been contained in the answer to this question.

8. Similarly, the usual powers are contained in Section 6, points 6.3. to 6.5 which should be referred to for guidance.

9. There is very little regulation at the present time concerning the provision of offshore pension fund services. Indeed, there is also a lack of regulatory controls in onshore centres as well. This lack of regulation means that an offshore pension funds will be able to take a more flexible approach to the investment of the assets and also to the payment of pensions and benefits. However, it also adds to the possible risks.

    Some centres have implemented measures which prevent corporate trustees from acting in any type of trust (including pension funds) unless they are licenced locally. This licencing requirement does at least provide some degree of control over those who can act as trustee of an offshore pension fund.

10.   It is very important that a reputable and experienced trustee is appointed to act in an offshore pension fund. Usually, a locally incorporated or locally licensed bank or trust company would be the ideal choice of trustee (and the chosen administrator and investment manager would often be a similarly licensed local institution).

The bank or trust company which is chosen would usually be of international standing and have operations in a number of offshore (and possibly onshore) locations. In view of the size of funds which will be under management it would also be reasonable to expect that the service provider chosen has a proven track record of high quality asset management.

Unit 14

1.   A unit trust is a type of trust. A promoter (the entity who wants to create the fund) executes a trust deed which will set out how the fund is to operate. A trustee and manager will be appointed and the trust property will represent the funds which have been received from the investors and the investors themselves will be the beneficiaries, although their interests will be in proportion to the funds which they have invested.

2.   The trustee will be responsible for the safe keeping of the assets of the fund and for ensuring that the terms of the trust deed are followed. He will also owe certain duties and have certain powers (which will be similar to those of a trustee of a private trust).

The manager will be responsible for the day-to-day administration of the fund and will report back to the trustees. The manager will usually advise on the investments and make a market in the units.

3.   Distributor funds are unit trusts which pay a dividend to unit holders, whereas roll-up funds are unit trusts where income is not distributed but is instead added to capital (which is why they are sometimes referred to as accumulation units).

Many investors prefer to invest in roll-up funds because if no dividends are paid, income tax will not be an issue for the investor and if there is any capital gains tax (or equivalent) to pay it will be deferred until such time as the units are sold. However, some onshore centres, such as the UK, have introduced legislation which has reduced the taxation benefits previously offered by roll-up funds.

4.   This is a corporate vehicle with separate legal identity. Instead of units, this vehicle will issue redeemable shares and may also issue founder shares, usually to the promoters or management company, which will generally have voting rights but no rights to participate in the profits of the company. There will not be a trustee controlling the fund as the management and control will be vested in the directors. In addition, there will not be a trust deed but instead the memorandum and articles of association of the company will govern the fund.

The directors will usually appoint a management company to assist with the administration and possibly to manage the investments. Often an accountant will be appointed to assist with the preparation of financial information. A custodian may also be appointed.

5. The structure will be similar to that mentioned for open-ended investment companies. The directors will be responsible for the management of the company and they will usually appoint a management company to administer the fund. The administrator will usually be responsible for holding the assets and will perform a function similar to that of a custodian. However, these funds do not offer redeemable shares.

    Such vehicles can borrow and also gear up which has created the possibility for greater returns.

6. The list should have included possible taxation benefits, the potential for greater returns and more flexible investment strategies.

7. Offshore funds generally provide promoters with the benefits of less stringent regulation, taxation advantages and the potential for increased revenues.

8. The issue of regulation is covered in Section 6 and the answer should have centred on the points which were covered under the various headings in that section.

9. The Undertaking for Collective Investment in Transferable Securities (UCITS) was a European Union initiative which intended to harmonise the regulatory controls of EU member states with the objective that collective investment funds could be freely marketed between those member states. These funds must be set up in an EU member state.

    The features (and indeed requirements) are that the assets must be held by a custodian who is authorised to act in this capacity in the centre where he is based, the investments in the fund must be transferable securities listed on a recognised stock exchange and it must meet certain reporting and liquidity requirements.

10. This question called for an understanding of the issues a prospective investor may want to consider before investing in an offshore fund. These would include the regulation of the fund, reputation of the service provider, the marketability of the fund, its taxation treatment and the cost.

Appendix 2

Mock Examination 1

Answer **FIVE** questions.

> **Section A** – Question **1** and **ONE** other.
>
> **Section B** – Question **4** and **ONE** other.
>
> **Section C** – **ONE** question.

Answers in note form are acceptable, where appropriate, provided they are clearly and logically presented and the points made are adequately developed.

Time allowed: three hours.

The total number of questions in this paper is **EIGHT.**

SECTION A

Answer question ONE and ONE other question.

1. Mr Jensen, who is not a client of your Trust Company, has called into your office to discuss his financial affairs with you, and in particular how they could be restructured to his best advantage.

    He advises you that he was born in Sweden 30 years ago, but that he left there when he was 16 to make his fortune abroad. He is married with two young children and is resident in Spain.

    Mr Jensen's main business activity has been exporting chemicals from South America to Europe and importing the finished goods back into South America. This expanding business has made him very wealthy and his personal assets now comprise:

    ● property and land in Spain valued at approximately £750,000;

    ● property in Denmark valued at approximately £1 million which he currently lets at a commercial rent;

    ● a flat in London worth in the region of £2 million which he maintains for his use when he visits London with his family;

    ● bank deposits in joint names with his wife held with three banks in the Cayman Islands with total balances in the region of £3 million;

    ● a portfolio of stocks, shares and mutual funds which he currently manages, worth approximately £5 million. He views this as his 'retirement fund'. Mr Jensen receives his share of the business profits on a quarterly basis and adds it to this fund.

    Mr Jensen does not know much about the type of services which your company can provide, although he has been told by friends that offshore services can be used to reduce tax and prevent probate problems whilst at the same time retaining benefit from one's assets.

    Advise Mr Jensen on the following:

    a) The structures you would recommend for holding his assets and how those structures would be operated;   [7]

    b) Which assets you would transfer into those structures, and why;   [5]

    c) The possible taxation advantages which could result from the structures suggested;   [4]

    d) How provision for family succession could be achieved and possible probate problems solved;   [2]

    e) How, if possible, he could continue to receive income or capital from the structures you have suggested.   [2]

                                                                         [Total – 20]

2. The number of offshore centres which have introduced and developed local legislation to attract offshore business has increased considerably over the last few years, and there is a wide range of trust companies and similar institutions which can offer the administration functions required to service this business.

    a) What factors do you think a potential client would consider when selecting an offshore location in which to base his financial planning structure?   [14]

    b) What factors do you think a potential client would consider when selecting a service provider to administer and manage his offshore structure?   [6]

                                                                            [Total – 20]

3. One of your existing clients, Mr Furrillo, has approached your trust company to provide full company management services for a new company which he would like you to incorporate to receive royalty payments.

    Mr Furrillo has no particular preference for the jurisdiction to be chosen although he does have a number of requirements concerning the entity to be used. Prepare a letter to Mr Furrillo highlighting any possible problems or difficulties which your trust company might have in meeting his specific requirements as follows:

    a) His ownership of the company is to be anonymous;   [3]

    b) He would like to have two of his professional advisers appointed to the Board to act as directors alongside officers of your trust company;   [5]

    c) The company should issue a power of attorney in his favour to enable him to negotiate new royalty contracts on behalf of the company;   [5]

    d) The issued share capital should be a single bearer share of nominal value and the bearer share certificate should be sent to him for safe keeping;   [3]

    e) He would like the company to issue a credit card for his personal use.   [4]

                                                                            [Total – 20]

SECTION B

Answer question **FOUR** *and* **ONE** *other question.*

4. You have been asked by your Trust Manager to present a series of training sessions to trust administrators on certain trust related matters. Write notes on the main points which you would cover on the following, commenting on possible problems or practical difficulties which the trustees might encounter:

 a) The use of a letter or memorandum of wishes in discretionary trusts; [5]

 b) The role of a Trust Protector; [5]

 c) Corporate Trustees' ownership of underlying private limited companies; [5]

 d) The provision of trust accounts for beneficiaries. [5]

 [Total – 20]

5. A prospective new trust client, Mr Popodolis, has called into your office in the Cayman Islands to discuss with you his requirements for an offshore discretionary trust, which he would like your trust company to establish and administer.

 Mr Popodolis is a Greek citizen, although he has not been resident in Greece for many years because he has spent most of his time travelling round the world on his yacht.

 He tells you that he has assets with a bank in Bermuda of approximately US$3 million and an account in Luxembourg of approximately US$1 million. In addition to his yacht, which he bought for US$1.5 million 2 years ago, he also owns a beach front apartment in Miami (worth approximately US$1 million), and a substantial vineyard in Greece which has been in his family for generations.

 Mr Popodolis has three grown-up children, two of whom are undergoing training in land management and commerce in America with a view to one day taking over the family business. The third is, in Mr Popodolis' opinion, a time and money waster who spends too much time travelling around Europe with his mother.

 You establish that Mr and Mrs Popodolis are separated although not divorced and that Mrs Popodolis (who is also Greek) owns a property in Greece. Mr Popodolis currently has a girlfriend who accompanies him on all of his travels and she was also in the meeting with you.

 Mr Popodolis is keen to establish an offshore trust to provide provision for himself, and on his death for his children in America and his girlfriend. He wants to make sure that his wife and other child do not receive any share of his assets on the basis that he has already provided for them by establishing a separate account with your bank in Athens, which his lawyer knows about.

 Required:
 Discuss, with an emphasis on possible problem areas, the impact which forced heirship rules in Greece are likely to have on Mr Popodolis' requirements and suggest ways in which potential problems may be overcome. [20]

6.   A financial intermediary in New York has contacted you concerning the possibility of your trust company providing offshore trusts and company services for a group of his high net worth clients.

The intermediary has asked you to provide him with answers to a few questions which his clients have raised. Prepare a response to him in relation to the following:

a)   The information which you would require about his operations and his clients, explaining why you would want this information;   [7]

b)   The documentation which your trust company would require;   [7]

c)   A summary of the provisions in your jurisdiction concerning client confidentiality (please state in your answer the jurisdiction covered).   [6]

[Total – 20]

SECTION C

Answer **ONE** *question.*

7. An international computer company with operations in America, the Far East and Europe, has approached your bank with a view to establishing an offshore pension fund for its employees.

    You are required to prepare a report for the Managing Director of the company explaining:

    a) The principle advantages in basing a pension fund in an offshore centre; [6]

    b) The parties which would be involved in the pension fund; [3]

    c) How you would structure the investments in the fund; [6]

    d) The services which your bank would expect to provide. [5]

    [Total – 20]

8. You have been asked to give a talk to a group of visiting professional intermediaries on the investment services which your bank can provide, with particular emphasis on the strategies you would recommend for the different types of offshore clients mentioned below.

    Prepare an outline of the main areas you would cover in respect of these clients on the assumption that they each have US$500,000 to invest. Include not only your preferred strategies, but also your proposals for the portfolio mix, any concerns you might have with regard to the trust situations in (c) and (d) and the additional information which you would require to formulate detailed investment recommendations. You are not required to recommend specific holdings.

    a) Client 1 An individual, aged 65, with a wife and two grown-up children; [5]

    b) Client 2 An individual, aged 30, with a wife and a young baby. The person concerned runs a successful business; [5]

    c) Client 3 Trustees of a discretionary trust, where the trust deed provides them with wide investment powers; [5]

    d) Client 4 Trustees of an interest in possession trust, where the life tenant has a high standard of living and demands as much income from the trust fund as possible. [5]

    [Total – 20]

Appendix 3

Answers to Mock Examination 1

Question 1

The following were the key points which were required.

a) ● At the heart of the structure should have been a discretionary trust with your Trust Company acting as the sole trustee. Trust Protector provisions could have been included in the trust deed if Mr. Jensen preferred although a Protector is not essential.

● The trust would hold the issued share capital of a series of offshore companies which your Trust Company would arrange to be incorporated and those companies would in turn hold the various assets. You might use companies from different centres or decide to use companies from just the one.

● Your trust company would control, manage and provide the administration services for the underlying companies. This would be achieved by providing:

  – nominee shareholders (who would execute declarations of trust in favour of the beneficial owner, in this case the trustees of the discretionary trust) to secure the ownership of the companies;

  – directors (to secure the management and control) and other officers;

  – the registered office and, if required, the registered agent or similar position;

  – maintenance of the accounting and general corporate records;

  – Depending on your trust company's policy, directors might not be provided for the trading company which could be used for the import/export activities. The policy may be not to become involved at all and the relevance of taking the trading operations offshore would have to be assessed.

● The management, administration and control of the structure would therefore be handled by your Trust Company (although you might prefer Mr. Jensen to manage the trading entity subject to him reporting details of the activities back to you). You would operate the bank accounts (by providing signatories on the accounts) and, where necessary, appoint agents to provide specialist assistance with regard to the management of certain assets such as the investments and property.

● Mr. Jensen's advice would be sought on the general activities and policies in relation to the structure and the assets, and in this regard he should be asked to consider preparing a letter or memorandum of wishes setting out his views and preferences on how the trust could be administered, particularly with regard to distributions.

b) Companies should be used to hold the various assets and the trust would only own the shares in the individual companies, not the specific assets. The reason for this should have been given along the lines that ownership of the assets through companies provides a layer of protection for the trustees, as it avoids the possible problems which direct (registered) ownership in the name of the trustees can cause. Reference to the possible problems with trustees holding land in their name and trying to register quoted investments should have been included.

The recommendations should have been along the lines of the following:

● The property and land in Spain could be held through an offshore company after Mr. Jensen takes up residence in Scandinavia. Until he leaves Spain it might be advisable for him to retain the ownership, when you consider the local taxes which might be payable on transfer and the tax levied on foreign corporate entities which own Spanish realty.

● An offshore trading company, perhaps maybe two companies, could be used for the import/export activities and the profits could be channelled into a further company.

● The property in Denmark could be held by a separate company although the 'look through' provisions under Danish tax law might reveal the trustees and subsequently the discretionary objects as the 'true' owners. In view of this, Mr. Jensen may wish to continue to hold the Danish realty outside of the structure, especially if he plans to take up residence there.

● The flat in London could be registered in the name of a separate company.

● A further company could be used to hold the cash deposits and this company could also be used to hold the investments, although it might be preferable to set up another company to own those assets. However, his wife would have to agree as they are joint assets.

c) Mention should have been made of the following:

● Possible tax advantages stem from the fact that Mr. Jensen would be giving up the ownership of assets which would mean that, in theory at least, he would not be liable to either income or capital taxes on assets once they are transferred out of his name and into the structure.

● Profits and income generated by offshore companies arising from international operations (export/import activities, investment trading) would not be subject to taxation in the centre where the company is based (although a nominal sum might be payable to the authorities for this special taxation status).

- Holding UK realty through an offshore company which is, in turn, owned by an offshore trust has been used as a means of avoiding UK IHT on that realty by making the asset excluded property.

- Death duties/taxes would not be payable on assets which do not form part of Mr. Jensen's estate on his death and such taxes should therefore be avoided by transferring them into the structure.

d) This would be achieved by letter of wishes or by Mr. Jensen including suitable provisions for himself and his family in the terms of the trust deed. In addition, assets contained in the structure would not form part of Mr. Jensen's estate on his death and so they would not be included in any applications for probate.

e) Mr. Jensen would need to be included as a discretionary object under the terms of the trust and could receive capital or income as a result of the trustees exercising their discretion in his favour.

Loans (secured or unsecured) could also be made to Mr. Jensen from the trust and/or the companies, provided suitable provisions were included in the trust deed/articles of association.

Question 2

a) There are a number of possible factors which a potential offshore client might consider before choosing a centre and, although the list will vary between clients, most of the following points should be covered:

- **Taxation Considerations**

  - no (or nominal) taxation on income from international businesses;

  - no capital taxes on gains/profits;

  - no death/lifetime transfer duties;

  - no (or nominal) stamp duty;

  - possible existence of tax treaties with other states;

  - government issues certificate confirming exemption from local taxes.

- **Confidentiality**

  - no public disclosure of beneficial ownership of companies;

  - no central register of trusts;

  - minimal reporting requirements to local authorities;

- local secrecy laws;

- contractual obligations of trust company or bank to maintain confidentiality.

● **Legal System**

- independent developed (modern) laws;

- no bureaucratic regulations;

- independent local judiciary;

- availability of local legal expertise.

● **Political Situation**

- history of stable government;

- no political tension locally or in the region;

- ability to govern locally;

- politicians willing to develop and support offshore business.

● **Economic Situation**

- no exchange controls;

- strong local economy;

- no (or little) local unemployment;

- good/high local standard of living;

- availability of local skilled workforce;

- few restrictions on employment.

● **Geographic Location**

- same time zone;

- easy to access;

- proximity to market-places.

● **Infrastructure**

- good and reliable communications;

- local financial expertise (banking, law, accountancy, insurance, trust/company management etc.).

b) It is not only important to appreciate why a client might choose a particular centre in preference to another but also how that client might decide on which service provider to appoint in his favoured location. Most of the following points should have been covered:

● Range of services offered (many different services might appeal to some while other clients might prefer concentration on a small number);

● Fees and costs;

● Number of and/or geographic spread of branches/offices in the organisation;

● Competent, highly trained and skilled staff;

● Location (appearance) of the premises;

● Appeal of using a prestigious name;

● Technology/systems employed;

● Customer has a relationship with the organisation in another location (e.g. UK);

● Reputation of service provider;

● Recommendation from a third party (word of mouth);

● Financial strength of international institution.

Question 3
The following is a summary of the key areas required.

a) Mr. Furrillo should have been advised that a location should be chosen where there are no requirements to disclose the beneficial ownership of companies (naming a jurisdiction which offers this). Your company could then provide the nominee shareholders and execute a declaration of trust confirming that they hold the shares in favour of Mr. Furrillo or in such manner as he directs.

Another option would be to incorporate a company with shares issued to bearer. This option is considered in more detail in section (iv).

b) Although such an appointment would probably not exceed the maximum number of directors as set out in the company's articles, your trust company might have a policy which prevents client companies having split boards where your company provides directors alongside clients or their advisers. In any event, the possible disadvantages of a split board should have been covered, the main ones being:

- The risk that the management and control is not with your trust company which could affect the residence status of the company and, in turn, create tax problems.

- The possibility of the 'outside' directors passing resolutions, executing contracts etc. or generally being able to bind the company without the knowledge or approval of your directors.

- If Mr. Furrillo insists on having representation on the board, perhaps you could offer a compromise solution in that you might be prepared to allow 'outside' directors but only if your trust company provides the majority of the directors (to include a managing director) and that the notice and quorum provisions in the articles are altered to prevent the 'outside' directors passing resolutions without the approval of the entire board.

c) Although trust companies who provide full company management services, in particular director services, are reluctant to issue general powers of attorney in their client companies, they are usually more relaxed when it comes to issuing specific powers of attorney, provided they are comfortable with the reasons for the request and have carried out due diligence checks on the attorney chosen.

In this case, it would appear that a specific power of attorney is required and there should not be a problem with agreeing to this request provided the trust company has full details of the nature of the intended contracts and that copies of the documentation completed by Mr. Furrillo is produced to the board in due course. His appointment should also be minuted. The bona fides of Mr. Furrillo should already be on your file as he is an existing client. However, Mr. Furrillo should check that his association with the company as its attorney will not compromise his anonymity.

d) Depending on the jurisdiction and type of company chosen, a single member will be sufficient and bearer shares could be issued. However, your concerns over the security of the share certificate should have been mentioned to Mr. Furrillo (i.e. what if he loses it or it is stolen?).

In addition your trust company might not want to deliver/send bearer shares to clients because of the possible exposure to your company, as the ownership could pass without your knowledge and you would have no background on the new owner (who might not be a suitable person to have as a beneficial owner of a client company). The client could also use the shares as security without your knowledge and create financial problems for the company.

e) Although the company could apply for a credit card, there is the possibility that the client's purchases might exceed the available cash, or indeed the assets of the company, which could result in serious problems for the directors. There might also be an argument that the client has a certain amount of control over the company's funds by being able to incur debts which the company would be liable for and this in turn might create possible taxation problems for the client.

A solution might be that the client applies for a card in his own name and the directors of the company then agree to pay the accounts out of company funds.

Question 4

The following is a summary of the points which should have been covered. You would not be penalised for not stating the names of the legal cases involved, but would be expected to show an understanding of the main issues which were highlighted by those cases.

a) Settlors of discretionary trusts are usually encouraged to provide the trustees with their views (wishes) on how they would like them to administer the trust and in particular the basis on which they would like them to make distributions.

The difference between a letter (being a written expression of wishes by the settlor) and a memorandum (which is usually a file note prepared by the trustees) should have been mentioned.

The advantages to the trustees in having a letter/memorandum available (i.e. having additional information which they can call on to help them reach decisions relating to distributions etc.) should have been included together with a note of the possible problems associated if the wishes are followed blindly (i.e. accusation of being a sham trust). You should have covered the need for an active mental process in exercising discretions and that the trustees are not bound to follow the settlors wishes, nor can they be made to (wishes are not legally binding).

b) The purpose of a Trust Protector should have been included (i.e. to protect the trust assets and interest of the beneficiaries by overseeing the actions of trustees etc.) and the fact that settlors often feel more comfortable in creating a discretionary trust if there is a protector appointed. The mode of appointment (usually by the settlor although often trustees and protectors can have the power to appoint/remove) under express power in the deed should have been mentioned – there are no statutory powers relating to protectors.

The type of powers protectors are given (i.e. consent to distributions, remove trustees etc., which amount to powers of veto) should also have been mentioned and the possible problems associated with the protector having administrative or executory powers which are too wide/substantial should have been noted (i.e. the protector might be considered to be a constructive trustee and if the protector has power to remove the trustees and the settlor has power to remove the protector, the trust might give the impression of a sham).

You should have gone on to point out that a protector has a duty to the beneficiaries to exercise their powers in the best interests of the beneficiaries and in this respect they will have fiduciary responsibilities, depending upon the powers given to them. The recent case in Bermuda (*Re Star Trusts* (1994)) covering protectors fiduciary responsibilities could have been mentioned to emphasise this point.

c) In most offshore structures assets will be held by a company which in turn will be held by a trust. Brief reasons why this might be the case should have been mentioned although the answer should have concentrated on the duties and responsibilities of the trustees in these structures.

Reference should have been made to the cases of *Lucking's Will Trusts* (1967) and *Bartlett* v. *Barclays Bank Trust Co. Limited* (1980) with a summary of the main findings relating to trustees' duties (i.e. they should obtain regular copies of financial reports as well as annual accounts, obtain copies of minutes of board meetings or be represented on the board).

The fact that professional trustees owe a higher level of care should also have been noted and that the usual indemnity clauses relating to underlying companies cannot be relied on, especially if the trust company provides directors of the underlying company.

d) Beneficiaries often approach trustees for information and often they will ask for copies of the trust accounts. You should have mentioned that although trustees are under a duty to maintain full and accurate accounting records, that does not mean that they are under a duty to furnish beneficiaries with copies and each case should be considered on its merits.

The judgement in *Re Londonderry Settlement* could have been mentioned, which provided guidelines on which information trustees should disclose. The rights of beneficiaries of a fixed trust to receive copies of accounts should have been mentioned but that the position relating to discretionary objects was far from clear and that each trust would have to be considered on its merits. However, an Irish case, *Chaine-Nickson* v. *Bank of Ireland*, could also have been mentioned which found that a beneficiary of a discretionary trust should be treated the same as a beneficiary of a fixed trust in relation to information rights.

You should also have mentioned that trustees should not release details which might lead to proceedings against the trust.

Finally, reference to who bears the cost of the preparation of accounts should have been covered.

Question 5
This question was based on the circumstances surrounding the case of *Lemos* v. *Coutts & Co. (Cayman) Limited* and generally called for a discussion of the factors to be considered when a person from a civil law centre wants to create an offshore trust with a view to avoiding forced heirship constraints. The following points should have been included.

Opportunities
Provided Mr. Popodolis has the necessary capacity and that the trust is validly created and constituted under the laws of the jurisdiction chosen to be the proper law of the trust, there is nothing to prevent a trust being established.

The opportunities available in establishing common law trusts for settlors from civil law countries should have been mentioned (i.e. trusts offer persons the freedom to be able to dispose of property as they see fit without being restricted by local inheritance laws). The opportunities for trust companies to market such an expansive and often wealthy target market should also have been covered.

Possible Problem Areas

You should have referred to the case of *Lemos v. Coutts & Co (Cayman) Limited* (1994) which highlighted the possible problems which could be associated with forced heirship trusts. In addition, the following points should have been made:

- Mr. Popodolis appears to have retained his Greek nationality and, as such, the trust would not be recognised under Greek law.

- Greek succession law will apply to Mr. Popodolis' estate on his death which will mean a certain percentage of his assets will have to pass to his wife and children (forced heirship).

- Greek law will not recognise any attempt to defeat the wife's and the children's claims.

- If Mr. Popodolis makes at least the same provision for his family under the trust as local inheritance law requires there will be less likelihood of a challenge to the trust on his death. However, the wife and one child will not be beneficiaries under the terms of the trust.

- The funds in the account in Athens may not be sufficient to cover the indefeasible shares of the wife and excluded child.

It is likely that the wife and one child would attack a trust which failed to cater for them sufficiently. A discussion of the possible areas of attack should have followed, namely:

- Mr. Popodolis' realty in Greece would be subject to the lex situs and not the law of the trust and a Greek court might be able to seize those assets on behalf of the family and distribute it accordingly.

- Luxembourg is a civil law centre and the courts might be sympathetic to claims from a Greek court in respect of the cash held in the bank account.

- If the trust company has assets in Greece, an order might be made against it in respect of those local assets.

- Attempts might be made to claw back distributions from the trustees and/or the beneficiaries.

- It is unlikely, although possible, that an attack might be made on Mr. Popodolis' capacity to make the trust and his title to the assets, and these too could have been mentioned.

Possible solutions could be:

- Establish the trust in a jurisdiction which bars claims by forced heirs (e.g. Cayman Islands).

- Do not include assets in the trust held in the civil law centre where a claim is likely to come from (in this case Greece).

- In addition, try to avoid including assets held in any civil law centre (close the account in Luxembourg and transfer the funds to the account in Bermuda or to an account in Cayman).

- Suggest to Mr. Popodolis that he considers the provisions made to his wife and estranged child and perhaps increase their benefits on his death.

- If the trust company or its affiliates has assets in Greece, obtain a policy decision from the parent/head office, perhaps even legal advice, before agreeing to provide the services.

Question 6

a) Your trust company should request information on each one of the clients on whose behalf it will be providing services. The information required will vary depending upon the type of structure required but the list should have included a combination of the following (together with brief notes on each point made):

- References from the intermediary and from another professional source, such as the client's bankers;

- Confirmation as to the source of funds to be introduced;

- Proposed use/purpose of the trust/company;

- A copy of their passport;

- Confirmation of their home address (e.g. a copy of a recent utilities bill);

- Copy of any tax/legal advice obtained relating to the client;

- Copy of their latest tax return;

- Full details of their assets and liabilities;

- Family details (possibly with supporting copy birth certificates etc.).

You should also request information on the intermediary to make sure he is the type of person your company would be comfortable doing business with. This would involve obtaining references on him etc.

b) The documentation would probably include:

- **Trusts**

  - trust request form;

  - draft trust deed;

  - letter of wishes (discretionary trust);

        – declaration/proof of solvency.

- **Companies;**

        – company request form;

        – company management agreement;

        – release and indemnity;

        – declaration/proof of solvency.

c) You should state the jurisdiction concerned prior to covering the confidentiality provisions. Although the provisions will vary between centres, your answer should include such matters as whether there is any specific legislation dealing with secrecy/confidentiality, what the position is concerning disclosure of beneficial ownership of companies, whether there is a central register of trust deeds, bank secrecy, laws relating to professionals/banks/trust companies, regulatory requirements etc.

Question 7

The following summarises the key points which should have been covered.

a) The advantages which could have been mentioned include:

- Flexibility;

- Provide uniform benefits to all employees regardless of legal conditions in countries where they are;

- Not restricted by onshore pension fund rules;

- Not restricted by having to hold certain investments;

- No restrictions on extent of benefits;

- No funding restrictions;

- Fund can be structured in more than one currency;

- Fund not subject to political/economic forces which may affect employers;

- Free of taxes except withholding taxes.

b) The parties involved would probably be:

- Offshore independent corporate trustees of international standing;

- Actuaries (to value the fund and calculate benefits);

- Investment managers (to manage the investments);

- Accountants and auditors (to prepare/audit accounts);

- Banking services provider (to arrange payments etc.);

- Administrators (to maintain records and administer the scheme);

- Legal adviser (to provide advice on the structure as required).

c) A long-term view will usually be required with the objectives set before any holdings are acquired. An estimate of the liabilities (pension and benefit payments) both now and in the future would be required together with an idea of the contributions which will be due.

The liquidity will have to be sufficient to cover benefits currently payable. Bonds/gilts provide regular income and predetermined redemption dates, which would help achieve the cash requirements in the short-term as well as allow for anticipated cash requirements in the future. High interest earning accounts should also be opened.

As the scheme will have a long-term view, a conservative approach to risk would be required to ensure there will be sufficient funds available not only to meet actuarial requirements but also to cover pensions and benefits in the years ahead. Unit trusts/mutual funds and bonds/gilts would be held to protect the capital. In addition, the fund should be diversified to spread risk. Capital appreciation is also important, as the value of the fund should at least match inflation, and usually a pension fund will contain a small percentage of speculative investments hopefully to improve the return. There will also be an equity content for capital growth and usually a spread of currencies.

A division of 15% liquidity, 45% bonds and 40% equities would not be unreasonable although the division will vary depending on the nature and objectives of the scheme concerned.

d) You could have mentioned the following services:

- Advice on the setting up of the structure;

- Trustee services;

- Provision of banking facilities such as payments, money transfers, foreign exchange, deposit taking, safe custody etc.;

- Investment management;

- Maintenance of the administration records for members/pensioners;

- Accounting services.

Question 8

a) In view of the client's age and his lack of current dependants, a conservative policy would probably be the most suitable. Regular income would be a requirement to top up any pension monies which the client may be in receipt of and the portfolio should be diversified to reduce risk. The mix would be likely to be 5% liquidity, 50% fixed interest holdings (bonds and gilts), 25% mutual funds with 20% in equities.

Additional information required from the client would include such things as sources of other income and other assets held for both the client and his wife, pension provisions, age of the wife, general attitude to risk, cash requirements, currency preferences, preferences/objections to types of investments etc. The client should also make sure he has made suitable and adequate provisions under his will.

b) In view of the client's age, his dependants and the likelihood that he receives a regular and reasonable income from his business, a more aggressive strategy could be followed to provide capital appreciation over a long period of time to cover such things as his child's school fees and enable him to save for his retirement. The mix would be biased towards equities, perhaps 80%, with the balance in below par bonds with a liquidity balance of around 10% (to take up new issues).

Additional information required would be similar to (i) above although other factors would have to be considered such as the extent of his business earnings, the age of his child and his plans for his family's financial security over the coming years.

c) You should have referred to the duty of the trustees to exercise due care when investing trust funds and that speculative investments are not to be recommended, even if indemnity provisions are included in the trust deed. Trust companies will be expected to provide a higher duty of care and it is unlikely that indemnities would afford much protection if a claim of breach of trust was brought against them for a loss arising from investment in speculative holdings.

Generally, trust funds should be invested with a long-term view and a conservative approach would be usual with sufficient diversification to spread the risk. A policy providing income but not at the expense of capital would be common although if there is a likelihood of the trustees making capital rather than income distributions, the emphasis would be more towards capital growth. In such a case, mutual funds offering capital appreciation yet maintaining stability would form the bulk of the portfolio, perhaps 45%, with say, 30% in fixed interest, 20% in equities and the balance as liquidity.

d) Again, you should cover the duty of the trustees in exercising reasonable care when investing trust funds. The need to balance the requirements of the income and capital beneficiaries would be paramount and the trustees would be at risk if they invested to maximise income at the expense of capital. A charge of breach of trust by the remaindermen would also be likely. The issues for trustees arising from the *Nestle Case* should have also been mentioned.

It is likely the mix would be 5% liquidity with the balance divided between income producers (fixed interest, bonds, income units of mutual funds) and capital growth holdings (equities, capital mutual funds etc.).

The additional information required for (iii) and (iv) above would include details of the provisions of the trust in relation to the investment of trust funds and the beneficiaries interests. In addition, in part (iv) the details of the financial position and age of the life tenant as well as the ages of the remaindermen would also be required.

Appendix 4

Mock Examination 2

Answer **FIVE** questions.

> **Section A** – Question **1** and **ONE** other.
>
> **Section B** – Question **4** and **ONE** other.
>
> **Section C** – **ONE** question.

Answers in note form are acceptable, where appropriate, provided they are clearly and logically presented and the points made are adequately developed.

Time allowed: three hours.

The total number of questions in this paper is **EIGHT**

SECTION A

Answer question **ONE** *and* **ONE** *other question.*

1.   Mr Mendes is a wealthy Peruvian business man who is interested in establishing an offshore structure with a view to reducing his taxation liabilities, making financial provision for himself and for his issue and protecting his fortune from his wife who left him a few years ago, taking with her the joint property worth US$2 million.

You are informed that he owns real estate in Peru worth US$3 million, a property in Spain worth US$2 million, investments held and managed by a London based private bank worth US$1 million, cash on deposit with a bank in Mexico of US$1.5 million, 55% of the issued share capital of a Brazilian company (which trades in local commodities with turnover in excess of US$10 million per annum) and an art collection held by a bank in Switzerland worth US$4 million. All of his assets are held in his personal name with the exception of the Brazilian company shares which are held through a Guernsey resident company.

Mr Mendes has already taken advice from one of your competitors who suggested he should establish one trust to hold all of his assets, but as he explained to you, he would prefer to retain control of his funds and was not keen to transfer ownership of his assets to strangers.

a)   Comment on the suitability of the present arrangements and the advice received from your competitor.   [5]

b)   Advise Mr Mendes on how you would structure his assets.   [10]

c)   What, if anything, could be done to enable the client to retain control over the assets in the structure?   [5]

[Total – 20]

2.   Write brief notes on the following types of corporate vehicle commonly used in offshore structures:

a)   Limited Duration Companies;   [5]

b)   Hybrid Companies;   [5]

c)   International Business Companies;   [4]

d)   Limited Partnerships.   [6]

Your answer should include a brief description of how each type of vehicle is usually structured, their common uses and examples of which offshore centres they can be found in.

[Total – 20]

3.   Your employers, an international private bank with offices in New York, Switzerland and London, have asked you to investigate the possibility of establishing an office to provide offshore company management services for their private clients. Prepare a report to the executive of the bank setting out your plans for the creation of this operation to include such topics as your choice of location, the type of services which could be provided, the possible problems or risks involved and any other issues which you feel would be relevant to enable your executive to reach a decision.   [20]

SECTION B

Answer question **FOUR** *and* **ONE** *other question.*

4. ABC Trust Company are the trustees of the Alan Walker offshore discretionary trust created 6 years ago with the settlor (Mr Walker), his spouse and their issue as discretionary objects.

   The trust deed contains the usual wide investment powers giving the trustees absolute discretion over the assets and there is an indemnity clause protecting the trustees from loss. On the advice of the settlor, the trustees appointed a small private bank in the Far East to act as the investment managers. This bank was chosen because of their aggressive investment philosophy and the settlor wanted capital appreciation in the short-term to help finance his business activities which involved buying and selling computer software.

   The initial trust property comprised cash of US$3 million which was invested mainly in equities and futures contracts. The portfolio was also geared to the extent of two times the value of the fund. A Turks and Caicos company was later incorporated by the trustees and owned by the trust to run the settlor's trading operations with the settlor as sole director.

   Until recently, the portfolio had performed well and at its peak was worth US$8 million. At that time, Mr Walker asked the trustees to lend US$5 million to the underlying company and on the basis of his request, the trustees granted the facility interest-free with no fixed date for repayment. However, shortly after the loan was made it became apparent that the company was experiencing financial difficulties and was liquidated soon after with assets, after debts, of US$1 million.

   Required:

   Comment on the actions of ABC Trust Company Limited in relation to the investment and management of the trust funds. Explain how the trustees might have contravened their duties and responsibilities and suggest ways in which they could have acted differently to reduce their possible exposure to risk. [20]

5. a) Comment on how the regulation of offshore banking, investment and trust business has developed in recent years and how onshore regulations might affect the conduct of business in offshore locations. [8]

   b) What do you see as being the main advantages for an offshore centre to have regulation and, conversely, what do you see as being the main disadvantages?
   [5]

   c) Choose an offshore centre which has introduced formal supervision and describe how it has been implemented, what activities it covers and what effects it has had.
   [7]
   [Total – 20]

6.   Most offshore trust deeds usually contain provisions relating to the law, often referred to as the proper law, which will govern the trust.

   a)   What areas are governed by the proper law of a trust?   [6]

   b)   How can the proper law be changed, under what circumstances might this be required and what might be the effect of making a change?   [6]

   c)   Under what circumstances could the law of the administration of trust assets differ from the proper law of the trust?   [2]

   d)   With reference to an offshore centre of your choice, describe the factors which would be taken into account in order to determine the proper law of a local trust if there were no provisions relating to this in the trust deed.   [6]

[Total – 20]

SECTION C

Answer **ONE** *question.*

7. You have received a request for information from Mrs Smith, a prospective client who is interested in your bank's offshore investment services. Write a letter to Mrs Smith covering the following points:

    a) What information your bank would require to enable it to open and manage an investment account for Mrs Smith; [7]

    b) What the difference is between your discretionary and non-discretionary investment management services; [3]

    c) The benefits of using your bank's custody services; [4]

    d) Assuming Mrs Smith has US$3 million to invest, how would you structure her portfolio if you were to:

        i) minimise risk;

        ii) maximise capital appreciation.

        (Specific recommendations are not required.) [6]
        [Total – 20]

8. You are the Manager of the Investment Department of an offshore trust company. Your department is expanding both in terms of the number of clients and revenues and because of this growth, you have had to recruit new members of staff into your team. Some of these recruits have not had much relevant work experience and, as a result, you have decided to organise a series of in-house training sessions on various investment related topics to improve industry and job-related knowledge.

Prepare a summary of the main points which you would cover in respect of the following topics:

    a) The benefits usually associated with an individual investing funds offshore as opposed to investing onshore; [2]

    b) The benefits and possible disadvantages associated with investing in offshore unit trusts, from the perspective of both the promoters and the investors; [6]

    c) The features and possible benefits of the following investment mediums commonly found in offshore portfolios:

        i) umbrella funds; [3]

        ii) eurobonds; [3]

        iii) zero coupon bonds. [3]

    d) How exposure to currency risk in a portfolio can be minimised. [3]
    [Total – 20]

Appendix 5

Answers to Mock Examination 2

Question 1
The following were the key points which were required.

a) As the client has substantial assets in his sole name this could create substantial taxation liabilities during his lifetime and possibly on his death. In addition, there will eventually be probate issues to consider which, in view of the nature and extent of his assets, could create additional problems and certainly time delays for his family.

The rights of the family under local forced heirship laws should be considered as these could have an important bearing on the nature of the structure required. In particular, the likely entitlement of the estranged wife, taking into account funds she has already received.

Although an offshore structure could provide scope to reduce some of these possible problems a single trust would not be advisable to hold all of the assets because of the liabilities attaching to the trustees. In addition, the trustees would probably have a policy preventing them from holding certain assets, such as realty, directly in their name.

b) Peru Real Estate: As the lex situs would apply, there will be limited scope for international financial planning although the client could transfer part of the land to his issue to reduce his ownership and at the same time act as a transfer in specie in respect of their entitlement under local forced heirship provisions.

Spanish Property: This property could also be transferred into the ownership of an offshore company. It can be assumed that the beneficial ownership has already been declared to the Spanish authorities and so there should be no objection to providing similar details in respect of the ownership by the company. Indeed, if this information was not provided, local property tax would be levied in view of the corporate ownership.

Investments in the UK: The investment management should be moved offshore and the assets held through an offshore company. Realised gains and income should be retained offshore until such time as funds were required by the client, thus deferring taxation.

Cash in Mexico: Too much liquidity is held in one source and consideration should be given to switching part or all of this cash into the investment portfolio.

Brazilian Trading Company: The shares should be held through an offshore company but not through a Guernsey resident company because of the taxation implications. If possible, the status of the company should be changed to an exempt company otherwise the company should be terminated and the shares in the trading company transferred into a new offshore company with a favourable local taxation status. Perhaps 6% of the shares could be transferred to the client's issue so as to reduce his ownership to below 50% which would reduce the overall value of his ownership which might create some benefits for local tax purposes. This could also be considered to be a further transfer in specie of their statutory entitlement to the client's assets on his death.

Art Collection: Consideration should be given to transferring the collection to another centre as Swiss law recognises claims of forced heirs. For added protection, the collection should be registered in the name of an offshore company.

Offshore Trust: The various companies which would hold the assets should be owned by an offshore trust. A separate trust might be considered to own the company which owns the shares in the Brazilian trading company.

The trust should have the proper law of a centre which offers forced heirship protection and the trustees should also be resident in such a location. Examples of where this could have been should have been quoted.

c)   It would be difficult for the client to retain control over his assets as the structure created would require control to pass to the directors of the various companies, and ultimately to the trustees of the overlying trust(s), otherwise the validity and potential benefits of the structures could be undermined.

The client could, however, be appointed a director of the Guernsey company which holds the shares in the trading company. In fact, not many corporate trustees are willing to provide officers for trading companies and so the trustees might insist on the client being appointed to the Board of the trading company.

In addition, the client could be appointed investment adviser to the company which will hold the cash and investments.

With regard to the trust, he could be appointed as the Protector but only with passive powers and if he insisted on a greater level of control, consideration could be given to appointing him co-trustee and/or investment adviser (if the later is favoured, the appointment should be contained as a provision under the terms of the trust deed). However, such appointments might bring into question his level of involvement, his intention to create a trust and the management and control of the trust funds which might in turn give rise to the trust being attacked as a sham.

The preparation of a letter or memorandum of wishes should have been covered and the possible peace of mind this could bring to the client in giving him the opportunity to set out his thoughts on the way he would like the trust to be administered. However, the effect of such a letter should also have been touched upon as it would not provide any 'control' over the trustees, merely advice and guidance.

The client's general concerns over passing control to 'strangers', which in effect means the trustees, should be discussed with him and the importance of choosing an established, reputable and financially secure trust company should be at the forefront of this discussion.

Alternative structures to a trust in view of the client's concern over losing control could have been suggested. A foundation, with the client acting as the founder with wide powers, could have been suggested although if this was, the potential pitfalls associated with foundations for clients with possible forced heirship problems should have also been covered. A Bermuda private trust company to act as trustees of the structure or a hybrid company were other possible options to act as the holding vehicle of the structure.

Question 2

Although specific aspects of these vehicles will vary between centres the following are the main points which will usually apply.

a) These are companies, often referred to as Limited Liability Companies, which have a limited duration of a certain number of years (usually 30 years). Upon expiry of that duration the company is deemed to have commenced voluntary winding up and dissolution, although compulsory winding up is also available if necessary.

The company will have limited liability as well as a separate legal personality. Usually the articles will specify that the management of the company is vested in the members who will be considered to be the directors and as a result there will be no central management.

Often the company will terminate on the happening of a specified event, such as the death or bankruptcy of a member.

Limited Duration Companies can be used to take advantage of present IRS rulings in the USA by which such a company is treated as a partnership and therefore transparent for tax purposes.

Examples of centres which have LDC legislation are the Cayman Islands, Bahamas, Bermuda and Turks and Caicos.

b) These are companies which are limited by guarantee but which also have a share capital. This two-tiered ownership could, for example, enable the shareholders to manage the company (through their voting rights) alongside the directors whilst the guarantee members could have the right to receive distributions. This creates a 'quasi' trust situation where the shareholders are trustees and the guarantee members the beneficiaries. Such an arrangement might appeal to persons from civil law countries who require a structure to protect their assets but do not like or accept the trust concept.

Hybrid companies can also be structured to act as family foundations and they are often used in timeshare resort structures.

Examples of centres which have legislation in place are the Bahamas, BVI, the Cayman Islands, Cook Islands, Cyprus, Hong Kong, Isle of Man and Turks and Caicos.

c) International Companies are sometimes referred to as International Business Companies (IBCs) and are found on the statute books of most offshore centres. They are essentially companies which make an application to their local centre's tax office to pay a nominal amount of local taxation (e.g. US$500, £600 etc.) rather than be categorised as a resident company and therefore liable to local tax on their profits/income.

Some centres give IBCs the choice to pay local taxation up to a certain figure (such as 35%) rather than pay the nominal sum, thus enabling the company to take advantage of tax savings under Controlled Foreign Company legislation.

The BVI is the centre which has the most registered IBCs.

d) Limited partnerships are unincorporated entities in which the limited partners enjoy limited liability whilst the general partner assumes unlimited liability. However, it is usual for the general partner to be a company and as such, there is limited liability available in respect of their interest as well.

They are tax transparent and can be used as collective schemes as well as tax planning vehicles in the UK and the USA.

An increasing number of centres offer limited partnerships, including the Bahamas, Cayman Islands, Guernsey and Jersey.

Question 3

The following are the main factors which should have been covered.

Choice of Location

Matters such as geographic location; political situation; communication systems; availability of suitable accommodation for siting the office; availability of workforce; employment control (work permit requirements); infrastructure; local tax regime for local and international business; tax treaties or reciprocity with other centres; exchange controls; regulatory system; local company legislation; anticipated standard of living for workforce; availability of private accommodation (any restrictions on purchasing); climate; local language; licensing requirements; attitude of local government to international business could have been covered.

Type of services

The following is a list of services generally offered by offshore company agents:

Incorporation of local companies; assistance with regard to incorporation in other centres; provision of directors; provision of secretary and other officers as required; provision of shareholders; provision of registered office; acting as agent for the receipt of documentation; maintenance of corporate registers and records; filing of forms and returns required by local Registrar; preparation of financial statements; preparation of minutes of meetings; asset management (perhaps by providing investment management and/or banking services under separate licence); safe custody.

Possible problems and risks

The possible problems associated with the nature of the services provided should be considered. These would include the risks associated with providing directors for client companies (personal liability aspect) and the need for suitable indemnification from both the client and the bank; the possibility of accepting new business which could later harm the reputation of the office and bank, and having the resources in place in terms of both technology and people to handle the influx of business and to continue to service new business as the client base grows.

There could also be a risk if the office has insufficent or out-of-date information on its clients and there could also be problems associated with any asset management undertaken (liability for wrong choice etc.).

The reaction of the competition to the setting up of the new office might be a problem as if they reduced fees it might affect both the credibility and profits of the new office. In addition, a decline in the popularity of the centre chosen could be a problem, as too might a decline in the features which first made it attractive.

Other issues

Although the previously mentioned areas are important considerations there are a few more issues which should have been covered and these are summarised below.

How the offshore company's finances should be recorded in the Group's accounts; how the office is to be regulated by the parent (i.e. will an internal audit be required); personnel issues, such as location and relocation packages, grading, salary structures and career development; budgets and targets; how to develop the business; how to monitor the growth etc.

The bank's objectives in offering offshore company services must be examined (i.e. is such a move in line with its general approach to private client services or is the aim to make a short-term profit). A medium to long-term view would usually be taken as the initial start-up costs would outweigh revenues in the short-term.

The attitude of the parent company to the nature of offshore business should also be considered as onshore solutions might be applied to offshore situations (which is not always appropriate).

Question 4

These are the main issues and arguments that should have been raised.

Although it seems likely that the trustees failed in their duties and responsibilities, the extent of their investment powers in the deed should be reviewed as this may have an important bearing on the situation. It was mentioned that the deed contained the usual wide investment powers but the trustees might have been specifically authorised to follow a highly aggressive and speculative investment policy which would have provided them with some defence for their actions. Similarly, the extent of the indemnity clause should have been raised by candidates as this too might have afforded the trustees some protection.

In addition, the proper law of the trust might have been important as not all centres have statutory investment duties imposed on trustees (i.e. the Bahamas and Guernsey) and in some centres there are no requirements to take professional investment advice.

Having said that, trustees are always under a duty to act prudently and in the best interests of the beneficiaries and although they are not expected to guarantee investment performance they must adopt a reasonable approach to the investment of trust property. The trustees did fail in their duties and responsibilities on the following grounds:

i)   Appointment of investment manager and policy followed

     Subject to the terms of the deed and the proper law, the managers were not a prudent choice because of their attitude to risk. In addition, the policy followed was contrary to what would be expected of a trust portfolio in that it was highly speculative and aggressive. The gearing should also have been of particular concern to the trustees.

ii) Activities and Control of the Underlying Company

     The company represented a risk, not only in terms of its trading activities, but also in respect of the extent of the funds transferred to it. The trustees failed to involve themselves in the management and operation of the company and there is little doubt they failed to request financial statements as otherwise they might have spotted the financial difficulties.

     The deed might have contained an indemnity negating the need for the trustees to take an interest in the company but it would be unlikely that such an indemnity would have any effect if challenged in a court of law as it would be contrary to the trustees duty to act prudently.

iii) Intention of the Parties in Creating the Trust

     It could be argued that neither the settlor nor the trustees intended the trust to take effect so as to benefit the discretionary objects. The settlor required the trust property to finance his trading activities and the trustees failed to exercise their discretion in the interests of all of the beneficiaries, leaving the decision-making to the settlor. There is, therefore, an argument that the trust was a sham, not least because of the passive actions of the trustees.

There were a number of areas where the trustees could have acted differently to meet their duties and responsibilities:

i)   The Investments

     The trustees should not have sanctioned the appointment of the investment manager and they certainly should not have allowed a high risk policy to be followed. Alternatively, the settlor (or the bank) could have been appointed investment adviser under a clause in the trust deed and a clause could have been inserted authorising high risk investments. This would not have removed the duty to act prudently but at least the deed would have authorised their actions.

Generally for trust portfolios a low risk, diversified middle-of-the-road policy is adopted in line with the prudent policy expected of trustees, particularly corporate trustees who are expected to show a higher standard of duty. Care should also be exercised in appointing investment agents and the trustees would be expected to consider their advice and monitor the investments on a regular basis.

ii) The Trading Company

The trustees should have taken an active interest in the underlying company which would have included receiving regular financial statements and if possible having representation on the Board of directors.

The loan should not have been sanctioned although there would probably have been scope for a scaled down payment provided the risks were adequately considered and thought to be reasonable in the circumstances. If financing was required, instead of a loan perhaps a capital distribution could have been made from the trust funds to minimise risk.

Perhaps the company could have been held in a separate structure to separate the risk from the remaining trust property or perhaps the settlor could personally indemnify the trustees in respect of the loan.

iii) Control by Settlor

The trustees should have advised the settlor not to retain, or be seen to retain, control over the funds which would affect or diminish their discretion. The importance of intention to create a trust should have been explained to the settlor prior to the trust being set up.

The settlor could have completed a letter of wishes covering such matters as his views on the investment policy and funding of the company, and perhaps a protector (though not the settlor) could have been appointed to offer advice to the trustees on the family's requirements.

iv) Exercise by the Trustee's of their Discretion

The trustees should have acted in the interests of all of the discretionary objects and exercised an active mental process in deciding on such matters as the appointment of agents, investment of funds and distributions/loans from trust property. Recording their decisions by the use of a trustee minute would be advisable to support such decisions although this in itself would not afford protection if the action taken was not what a prudent trustee would have been expected to take.

Question 5
The following is a summary of the points which could have been made.

a) **Banking Regulation**
It must conform to the Basle Committee on Banking Supervisors Concordat which are the guidelines set by the Basle committee of banking supervisors.

These guidelines set minimum standards which must be met if banks in a country are to be regarded as adequately supervised. Such matters include 'four eyes' management and control; suitable ownership, usually by a parent bank which is supervised in another approved country; free exchange of information required for supervisory purposes with other supervisors; minimum levels of capital, liquidity, debt ratios etc; limitations on large accounts; submission of periodic status returns; rights of inspection and enquiry.

There are now 19 members of the Offshore Group of Banking Supervisors covering such centres as Jersey, Guernsey, Bahamas, Cayman Islands, Netherlands Antilles and Panama.

Investment Funds

Regulation offshore must be comparable with onshore regulation in the country in which it is proposed to sell or market an offshore fund.

For example, within the European Union, the UCITS Directive provides a uniform regulatory structure and in the UK, SIB and other SROs implement regulatory requirements based on UEU directives.

Control is exercised over unit trusts and investment trusts, their promoters, managers, trustees, custodians, investment policies, promotion and marketing by setting in each case minimum requirements.

In the USA, SEC controls and monitors securities offerings and mutual funds.

In each onshore country, its tax laws will also have a bearing on how offshore investment schemes are treated, either as an investor in stocks and bonds in that country or when its shares are purchased or disposed of by a resident.

Many offshore centres have also developed specific regulatory law in relation to publicly offered investment funds, usually by implementing specific laws administered by a Financial Supervision Commission or equivalent agency. Examples should have been included referring to the type of legislation introduced in centres such as Jersey, Guernsey, Bahamas, Bermuda and Hong Kong.

Trust Company Regulation

There is regulation concerning the role of the trustee in relation to investment schemes but nothing to cover trustees generally. Some offshore centres have discussed the possibility of regulating both trustee and company management service providers but to date no legislation has been passed. There is no specific regulation onshore.

b) The advantages could include – regulation provides the rule book for the conduct of business, and businesses who are not prepared to be subject to those rules would not necessarily be wanted/welcomed by the centre concerned; they encourage quality business; provide protection for clients and their assets/structures; centres receive higher level of respectability from onshore advisers etc.

The disadvantages would probably centre around the fact that if regulation is too far reaching it might negate the advantages of conducting business offshore. There is also the danger of applying onshore solutions and regulations to the offshore market.

c) The answer would depend upon the centre chosen but should cover the type of regulatory body or bodies in existence and the nature and extent of the regulation in place before commenting on the effects of regulation.

Question 6

a) The areas include the rights of the beneficiaries; the duties of the trustees; the interpretation of the terms of the deed; the appointment and removal of trustees; whether the terms of the trust can be varied and the duration of a trust. There is also an argument that the proper law determines the validity of a trust.

b) Most trust deeds contain provisions concerning how the proper law can be changed. However, the only legal authority on this issue suggests that it cannot be changed by a specific power in the deed without the consent of the beneficiaries. Most trustees tend to rely on the specific power.

A change might be required if the 'home' country experiences a change in its legislation or its attitude to foreign trusts which would negate the benefits of using the proper law originally chosen. Civil unrest is another possible reason to move the proper law to a more stable location. Provisions in the deed to change the proper law on the happening of certain predetermined events are often referred to as 'flee' or 'emergency' clauses.

Before a change in the proper law is made, the trustees must make sure that the proposed change would not affect the words, expressions or even the validity of the trust. This could happen if the new forum does not use the same definitions or applies different principles to the original law.

Of equal importance will be a check to make sure that the new law recognises trusts.

c) It is possible for the law of the administration to be different from the proper law. For example, an asset might be administered in accordance with a particular law (such as the lex situs) but the proper law governing wider issues such as the rights of the beneficiaries might be different.

d) The answer will vary depending upon the centre chosen and a detailed summary of the provisions of that centre would be required. However, it would be usual for the place of administration, the situs of the assets, the place of residence of the trustees and the objects of the trust and the places where they are to be fulfilled to be important deciding factors.

Question 7

a) The type of information required on the client would include details of her assets, age, possibly details of her family and dependants, attitude to risk, requirements for income/capital, tax position, anticipated capital withdrawals, income from all sources, relationships if any with other offices of your bank, investment preferences (i.e. are there any companies which the client does not want to have in her portfolio), life assurance arrangements etc.

With regard to the account opening requirements this could include completion of a 'know your client' questionnaire, taking up of references, obtaining a copy of her passport, proof of her home address, a copy of her latest tax return and the completion of a management agreement (possibly containing an indemnity designed to protect the bank).

b) Most service providers offer discretionary and non-discretionary investment management services. A discretionary service involves the bank having complete control over the investment portfolio enabling them to buy, sell and retain investments at their discretion without having to refer to the client. A non-discretionary service is where the client provides instructions to the bank or where the bank refers possible changes to the client for their approval.

The risk to the bank in providing a discretionary service should have been mentioned and the fact that the fees would be higher for such a service.

c) Many international banks now provide custody services for their private and corporate customers and the benefits which they tend to boast are: sophisticated technology to record trade settlements etc; network of sub-custodian agents covering most international and all of the major markets; the ability to achieve effective settlement of trades; the prompt production of supporting paperwork (contracts etc.); tracking of cash dividends to improve income collection; prompt advice of corporate events requiring action (such as scrip dividends etc.); detailed reporting; banking services in relation to funds held (demand and term accounts) as well as foreign exchange capabilities.

d) Specific investment recommendations were not required, only a discussion of the type of investments which candidates would choose to meet the objectives required by Mrs Smith.

A low risk policy would generally necessitate holding a substantial part of the portfolio in mutual funds and government issued fixed interest securities with the balance in liquidity, such as on term deposit. However, a policy to maximise capital appreciation would usually require a high equity content with the balance in stocks and bonds.

Question 8

a) The benefits which could have been included were confidentiality/secrecy provisions, possible taxation savings, investment expertise which is generally available in most offshore centres, no exchange controls, proximity of the centre to a particular market, investment in an offshore unit trust/mutual fund might suit the investor's particular requirements better than an onshore trust/fund.

b) The benefits/disadvantages could have included the following: regulation offshore tends to be more flexible or not as strict as that found onshore. This might deter some investors but it might appeal to promoters and those investors with a more aggressive approach to risk; the fund would not be subject to direct or indirect taxation on its asset value; the fund would not be subject to taxation on the income or gains realised or retained in the fund; the fund will not be liable to withholding taxes on distributions made from it; management fees are generally higher in offshore funds; the lack of taxation within the fund enables the fund to build in value and enjoy economies of scale; not all of the centres which provide fund management have the same level of expertise or support services and as a result investors and promoters must chose their centre carefully.

c) A brief definition of each type of investment was required, together with a summary of their attractions for investors. Most investment text books would have contained this information and it is likely that most candidates would have come across these vehicles in their place of work. The main points which should have been made concerning the features and benefits are as follows:

(i) Umbrella funds – These offer the managers cost-effective administration as one fund is run (which contains a variety of sub-funds holding different shares) rather than separate funds. The investor also has the ability to switch, cheaply, between different investment areas within the fund.

(ii) Eurobonds – They developed from the market in Eurodollars and eurobonds are now issued in most of the world's major currencies. They are issued by a consortia of banks mostly on behalf of large corporations or governments and the banks may then sell them to investors, usually institutions. They are attractive because they are usually issued in bearer form and the interest is paid without the deduction of tax. They can also be readily purchased through brokers or banks.

(iii) Zero Coupon Bonds – They do not pay a rate of interest but instead are issued at a price below their face value and the investor's return comes in the form of a capital gain on redemption. The gain is often expressed as a compound annual rate of interest. Eurobonds are often issued with a zero coupon.

d) You should be aware that when an investor buys into the shares of a foreign country he is also buying into its currency as well. There is, therefore, a risk that gains made on the investments could be cancelled out by adverse currency movements.

The choice of market is important and the factors to consider are the likely performance of the economy, the level of interest rates and likely changes, the valuation of the stock market and the likely movement in foreign currencies.

The risk could be reduced by hedging against exchange rate movements, perhaps by currency swapping (as offered by some investment trusts) or by using foreign currency loans for overseas investments (as practised by some offshore unit trusts).

Another method of reducing the risk would be to invest in securities which are quoted in the investor's 'home' currency as exchange rate changes would not affect the value of the portfolio. However, exposure to only one currency might not suit clients who are looking for diversification.

Subject Index

Case Index

Statutes Index